Position Rifle
Shooting

POSITION RIFLE SHOOTING:

A HOW-TO TEXT
FOR SHOOTERS AND COACHES

by

Bill Pullum
and
Frank T. Hanenkrat, Ph.D.

WINCHESTER PRESS

Published by Winchester Press
460 Park Avenue, New York 10022

Printed in the United States of America

Contents

Preface

by Gary Anderson

In the world of international target shooting competition, United States rifle teams are generally accorded the honor of having been the world's best during two periods, the early 1920's and the middle and late 1960's.

The explanations given for outstanding team and individual performances by athletes from any nation in any sport invariably focus on personalities. Every sports success story has to have its heroes—the athletes who turn in championship performances and set records. But every sports success story also has to have its unsung heroes—the coaches and team leaders who set the stage for these victories.

I am personally convinced that there are many young people in the world who have the personal ability and commitment to become world and Olympic champions. One of the reasons so few of them ever reach this level of athletic performance is that there are so few sports leaders and coaches who have been able to provide the organizational setting for optimum training, the technical knowledge that leads to superiority, and the motivation that keeps athletes willing to pay the price of victory.

When United States rifle shooters dominated the rifle events in the 1964 and 1968 Olympics, won the smallbore and centerfire world team championships in 1966, and defeated USSR national teams in smallbore and centerfire team meets in 1965 and 1968, two men were largely responsible for these victories.

The first of these men is U. S. Army Colonel Thomas J. Sharpe. Col. Sharpe had the vision to see that the lowly position of the United States in international shooting competition would never be improved unless special training programs were established for our marksmen that afforded them the same training opportunities European and Soviet marksmen were receiving from the training programs sponsored by their governments or national shooting federations.

It was out of this vision that Col. Sharpe hammered out the

military marksmanship training unit concept and created almost
singlehandedly the United States Army Marksmanship Training
Unit in 1956. Almost immediately, Army-dominated U.S. national teams rose from our also-ran status of the 1950's to a
position second only to the Soviet Union. The marksmanship
training unit concept not only improved the quality of Army
marksmen, but had a profound effect on all shooting in the
U.S.A. by encouraging other military services to adopt similar
programs and by teaching advanced marksmanship techniques
to shooters all over the country through a highly developed
system of training clinics.

Col. Tom Sharpe's efforts provided a training program that
could produce champions, but the final rise of the U.S.A. from
second best in international rifle competition to first had to
await the impetus provided by the coaching genius of the
second of these men, William C. Pullum, one of the authors of
this book.

Bill Pullum became the coach of the International Rifle Team
at the United States Army Marksmanship Training Unit in
1962. In that capacity he inherited a group of promising but
not yet successful marksmen and molded them into the team of
world-class competitors who dominated international rifle
meets from 1964 through 1969, when he left his job with the
Army International Team.

Pullum-trained riflemen won five of the six possible medals
in the rifle events of the 1964 Olympics. He was the coach of
the 1966 U.S. World Shooting Championship team, which won
five of eight World Team Championships as well as fourteen
individual medals including seven of thirteen World individual
championships. He was also the rifle team coach at the 1968
Olympics, where his shooters won a gold medal in 300-meter
and a silver medal in 50-meter competition.

I did not meet Bill Pullum until after I was discharged from
the Army and had left the Army International Rifle Team, but I
had many opportunities to train under him when I trained with
the Army prior to the international championship in the years
that he had that team as well as when he coached the U.S.
international teams on which I competed. His coaching had a
profound influence on my own shooting and my approach to
marksmanship training. I am sure he had an even greater effect

on the development of many of our younger shooting talents who rose to world-class level under his tutelage.

Bill Pullum's genius as a shooting coach does not lie in his knowledge or ability to teach the mechanics of shooting. During my own career I knew several shooting coaches, including Bill Pullum, who could teach the shooting positions and the techniques and tactics of shooting well. That was what we thought marksmanship coaching was. Bill Pullum's genius was in teaching us that positions, techniques, and tactics are really only a preliminary and rather minor part of championship shooting. He caused us to stop believing that we could become world champions by simply finding a set of ideal positions and a perfect trigger-control technique. He showed us that the real key, the most important part of championship shooting, is what goes on in the shooter's mind. Thinking, psychology, mental discipline—that is what really produces world-class shooters.

Indeed, when Bill Pullum took over the Army international squad in 1962, he did not even have the kind of background that would suggest the key role he was to play in leading U.S. shooters to the top. He had been an average Army service rifle shooter and a successful team captain of the Army Service Rifle Team, but he had never fired an ISU course of fire in his life. Perhaps his lack of direct experience in international shooting was a big advantage to him, however, since it gave him the kind of outside perspective that could provide us with the training breakthrough we needed.

Bill Pullum told us that 90 percent of a championship shooting score is mental and not physical. As you read this book, I am sure you will quickly come to this same important realization. The positions, techniques, and tactics of shooting are only a basis upon which to begin the psychological training of the rifleman. Bill Pullum taught us that the real key to training progress was the training of our minds, which in turn controlled the physical performance we made with our rifle and the score we fired.

Bill Pullum's approach to coaching is unique among shooting coaches. To me, it is significant to note the similarity between how he coached us and the client-centered psychological counseling techniques pioneered by Dr. Carl Rogers. In client-centered counseling, the counselor attempts through his own openness to and acceptance of the client to make it possible for the client to achieve an understanding and insight into his problems through his own efforts. When Bill Pullum tried to help us with our shooting problems, he used the same approach. He never gave us quick dogmatic answers. No one ever had a stupid question or a ridiculous problem. Each person was a valuable member of our team, and every problem he had or thought he had was worth listening to. When Bill Pullum finished with our problems, we usually found that we had come up with the solution ourselves, something that made the lesson much more valuable than if he had simply given us the answer.

Where many shooting coaches had the attitude that their function at matches was literally to tell their shooters how to shoot, Bill Pullum's approach was different there too. For him, the coach's teaching function should have been completed long before the match. At matches, he considered that it was his function to create the conditions that would make it possible for the shooters to perform at their very best. It always amazed me how much less harassment and distraction we had to endure at international competitions when Bill Pullum was coaching. He obviously believed very strongly that marksmanship training and performance in competition are directly related to the atmosphere provided the shooter, and that the coach can do a lot to make the shooter's job easier.

Through my experiences as a competitive shooter who has competed under Bill Pullum's coaching leadership, I have developed the firm conviction that he is the best competitive shooting coach in the world. When he told me that he planned to write a book about target rifle shooting, I couldn't hide my enthusiasm, because I know how much he has to share with the shooting world. His knowledge of target rifle shooting and his sensitivity for what the competitor actually feels when he is all alone on the line are qualities that make anything he has to say about shooting invaluable not only to the world-class competitor but also to the beginner. I am certain that anyone who studies this book carefully cannot help but achieve a tremendous improvement in his scores.

—GARY L. ANDERSON

Acknowledgments

We are indebted to large numbers of people who have contributed in one way or another to the preparation of this book. They are too numerous to mention individually, but they include friends from all over the world who have freely shared their experiences as technicians, designers, and manufacturers of arms, ammunition, and shooting equipment; as shooting organization officials and members; as researchers in various fields; and as coaches and shooters. It is to the shooters in particular that we are most indebted, for many have made important discoveries by dint of hard labor and personal sacrifice, but have freely shared their findings with others, and given up what personal advantages they could have gained, in the interest of promoting the shooting sport. We are indebted also to the United States Army Marksmanship Training Unit, Fort Benning, Georgia, which was our home for a period, and provided facilities and personnel that made possible a great number of the findings presented in this book. Ellen and David Ross III and Gary L. Anderson read early versions of the manuscript, made helpful suggestions, and gave valuable encouragement. For kind permission to use photographs, we are grateful to Gary L. Anderson and to the U.S. Third Army. Especial thanks are due to Jo and Kathy; their patience and encouragement through many long months of writing have earned a gratitude too deep to be expressed.

—W. C. P.
—F. T. H.

How to Use This Book

This is a book about the endlessly fascinating sport of rifle marksmanship. It contains information of some interest and value to all kinds of rifle shooters, from weekend plinkers and hunters to those who regularly engage in one of the several types of stylized competition. It is, however, directed primarily toward those who engage in formal position events, and is designed to carry such readers from the basic fundamentals to the most advanced concepts such as might be applied in Olympic competition. We have found that the most practical way of organizing the discussions is to orient them toward international-style smallbore free-rifle shooting. If one considers the sport on a worldwide scope, this is the most widely practiced form of competition rifle shooting. International smallbore shooting is also among the most challenging forms of riflery, demanding of a shooter the utmost concentration and physical effort. The experience of years has shown that a person who understands the principles of international free-rifle shooting and can put them into practice is invariably able to adapt to other forms of shooting with surprising ease and confidence— even to handgun and shotgun shooting.

We considered carefully whether we should include in this volume discussions of other forms of competition, but decided against it; such material would make the book unpleasantly long and expensive. Instead, we chose to rely on our readers' good sense to enable them to reduce or modify training schedules or goals to suit their own purposes. If you are interested in another, less demanding form of competition—such as a modified international course, or even just informal weekend competition with some friends—then the rule is simple: modify the training requirements set forth in this book to suit your own needs. The principles of shooting will remain unchanged, but the training effort can be anything you want it to be. We give a training program that would be suitable for an aspiring Olympic champion. If you are not quite willing to go that rather strenuous distance, then design yourself a training program to meet *your* needs, *your* aspirations, and *your* particular shooting interests.

Particularly if you are serious about competition, the way you use this book will be of great importance. It presents a complete program or system of shooting, with each element of the system integrated with every other element. To get the most benefit from the book, then, follow these simple rules. First, *read the book completely through.* The chapter on mental discipline, for example, will be of little value unless you have also read the chapters on positions and training. And the opposite is true—the chapter on positions will be of little use unless you have a fair knowledge of mental discipline. Second, *reread the book at reasonable intervals to refresh yourself on fundamentals.* Shooting is an amazingly complex activity, with numerous fundamental principles, no one of which can be violated. In the act of concentrating on various of these principles, most people will overlook and forget others, usually without being aware of what has happened, or of what has gone wrong with their performance. A thoughtful survey of this book at such time will draw attention to all the fundamentals and keep your scores advancing steadily upward.

A complete reading of the book is necessary to see in entirety the system it presents. After one complete reading, the book may then be used as a reference work—that is, the reader may turn to the chapter that deals with a subject he wishes to review and find there a relatively self-contained discussion of that topic. Because the book has been designed this way, the reader will notice when reading the book completely through that certain matters are discussed more than once. The subject of shooting can be likened to a spiderweb in which every element is somehow connected to every other element. The various topics which constitute the subjects of individual chapters are like the spokes that radiate out from the center of the spiderweb. The fundamental principles of shooting are like the rings that form concentric circles around the center of the web, intersecting all the topics, or chapter discussions. To minimize the repetition of discussions of basic principles, we have discussed a principle fully only once, and resorted to short summaries whenever it became necessary to refer to the principle again. This method serves the purpose of making each chapter complete while keeping repetition as unobtrusive as possible.

A word needs to be said about the method of documenting sources used in this book, and about the sources themselves. Occasionally you will see at the end of a particular passage a set of parentheses containing a name and a page number—for example, "(Morgan, p. 28)." This means that the information just preceding the parentheses was taken from page 28 of Clifford T. Morgan's book, *Physiological Psychology.* Complete bibliographical information on Morgan's and others' books is given at the end of this volume in Appendix C. The books cited there are by no means an exhaustive list of additional information pertaining to shooting. However, books cited have been carefully selected for authoritativeness and completeness, and each is briefly described and evaluated. Most contain quite thorough bibliographies of their own. Thus if a reader wishes to investigate a topic further, the books listed in Appendix C will provide him with a convenient place to begin. We have attempted to extract the most important information related to shooting from these books and present it here.

If we may say so without being vain or boastful, we would like to suggest that this book as a whole, and the individual chapters, probably need several readings. Any book worth its salt contains more information and more ideas than can be digested in a single reading, for all good books are the product of long, sustained efforts at gathering, sifting, clarifying, evaluating, and organizing information. Whatever the merits of this book, it is the result of years of experience and thinking and planning, and months of actual writing and revising. Consequently it is not an "easy" book with a low content of facts and ideas in relation to the number of words. Every effort has been made to make it as comprehensive and compact as possible without sacrificing clarity. We hope it is a book that people interested in riflery can read through with enjoyment, and that they can then turn to over and over again as they wish to refresh themselves on various elements of shooting. If the volume were not worth a second and third look, the reader would not be getting his money's worth.

Nevertheless, though we have put into this book almost all we know and consider worth communicating about shooting, it is still, compared to what remains to be known, merely a scratch on the surface. We urge you, the reader, to go beyond what is presented here. Read everything you can about shooting, talk to shooters and coaches, and judge and evaluate what others have to say. But most important, seek new knowledge on your own. We have suggested some ways of doing that in various discussions which follow. We hope this book will be useful, if only as a means of reviewing fundamentals. But we hope it will be more than that; we hope it will increase your present knowledge *and* enable you to go beyond what it sets forth. Use this book, and build upon it. The improvements in your scores will be satisfying to us, but most of all, they will be satisfying to you. Good shooting!

Position Rifle
Shooting

Introduction:
The Challenge and the Call

This book is about position rifle shooting as it is recognized and practiced around the world, particularly in such events as the Pan-American Games, European Games, World Championships, and Olympic Games. These major events, of course, are only the cream of the crop. Many thousands of matches are conducted each year at local, regional, and national levels throughout the world. Competitive rifle shooting, though relatively unpublicized, probably has more actually participating adults than many other of the more "popular" sports, such as baseball or soccer. Competitors try to outdo each other in various courses of fire involving one or more of the standing, kneeling, prone, and other positions. Many, if not most, of the competitors work quite hard at improving their shooting skills, and enjoy the sport immensely. This book is primarily about the hows of that style of shooting. But before dealing with the hows, it might be interesting and profitable to take a look at the whys—to learn why so many people are so completely dedicated to this unique sport.

If we were to poll all the members of the shooting fraternity and ask them why they engage in competitive shooting, probably a vast majority would give one or both of the following reasons: first, shooting is a pleasant, fun-filled recreation; and second, competitive shooting places one constantly in the face of a unique challenge—a challenge so intensely personal that only those who have wielded a rifle in serious competition can understand it.

The fun and recreational value of shooting is self-evident. Both training and competition frequently take place on outdoor ranges in undeveloped areas of the countryside where there is an abundance of fresh air and an opportunity to escape from the congestion and monotony of city life. Many shooters also have access to indoor ranges, and are thus able to train and compete all year. The value and desirability of a sport that is physically demanding yet free of violent exertion needs no comment.

Whole families may participate—men, women, youngsters, and oldsters. The investment a young person makes in shooting equipment and experience will last a lifetime, for shooting is literally a lifetime sport. This is evident at any match, where the top contenders are likely to range in age from sixteen to more than seventy, and will include both men and women. Probably no other sport can boast of such equality among competitors of both sexes and all ages. The atmosphere on a rifle range is notably open and democratic. And this democratic spirit is one of the most appealing things about the shooting fraternity. Its members include people from all walks of life who are bound together by a common interest in temperate living, in the outdoors, in friendly competition, and in precision shooting. The lifelong friendships that are formed on the range, and the camaraderie that exists there, make shooting one of the most socially enjoyable sports.

Moreover, we seem to enjoy marksmanship because it appeals to something deep in our nature, something perhaps buried in the desires of our unconscious minds. At some deep level, we seem to revere marksmanship ability. Great marksmen appear as admired figures in the myths and folktales of all people. The ancient Greeks told stories of the legendary Hector's skill with a spear and of Ulysses' ability with a bow; the Old Testament celebrates David's accuracy with a slingshot. In more recent times, Europe abounded with stories of men who excelled with the crossbow or bow, as witness the stories of William Tell and Robin Hood, among others. And the American West is rich with stories of such people as Lewis Wetzel, Wild Bill Hickok, Annie Oakley, Doc Holiday, and a host of others who could perform amazing feats with the Kentucky rifle or the Colt .44. Competition in marksmanship—whether with stones, spears, arrows, or bullets—has a history probably almost as old as the human race.

Psychoanalysts have attempted to explain the enduring fascination of marksmanship in several ways. Some of the explanations sound farfetched to the layman, as, for example, the argument that marksmanship appeals to our deep desire for magical powers—the gun acts as a kind of magical wand that enables us to stand in one place and make something happen in another place. Another theory is that a weapon is a means of expanding our potency or power, and thus appeals to our desire for the power to control others. But whatever the reason for its appeal, marksmanship does have a fascination all its own, and in addition provides an outlet for our enjoyment of sports and friendly competition. For these and other reasons, shooting very easily "gets in the blood," and has become a fascinating lifetime hobby for hundreds of thousands of people throughout the world.

But many shooters find, in addition to the enjoyments already mentioned, a special brand of personal challenge in the sport. Shooting a competitive course of fire, particularly an international course, whether in training or in competition, constantly affords the challenge of mastering oneself in order to better a previous performance. For a beginning shooter this may mean gaining a few points on his last score; for an Olympic competitor going after a world record it may mean performing in a way no other human being has ever done before. But both the beginner and the champion are faced with the same challenge—controlling their bodies and their minds in one of the most demanding forms of self-discipline known in sports. Both are trying to place every shot in a 10-ring not much larger than the iris of the human eye at 50 meters distance. The demands made upon one's body and powers of concentration in order to perform this feat are quite extraordinary. The ability to place shots in the 10-ring time after time, from three different shooting positions, is acquired only after a good deal of physical and mental training.

Many a non-shooter might question why anyone would go to so much time and trouble in the first place. "Why," he might ask, "does anyone make the tremendous effort necessary to break a world shooting record?" One fundamental reason is surely because *the challenge is there.* The whole history of human achievement reveals that man is simply geared to overcoming challenges. We have conquered the New World and walked on the moon for the same reason Mallory gave for trying to climb Mount Everest—because the possibility of the thing was there, and posed the challenge. The challenge formed by Mount Everest exists in the external world. Anyone looking at it can feel the challenge of the obstacle it poses if he has even the slightest spark of adventurousness in his soul. But the challenge of shooting championship rifle scores is not apparent to non-shooters, primarily because the obstacles exist almost wholly *inside* the body and mind of the shooter. An observer with no shooting experience sees a rifleman assuming his position, taking careful aim, and pulling the trigger—the act of shooting a 10 appears to be simplicity itself. Yet if the inexperienced observer were to pick up the rifle and attempt to shoot a 10 from the standing position, the task would suddenly seem nerve-rackingly difficult. His position would be unsteady, the rifle would feel unbalanced, he would have difficulty coordinating his mind and his trigger finger, he would probably flinch when he pulled the trigger, and very likely he would miss the bull's-eye altogether, for he would be forced to shoot at it "on the fly" as it appeared to swerve and dart around the sight picture like a bat hunting insects in the twilight.

The first attempt of shooting at a competition target from the standing position can be an unnerving experience. A few people react to the first experience by saying, "I can't do it. It takes some natural talent which I don't have." In reacting this way they are, unfortunately, denying themselves all the pleasure and satisfaction of learning to shoot well, which they could in all likelihood do. But the decision is theirs to make, and so we bid them a polite goodbye. Most people react differently to that first disconcerting attempt. They have seen other people shooting good scores; they understand from their first experience the challenge involved, and say, "It can be done, and I'm going to do it." They may work with a borrowed rifle for a while, but before long they want their own equipment which they can tailor to their own needs and use at their own convenience. They are "hooked" on shooting.

The challenges of shooting exist in two interrelated but nevertheless separable areas. The first is physical, and included in this area are all of the considerations of properly adjusted equipment, body positions, and the muscular, or motor, skills that go into shooting. The second area is psychological, and is not so easily delineated. It includes the logical analysis and reasoning that goes along with building and perfecting a position, the mental concentration that is necessary for perfecting performance, the ability to withstand the pressures of competition, and, last but very important, the desire to win. Each physical and psychological component just mentioned will be discussed in detail in the following sections of this book. In the remainder of this section, we will take a preliminary brief look at each one to see how it fits into the whole act of shooting. This overview will give us an idea of the function of each component in the coordinated act of shooting, and will make the later, more detailed discussions more meaningful.

THE PHYSICAL CHALLENGE

Adjusting the equipment.

The rifle and its accessories, and other equipment, must be properly fitted to the individual. Equipment should be adjusted to fit the position of the shooter, and not the position adjusted to the equipment. As the free-rifle and its accessories admit a wide latitude of adjustments, this would appear to be a simple matter, but it is not. The very small refinements which are necessary to improve a position are sometimes difficult to determine, and equally difficult to achieve. The standing position provides a clear (and the most dramatic) example. Like all positions, it is based upon maximum use of bone support. To minimize the involvement of muscles, the shooter bends his body back and to the right so that the weight of the rifle and upper torso falls upon the bones of the lower spinal column. The goal is to achieve as nearly as possible a perfect balance, with the weight of the rifle to the left-and-front of the feet equalized exactly by the weight of the body which is bent to the right-and-rear of the feet. It is difficult to achieve this balance with a structure as complex as the body-rifle configuration, and the task becomes immensely complicated by the fact that the balanced position must be adjusted so that the rifle points naturally at the bull's-eye. Many small adjustments, both horizontal and vertical, must be made in the palm-rest and butt-hook assemblies, and in all relationships between body components, before this position is achieved. The number of adjustments that must be tested and evaluated is large, and the process is frequently quite time-consuming. The standing position is more complex than the others, but all positions, in addition to producing a good hold that is aimed naturally at the bull, must be reasonably comfortable and must be legal by the rules governing competition. The requirements of comfort and legality further complicate the problem of correctly adjusting equipment.

Learning to hold still.

After a reasonably satisfactory position has been found, the rifleman must undertake to train the muscles of his body to hold still. This may sound absurdly simple, for it appears at first thought that holding still is merely the absence of activity—one holds still simply by not doing anything. Yet nothing could be further from the truth. Learning to hold the body still is probably many times more difficult than developing a good position. It is an observable fact that unless one is concentrating on being still, the body is almost constantly in motion. Watch the people around you and you will discover that they are usually moving some part of their bodies, and are seldom if ever perfectly still for scarcely more than a split second. Muscular activity seems natural to the body, for even in sleep, when the muscles are most relaxed, they still involve themselves in intervals of activity. In wakefulness, even when we consciously hold the voluntary muscles of the body still and suspend the action of the diaphragm by holding our breath, the internal organs are constantly in motion. The heart and arteries are pumping blood, the digestive tract is moving food and waste through the body, the kidneys are removing liquids from the blood and moving them to the bladder—and numerous other internal activities are going on as well. The effect of all of these activities is a constantly shifting center of gravity in the body—the changes are extremely minute, no doubt, but they nevertheless exist.

As a result of all of these combined internal activities, it is virtually impossible to hold the body absolutely motionless in any position. In the prone and kneeling positions, some pulse beat will inevitably be transmitted to the rifle. In the least stable position—standing—the effect of all these minute shifts in the center of gravity is a small, rhythmic, but perceptible oscillation of the body. This oscillation is tied directly to the reflexive righting action of the body—that is, to the body's built-in tendency to hold itself upright. The controlling mechanisms for this reflex are not fully understood, but appear to be spread throughout the body. One of the control centers is the inner ear (the organ technically called the vestibular apparatus), which senses the direction of gravity. If the pull of gravity is not offset by some means of body support—that is, if the body is "falling"—it appears that the inner ear sends messages to the brain, which in turn triggers reflex movements in the muscular system to restore the body to a balance point. Related control centers appear to be nerve endings in the ankles, and possibly in the knees, hips, and neck, which measure muscle flexion and likewise send messages to the brain to inaugurate righting actions.

The oscillations of the body in the standing position, then, probably result in the following fashion. A change in the center of gravity causes the body to begin swaying in one direction. The complex control mechanisms sense this drifting away from the point of balance and cause righting responses in appropriate body muscles. These pull the body back toward the balance point; but momentum then causes the body to begin drifting out of balance in the opposite direction. As a result, righting responses are initiated in the opposite direction, and the cycle repeats itself (Morgan, pp. 289-97).

Though these oscillations are reflexive, a shooter can learn to minimize their effect by building a position that makes maximum use of weight distribution and balance, and by refining the muscle responses involved in the reflex, thus holding movement to a minimum. The oscillations will not be completely eliminated, but, as an additional measure, one can learn to control the rifle in such a way as to compensate for the oscillations. This is done in the following manner: when the body sways to the right, the aim of the rifle is moved on the target a corresponding distance to the left; when the body sways to the left, the aim of the rifle is moved on the target a corresponding distance to the right. By this means, the aim of the rifle may be kept consistently in the 10-ring. This compensating movement, however, is effective only if the sway is relatively small, and is ineffective if the body sway exceeds a certain maximum limit. The compensating technique can be learned and employed, in short, only after the rifleman has first reduced normal body sway to acceptable limits.

The effort needed to hold still in the kneeling and standing positions, it can be seen, is of a double nature. First, muscles must support the body in a given position, otherwise it would collapse and fall to the ground. And second, muscles must correct and compensate for the shifts in gravity to the body structure in order to hold it in these positions.

Semi-conditioned responses.

If a shooter is to reach his full potential, certain muscle, or motor, skills must be learned to the point of becoming almost automatic responses. The type of responses we are talking about are frequently called semi-conditioned responses, and may be defined through the following distinctions. A *true reflex* response is one over which we have no control, such as the jerk of the foot when the knee is tapped with a hammer, or the ducking of the head that occurs when we hear an unexpected loud noise. A *conditioned reflex* is similarly automatic and beyond the responder's control, but instead of being an inherited, natural reaction to a given situation, the response is learned. Conditioned reflexes occur in everyday life, but usually in a very complicated form. An example would be the uncontrollable tension some people feel when they are forced to perform a task in front of observers. Theirs is not the usual tension associated with "normal" stage fright, but a more extreme form that results from some neurotic fear of failure or a feeling of inadequacy that was learned in earlier life. This tension, which is beyond their power to control, occurs whenever they find themselves under scrutiny by others, and, among office workers, for example, where observations by others are unavoidable, may result in the subject's developing ulcers. Simpler forms of conditioned reflexes are found in the laboratory, where for experimental purposes, for example, a dog may be conditioned to salivate at the sound of a bell, and will be unable to control his salivation response whenever the sound is presented.

It is not likely that the skills involved in shooting can be learned to the point of becoming truly reflexive and automatic, completely beyond the control of the shooter. However, some skills may be learned to the point of becoming almost automatic—learned to the point of having a borderline existence between the willed, consciously controlled response and the unwilled, automatic response. Such a skill is not fully conditioned, but is almost so; it is a semi-conditioned response.

Among the semi-conditioned responses found in a well-trained shooter is the compensatory response to body sway, discussed above, wherein the aim of the rifle is adjusted automatically to body oscillations. Others include proper procedures of target alignment, eye use, breathing, and trigger pull. These skills acquire semi-conditioned characteristics through constant, repeated training efforts until they become more or less automatic.

There are many semi-conditioned responses in everyday life. For example, while driving an automobile, many people perform a number of learned responses without being more than marginally aware of them, including starting, steering, changing gears, and braking. Conscious direction of the muscles is unnecessary for them to perform these tasks, though, it should be noted, the responses are always subject to the performer's will—unlike a reflex response, over which the performer has no control, a semi-conditioned response may be suspended or changed if the performer wills to do so. Semi-conditioned responses are common and extremely useful, for they free us from giving all our attention to ordinary tasks, but allow us at the same time to have control over those tasks. Without semi-conditioned responses, the muscular movements involved in such activities as walking, driving, eating, and writing would require all our attention; but because these are usually semi-conditioned responses, we can perform them and are yet free to think about other things. For the same reason, semi-conditioned responses are extremely valuable in shooting and are worth the repeated training efforts necessary to acquire them.

THE PSYCHOLOGICAL CHALLENGE

Consciousness and bodily states.

The basic problem posed to an analysis of the psychology of shooting is that we do not know what causes or what constitutes consciousness. It centers in the brain, apparently, and is perhaps the result of chemical and electrical activities in the neural cells. But beyond that we cannot go. Freud, the father of psychoanalytic medicine, still speaks for scientists and psychologists when he said years ago that consciousness is what we all know and recognize, but cannot define. We do know that it is vastly complex, existing on many levels which are subject in varying degrees to control by the will. At its first level, consciousness is awareness, what we are "thinking" at any given moment. But simultaneously, the brain is performing numerous other functions that are not part of our consciousness but may at any moment intrude directly upon consciousness, or affect it indirectly by producing emotions which alter mental processes. Some of the functions taking place in the brain which may affect shooting performance are memory, associative processes, reception of sensory input from the body itself, unconscious regulation of the involuntary muscles, conscious control of the voluntary muscles, unconscious regulation of body chemistry, and perhaps several other functions as well. Each function can be influenced by any other, because they are all regulated by parts of the brain that are interconnected by a complex system of nerve cells (Morgan, p. 25).

A hypothetical example can show how this works. You may be seated calmly in your chair reading, only vaguely aware that a small baby is asleep in an adjoining room. Some unusual sound or sight interrupts your concentration, and you look up and see a pair of window draperies on fire in the same room with the baby. This sensory input is instantly judged as posing a danger to both you and the child—a judgment that is made so quickly, in fact, that reasoning or even conscious thought seem hardly to take place in arriving at the judgment. This judgment at once affects other areas of the brain that trigger the release of certain glandular secretions that speed up the heart and breathing rates, cause the muscles of the digestive system to slow down, the voluntary muscles to tense, the speed of nerve impulses to increase, and the whole center of consciousness, or thinking, to be speeded up and possibly to spin out of rational thought into a state of panic. Something similar to this can happen when you begin shooting a match, especially if you should accidentally shoot a "snowbird" (the shooter's term for a shot completely out of the bull onto the surrounding white), or if you look at another shooter's target and find that his score looks for the moment unbeatable.

Concentration during shooting.

Because of the overwhelming complexity of the neurophysiological system, we do not know how to define consciousness or concentration in any precise way. We are not even sure what a shooter is "thinking" when he executes a perfect performance, or even if what is happening in his mind is thinking as we usually define it as "speaking silently to oneself." Something quite different may be going on, and perhaps the processes differ widely from shooter to shooter. What we do know is that attention is limited to, or concentrated on, performance. And we know for certain that anything that is not part of the positive shooting process is excluded. We will have more to say about this later. The things which definitely are involved in positive performance are basically four: sight picture, hold, trigger pull, and follow-through. The first three considerations are made in such rapid sequence that they sometimes appear to be made simultaneously. We do not know for sure that they are, or how the brain can put these functions together so that consciousness can deal with them all at once. We only know that sometimes it does, or appears to, though not always. Something is known about each of the three processes, however, and we believe that they are synthesized in an event that may be described accurately as an act of judgment. The fourth consideration—follow-through—is more an act of observation, and is the basis of an accurate analysis of the performance after its completion. Each of these four functions deserves further attention.

Sight picture.   The first mental process involved in shooting is evaluating the sight picture. This involves, in the beginning, selection of the right bull if the target frame contains more than one. Then comes the evaluation and correction of sight alignment. The next step involves judging whether the aim-point is satisfactorily close to the center of the bull. But "satisfactorily close" is a relative term. A champion shooter will be shooting for X's in prone and kneeling, and for 10's in standing. For him, the sight picture is satisfactory only if it is on or near dead center. Intermediates will sometimes judge a 9-ring sight picture satisfactory in standing, and beginners an 8- or even a 7-ring sight picture satisfactory. This is as it should be, for an inexperienced shooter simply has not acquired the techniques to enable him to hold dead-center aim. If he tried to limit his shots to 10's only, he would be unable to complete the course of fire within the time limit. The first and simplest process, then, is judging the sight picture to be satisfactory within the capabilities of one's techniques.

Hold.   Hold is, by comparison, much more difficult. Hold may be judged from two perspectives—steadiness and durability. A hold is *steady* when it is as free as possible of oscillation and pulse beat. The ideal hold settles into the 10-ring and has no movement perceptible to the unaided eye. A less steady hold will have perceptible movement around the inside of the 9-ring, say, but will not confine itself to the 10-ring.

From the instant a hold is judged satisfactory on the basis of sight picture and steadiness, it must also be judged on the basis of durability. A hold is *durable* if it will remain unbroken long enough to ensure proper trigger pull and follow-through. A hold may be steady, but not durable, as in the case of a 10-ring hold that is likely to disintegrate at any moment; or it may be durable, but not steady, as in the case of a hold that drifts around the 9-ring but can be maintained for an extended time. A shooter judges steadiness by what he sees through the sight picture. He judges durability by sensing his body. He evaluates whether or not all the muscles in the body can sustain the fixed position they are in long enough to allow proper execution of the shot. This process, which we will later discuss as *kinesthesia*, is a complex sensing process involving evaluation of *every* muscle in the face, neck, shoulders, arms, hands, back, stomach, legs, and feet. Exactly how one learns to judge this sensory feedback is unknown, but the ability seems to come naturally with experience and effort toward acquiring proper concentration.

Trigger pull.   When sight picture and hold are judged as satisfactory, then the trigger finger must be moved (or, as we say elsewhere, allowed to move) without disturbing any other part of the body. The remainder of the body must sustain the hold through the completion of the shot. This complex process seems to require a divided concentration, with part of the shooter's mental effort devoted to holding the body motionless, insofar as that is possible, and part devoted to controlling the trigger finger. It is difficult, if not impossible, to say how the mind accomplishes both of these functions simultaneously. Very likely, however, this kind of divided attention is present in most complex physical activities involving coordination of various muscles.

Follow-through. Simultaneously with the release of the shot, concentration should shift to follow-through. Follow-through is often talked about but we suspect that it is actually practiced in its fullest sense by only a few champion shooters. Most people feel that follow-through is simply "holding on" to the position until the bullet has cleared the rifle barrel. But complete follow-through involves more than this, for it involves a follow-through in mental concentration as well. A champion shooter concentrates on sensing and analyzing every aspect of his performance until after the completion of recoil, is precisely aware of the feel and direction of recoil, and is capable of predicting within minute limits where the bullet struck the target.

Coordination of physical and psychological activities.

For a fully developed shooter, the act of releasing the shot is far more complex than simply pulling the trigger. Sight picture, hold, and trigger pull all seem to be synthesized and treated simultaneously in a *single* act of judgment. Releasing the shot is in many ways an indescribable "psychological moment" in which the entire mind and body blend in a fully coordinated act. This is best illustrated by the curious, complex psychophysical sensation of loss experienced when one *intended* to pull the trigger, but somehow the trigger finger disobeyed and the expected recoil does not occur. The shock of that moment can cause all sorts of brief feelings of panic, accompanied by muscular jerks and changes in vision. In its broadest sense, releasing the shot is the coming together of mind and body in an instant of complete integration. This total blending of mind and body is not unique to shooting—it is sometimes experienced in other sports, as in the game of golf, for example—but we believe it is experienced more deeply and more consistently in shooting than in any other sport. It is indeed so complex a phenomenon that it defies adequate explanation in words, and must be experienced to be understood.

If you are an attentive reader, you have noted that several times now we have said that certain psychological processes are quite complicated, and that we do not know how to describe them precisely, or how they are accomplished. This was done because to do otherwise would be untruthful and misleading. Some of the psychological, and also some of the physiological, processes involved in shooting remain mysterious, though the sport has been around and has been studied for many years. But we may now dispel any mystery about the processes insofar as they concern you, the shooter. Though neither we nor anyone else can give an objective, scientific explanation of how certain things happen, you will know when they happen in your own experience. You will know you have been concentrating on the right things when you release the shot and it goes down the middle and you *know* it went down the middle and everything was done right. There is a deep-seated feeling of confidence that results the instant the gun begins to recoil and you see the sights centered perfectly in the X-ring and the follow-through feels solid and sure. When you have executed such a shot, you have achieved perfect concentration—you have coordinated body and mind in a single, perfect act. The next step will be to acquire the ability to duplicate that performance over and over again. This, perhaps, will be an ever greater challenge than producing the first perfect shot, for you must be able to reproduce—or very nearly reproduce—that perfectly coordinated act, with a minimum of deviation, for a minimum of forty shots in each position.

THE CALL

Obviously, shooting *is* complex and *is* a challenge of a rather unique kind. Its appeal, perhaps, is that any level of performance demands its own degree of self-mastery—mastery of the body, the intellect, and the emotions. Beginners, intermediates, and advanced shooters all face, at different levels, the same basic challenge of self-mastery. Throughout the history of mankind, men seem to have been called by any activity that required such self-discipline. In fact, if we looked closely at all of the great challenges that men have faced and overcome, we might find that they all posed a similar problem: before the obstacle could be faced successfully, man had first to master and discipline himself.

Hillary spoke of this when he descended from the peak of Everest. "Have we vanquished an enemy?" he said; and then answered, "None but ourselves." As humans, we want to master ourselves, to squeeze the greatest possible achievement out of our *selves*. We do this best when we face some difficult challenge, and most of us, at some time or another, feel the need, the call, to face some stirring challenge. Most of us cannot hope to scale Everest or go to the moon, but position rifle shooting lies easily within reach. The hobbyist can find a pleasant challenge in simply keeping his score up to par by only weekend practice. The more dedicated shooter will find a challenge in trying to win a local or regional match. The aspiring champion will find that breaking a world's record can provide an individual with just as much of a personal challenge, if not more, than was faced by any one man on the teams that assaulted Everest or walked on the moon. Shooting allows a person to aim for any degree of self-mastery. No matter how fine a score a rifleman has achieved, no matter how much self-mastery he has wrought, the possibility of a greater challenge is always there.

–/–

PSYCHOLOGY

THE CHAMPION'S SECRET WEAPON

It may seem strange to begin a "how-to" book with a discussion of psychology. The usual expectation is that a book such as this will begin with a discussion of fundamental physical skills. Yet it is just because of that expectation that we begin the book this way, hoping thereby to emphasize the importance of the role of psychology in successful shooting. The overwhelming importance of psychology has unfortunately long been overlooked except by the few very best shooters in the world. For years, the emphasis among the majority of coaches and shooters has been on position, and usually (and erroneously) on the position used by the then-current champion. The refrain has been, "If you change your position to look like X's position, you will then be able to win the match." If this advice proved true, it was only because of extremely good luck, not coaching or analytical skill. Of course, we do not deny the importance of good shooting positions; they are absolutely essential. But a position is to the act of shooting what the skeleton is to the living body—a mere physical support. Before a position can begin to function purposefully, it must be fleshed out by developed motor skills; and then it must be given consciousness and a life center by a developed psychology. Psychology, as will be seen, is utterly fundamental; it is the key to building a position, developing physical skill, and putting the whole complex to work to shoot a winning score. It is the very foundation of a good training program. Psychology is, in effect, the all-important "secret weapon" that enables champion shooters to reach and sustain the high levels of performance that make them champions.

The attention a rifleman gives respectively to equipment, positions, and psychology changes considerably during the course of his development from a beginner to a champion. A beginner is primarily concerned with finding basic positions and adjusting his equipment to fit the positions. After equipment is properly adjusted, it should cease to be a concern except insofar as it is properly maintained, and small refinements are made to improve the conformation of the rifle and its accessories to the shooter's position. The overriding concern with positions that characterizes the beginner diminishes as the shooter develops, until positions receive about 20 to 25 percent of his attention. As equipment and positions are more or less stabilized, the percentage of attention given to psychology by a well-developed shooter increases steadily to something like 70 percent; but a rifleman in the final stages of preparation for high-level competition, such as an Olympic match, may devote as much as 95 percent of his attention to developing a proper psychological state.

This section of the book will be divided into four chapters. The first will deal with concentration, the second with mental discipline, the third with match pressure, and the fourth with confidence and the will to win. The other area where the intellect plays an important role—analyzing and perfecting shooting positions—will be dealt with in a later chapter.

CHAPTER
1

Concentration

THE ROLE OF CONCENTRATION

Correct concentration during a shooting performance is absolutely crucial. Without it, even the best of shooting positions is of limited value. The first and most essential characteristic of concentration is that it be on performance. It must be focused on controlling the body and releasing the shot. It must not be on the score you might or might not get, or on the other competitor who might win, or on anything else that is not directly related to your own performance. Second, the entire mental process must be positive. The mind should be directing the body in what it should do. It should not be concerned with the negative side of performance, with thinking about what you should *not* do. In a word, concentration should be on *performance*, and it should be *positive.*

Perhaps an example would be the best way of illustrating these principles. Let's imagine two shooters, both of whom are halfway through the standing course in an important match. They are of equal physical ability. Both have just had their last shots drift out into the 7-ring at three o'clock. The first shooter is rattled by this loss of points and its possible effect on the outcome of the match. He begins to compute the number of

10's that he must pick up above his average in order to recoup this loss. With score still in his mind, he takes aim, thinking to himself, "I cannot afford to shoot another 7." Flustered by the fear of another mishap, he attempts to rush the trigger the instant the rifle moves into the 10-ring, and as a result upsets the hold and changes the angle of recoil. The consequence is another shot into the 7-ring.

Now the other shooter has learned the value of positive concentration on performance. When his last shot drifted into the 7-ring, he immediately began analyzing his performance. He recalled that he had slightly moved his foot before putting the rifle into place, and probably moved his natural area of aim somewhat to the right. He moved his foot the fraction of an inch back to its original placement, reloaded, and tested his position. It felt right, and the aim seemed to center naturally in the 10-ring. He concentrated on sight picture and hold long enough to judge both as satisfactory, then carefully released the shot, shifting his concentration to maintaining follow-through. The result was a shot dead in the center of the bull.

The important differences between the two shooters would not be apparent to an observer, for the differences are entirely mental. But these unobservable differences determine who will win a match. The first shooter thought about his score; the second thought about his performance. The first shooter allowed negative thoughts ("I cannot afford to shoot another 7") to enter his mind; the second was entirely positive in his approach to performance. Both riflemen have equal physical ability, but the first will lose the match, the second will win. He will win because he has developed the ability to concentrate exclusively on the positive aspects of performance and forget about score altogether. He knows that if he minds his performance, his score will take care of itself. The hidden, unobservable ability to concentrate is one of the most important "secrets" of the champion shooter.

The obvious question, of course, is *how* does one concentrate on performance? What does one "think about" while releasing the shot? Well, to answer that, we go back to the four primary principles of sight picture, hold, trigger pull, and follow-through. All of these, it must be noted, are results of, or products of, the shooter's control of his body. Sight picture is an indicator of "where" he must position his body. Hold is judged on feedback from the body which indicates "how long" he can maintain the position. Trigger pull involves releasing the shot without disturbing the "where" of the body during the time-frame of the hold's durability. Follow-through means maintaining the hold as fully as possible through the completion of recoil. In the most general terms, then, *concentration on performance is concentration on body control.*

But in actual practice, body control is not attained by concentration on any one particular muscle group. When the mind and body are performing at their best, shooters report that a kind of generalized concentration seems to be all that is necessary for peak performance. The mind seems to be concentrating on no particular part of the shooting process, a kind of rhythm develops, and performance appears to materialize with perfect ease and naturalness. When this happens, the shooter gets hot, in rifle range slang, and he is able to do everything right without undue effort.

These times are infrequent, however, and usually shooters report that they have to concentrate on some particular muscle group which is creating difficulty—the muscles which control the forward arm, for example, or the neck, or the shoulder, or a leg, or occasionally even the muscles in one of the feet. The focus of concentration is on the "trouble area" where extra effort is needed to hold the muscle motionless. At other times, the focus of concentration will shift to trigger pull, where it is almost always placed in the very stable prone position, or to some other component of the shooting process. However, the area of the body where concentration is focused may begin functioning satisfactorily, and concentration may have to be shifted to some other trouble area. In short, there is no one specific way to concentrate properly. Shooters find themselves changing the point of concentration several times during the course of fire in a single position. This is necessary and proper, as long as concentration remains on performance and is placed on the part of the body that is causing the greatest amount of difficulty.

One note here about a technique that may work for some people: a few shooters report that they select and concentrate on one area of the body even if there are no particular problems developing during their shooting. One excellent shooter concentrates on the muscles of the neck and shoulder adjacent to the gun stock. Another concentrates on cheek pressure. Having one thing to concentrate on helps them to keep their minds from wandering away from performance to other, unwanted thoughts. A similar technique may work for you.

LEARNING TO CONCENTRATE CORRECTLY

Proper concentration during shooting must be learned. We know of no one who has proved an exception to this rule, and it can be stated with reasonable certainty as a universal principle. How, then, does one learn to concentrate correctly, without experiencing stray thoughts? We must recognize first that mental control can be achieved only by effort. There are no short cuts. We cannot memorize a chart or a list of words, nor read a book, nor listen to a pep talk, and thereby acquire the ability to concentrate. All of the things just named are external, for they originate outside the mind. Mental control and concentration can come only from *inside* the consciousness, and must be developed there by training and effort. When we outline below a method for learning to concentrate, it should be regarded as simply that—a method. It might be described as a framework within which you can make the effort to concentrate properly, and you will achieve full concentration *only* with effort and with time. In fact, no matter how well you master the ability to concentrate, you will find that there is always room for improvement. If and when you master concentration sufficiently to fire a score of 1200 in international three-position competition (which has not yet been done, but probably some day will be), the course of fire will probably be changed and made more difficult. So there's no reason to fear that over-mastery of concentration will take the fun or the challenge out of shooting!

The following method of learning to concentrate has proved quite successful. It involves learning (or teaching) concentration in two phases. The first phase centers on the shooter's learning to describe verbally what physiological psychologists call the "internal environment"—the condition of the body and of consciousness—at the moment of firing the shot. The second phase involves learning to expand the frame of concentration to include follow-through. Let's examine each of these phases in turn.

It was said earlier that while concentrating on performance a shooter's "thinking" may not be verbal at all. It is more likely to be engaged in a nonverbal kind of sensing of the body, the sight picture, the wind, and the trigger finger. There are many kinds of evidence and a number of reasons to support this argument, but perhaps the most compelling is the one that follows. When a new shooter is brought into a training program, he is normally made to work exclusively on developing a good basic position. When his position becomes reasonably stable, the next step is to start him working on his concentration, and he is instructed to give his whole effort to this purpose. During successive training sessions, the coach will periodically walk quietly and unobserved up behind him, after he has fired a few shots, and ask him what he was concentrating on during the last shot. Almost invariably the shooter will be unable to describe what he was concentrating on. He will either say that he doesn't know, or will struggle to describe his internal environment but will be unable to do so. It will usually take four or five days of such activity, with the coach at unexpected intervals questioning the shooter, before he will be able to say what he was concentrating on. No doubt this phenomenon arises out of the difficulty of translating the nonverbal mental activities during shooting into verbal terms.

With repeated effort, however, the shooter will learn—usually very rapidly, once the process begins—to describe his internal environment quite accurately. He will be able to say, for example, that his point of concentration was on the sight picture, or on his right shoulder, or on the trigger, or on some other constituent of shooting; and he will as well be able to describe various sensations arising from his body, such as a tightening of a particular muscle group just before the shot was released.

Incidentally, a phenomenon that usually appears at some time during this process—and for that matter at any time during a shooter's career—is that he begins to concentrate on concentrating. It is always accompanied by a significant drop in performance. The shooter will be preparing to release the shot, and instead of concentrating on control of his body, he will be verbally thinking something like, "I've got to concentrate, I've got to concentrate." All shooters experience this at one time or another, and it can be difficult to shake oneself free of it. A good way to escape from it is immediately to take a short break from shooting, get out of position and walk around, and then come back to the position with a keen attention to details of the position and its "feel." Experienced riflemen usually have developed so well the ability to concentrate on performance that they can quickly overcome this phenomenon whenever it occurs.

Learning to describe verbally one's internal environment during shooting has several advantages. The most obvious is that it gives the shooter a means of being *aware* of his concentration. He can think about it verbally, and it thus enters fully into his consciousness for the first time. This in turn facilitates analysis of his shooting performance. If he is *aware* that he was concentrating on the trigger, but that the hold was disturbed in the last second by a tightening of a back muscle, then he will be able to focus his concentration next time on the real source of his difficulties—his back muscle. Still another advantage is that using this technique also appears to instill the ability to concentrate more deeply and completely. Why or how this works is unknown, but new shooters who have gone through this type of training procedure report—and exhibit—an ability to concentrate that they never knew was possible before the training.

We might note that a coach is necessary for the use of the technique described above. A fellow shooter or a close friend may act in the capacity of coach, for the primary function of the coach in this particular phase of training is merely to provide a sounding board against which the shooter can verbalize his sensations. But actually no one need be present except the shooter himself if he will form the habit of analyzing his performance by either talking aloud or writing down his sensations in complete sentences. This may seem unnecessary, for it is easy to say, "Why not just think through the performance silently to myself?" This technique has been tried in training programs and has been found to be generally unsuccessful. Apparently, only by externalizing—by talking aloud or by writing down his thoughts—is a shooter forced into verbalizing his sensations completely. Only complete, clear verbalization will effectively accomplish the desired end of forcing him into achieving full awareness of his sensations. When the technique of verbal analysis has been mastered, the shooter can then safely resort to thinking through each shot silently to himself. This, of course, is what champion shooters always do. This constant, continuing analysis of performance is another of the hidden "secrets" of championship shooting.

Concentration is not learned completely, however, until it embraces not only the moment of trigger pull, but also every detail of follow-through. After the rifleman has thoroughly mastered the ability to analyze verbally his performance up to the moment of release, he should then acquire the habit of extending his concentration through the completion of recoil. This is the second phase of learning to concentrate, and the training technique is exactly the same. The shooter must learn to describe *verbally* every aspect of the shooting process up to the completion of recoil. Again the results are the same. He becomes *aware* of follow-through, and can thus analyze performance with an eye to bringing about improvements. He may, for example, discover that the angle of recoil seems to vary widely from shot to shot, indicating perhaps a changing cheek pressure against the stock, or possibly a changing position of the stock against the shoulder, or possibly trouble with the forward arm support. These important details go unnoticed by shooters who have not learned to concentrate properly to the completion of follow-through, and who continue to wonder why their scores don't improve. Verbalizing all aspects of follow-through is absolutely essential to analyzing performance and correcting "hidden" problems. Its importance cannot be over-emphasized.

The test of effective mental follow-through is the ability to *call the shot.* A shooter who is effectively following through his performance should be able to call the shot—for example, "8 at three o'clock"—on the basis of sight picture and recoil only, within one scoring ring on the target and one hour on the clock. He will, of course, confirm his call by looking through the spotting scope. If he is unable to make accurate calls fairly consistently, then his concentration during follow-through is inadequate (providing, of course, that his rifle tests out to be accurate).

CHAPTER
2

Mental Discipline

MENTAL DISCIPLINE DEFINED

As we have seen in the previous chapter, no one way of concentrating is exclusively correct, because there is no single area of the body which should always be the focus of concentration. Therefore, we define mental discipline as *the ability to duplicate a successful performance.* Obviously, the application of mental discipline, as we use the term, assumes that the rifleman has already developed a reasonably successful position, as well as the ability to concentrate properly, during at least some of his shots. He has done so, in a limited sense, when his position first yields a shot into the 10-ring, not by luck but by his own conscious, deliberate control of the shooting process. Mental discipline is the ability to duplicate that perfectly controlled shot repeatedly, under competitive conditions.

At one level, mental discipline is the ability to concentrate solely upon performance to the exclusion of everything else. At a deeper level, it is the ability to think positively about, and thereby *control*, every step of the shooting process. At its deepest level, mental discipline goes far beyond concentration. It is the deep-seated feeling of confidence that one can, without doubt, duplicate or exceed one's best previous performance. It is an inner sense of certainty about one's ability to execute properly a series of shots; ultimately, it is an absolute, unquestioning belief in one's ability to win.

We believe—on very good evidence—that mental discipline is the final key to the inner circle of championship shooting. Like a shooting position, mental discipline is learned. A beginning shooter who is still working on mastering fundamentals should not be concerned with it. Only after the fundamentals of positions have been mastered does mental discipline begin to play an active role in the training process. But from then on, like the positions, it must be continuously refined, rehearsed, and relearned until it becomes literally a way of life.

WHAT MENTAL DISCIPLINE IS NOT

Mental discipline is often equated with such things as morality, patriotism, honor, and team spirit. Actually it is independent of all of these things. Conceivably, a shooter could be a criminal, or a traitor to his country or team, and still have the mental discipline to be a champion. This is not to say, of course, that a shooter cannot derive inspiration from his religion, country, family, or team. Such is entirely possible, and certainly desirable. Shooters who have set world records have said that the feeling of representing a certain team or a certain country gave them an added inspiration and desire to win. But primarily, inspiration comes from within the individual. A shooter's basic inspiration is simply the appetite to win; he is hungry for another victory; he wants to defeat the competition. He has come of age when he no longer worries about the other competitors on the range, but is after a new record score.

Nevertheless, what we have just described is not mental discipline. No matter how inspired a person may be by the desire to be a champion, he can never become one unless he has mental discipline. And the man who has the best mental discipline, other things being equal, is the man who will win. He is the man who has prepared himself to win by conscientiously training himself to shoot a winning score; and he goes onto the range confident that he can walk away with that score duly entered at the top of the winners' list. Inspiration, or desire to win, will be the driving force that propels him to the winner's circle; but mental discipline is the only road that will take him there.

THE PURPOSE OF MENTAL DISCIPLINE

The whole purpose of mental discipline is to enable a rifleman to reproduce or exceed, under competitive conditions, his best previous performance. Mental discipline is acquired during training, but is aimed at enabling the shooter to perform at peak ability during a match. Later we will talk about why and how match pressure affects a competitor. But at this point it is necessary to establish the basic premise which paves the way for the acceptance of the necessity of mental discipline. It is this: there is nothing legal or sportsmanlike a shooter can do to affect the scores of his opponents.

In most team sports certain defensive measures are possible which are designed to offset the opponent's offensive measures—shifting the position of the players, for example, or capitalizing upon an opponent's weakness. But in shooting, there are absolutely no defensive measures possible. Worrying about the opponent's score, or wondering what new techniques he is using, cannot possibly affect his performance, and can only result in a loss of points in one's own score. Therefore, the whole strategy must be to defeat the opponent by a superior offense. The offense consists solely of positive performance. Hence, a rifleman should develop the ability to concentrate fully and deeply on his own performance, without letting *anything* else enter his mind. To do this requires concentration that is both full and continuous.

THE KEY TO MENTAL DISCIPLINE: ATTENTION SPAN

The ability to duplicate a successful performance in competition requires continual concentration. And the ability to concentrate continually under match conditions is not inborn—it must be learned. The key to understanding continual concentration is the concept of *attention span.* Attention span is the length of time that one can devote attention exclusively to one subject. Young children have very short attention spans. This can be tested by trying to talk to a five-year-old about some subject, such as his favorite toy or cartoon character. Most five-year-olds are able to talk about one subject for only a few seconds, and then their attention and conversation will shift to another topic. A mature adult has a considerably longer attention span. But unless he has lengthened his "natural" attention span through training, he will probably not have enough mental endurance to last out a complete shooting match without some loss of concentration. Mental endurance, like physical endurance, is built up through training. If a person's physical training consisted of shooting only five shots in each position, he would naturally expect to be fatigued and shaky if he suddenly shot a complete match of forty shots in each position. The same would be true of his mental condition: his concentration would also be fatigued and "shaky" at the end of the course.

The procedure he should follow, then, is to lengthen his attention span through training, just as he strengthens his body through training. And the rule is this: he should train his attention span to exceed the requirements of a match. Later we will talk about how a person trains his body to shoot 140 shots so he can, in a match, shoot the required 120 shots without excessive fatigue. This gives him an extra edge, in physical performance and in confidence. A successful rifleman does the same with his attention span. He lengthens it so he can concentrate on performance for 140 shots. The result is increased mental performance and confidence.

DEVELOPING THE ATTENTION SPAN

To train the attention span, one begins by achieving perfect concentration during one single shot. He then attempts to duplicate physically *and* psychologically everything he did in that one performance. At first this will seem difficult. One may shoot two or three, or even twenty, shots before another perfect performance occurs. But with continued effort, deep concentration will be achieved more and more frequently. As improvement comes, the percentage of fully controlled shots will grow larger and larger. Ideally, of course, the percentage should be 100. But success does not come instantaneously; the position will probably need to be refined, and physical endurance increased, as the shooter goes along, to increase steadiness and durability.

But aside from these physical considerations, the attention span itself must be lengthened to permit the repeated efforts of concentration needed to shoot a perfect string of shots. It is a simple fact that each act of concentration requires effort, and at first the repeated effort involved in shooting a whole course will deplete mental endurance. Concentration will weaken, and eventually will be unattainable in a given training session if the individual exhausts himself psychologically, even though physically he may feel quite strong.

One of the most valuable training procedures to keep in mind is that a rifleman should not prolong training if he has exhausted his ability to concentrate. The reason is quite simple: If he has lost the ability to concentrate, he has lost effective control of his performance. If he continues to repeat a poor performance, some of the mistakes may become ingrained physical habits, difficult to detect or break, which may set back his training program. One can overtrain in a single session, but also over the long haul by having too many training sessions in close succession. Overtraining is indicated by a lack of interest, inability to concentrate, and the feeling often described as "being stale."

Everyone needs, of course, to push himself, both physically and psychologically, if he is to gain increased endurance. But he should be moderate, and use judgment. No one should ever push himself so far that a training session becomes merely an endless repetition of a poor performance. As a rule of thumb, never fire more than ten shots beyond the point where you lose the ability to concentrate effectively.

THE CONCENTRATION CURVE

If we were to evaluate realistically the performance of the best shooters, we would judge that they achieve full, deep concentration on about thirty-five out of every forty shots. This does not mean that full concentration cannot be achieved on forty out of forty shots—it simply means that no one is at present doing so. Perhaps some future champion will. But we find that there is a general pattern, a curve in the concentration during the shooting string (particularly during a match), and a knowledge of it will help in evaluating and understanding one's own performance.

Generally, concentration is weakest at the beginning and end of each position course. This is quite easy to understand. When a rifleman begins to fire for record, he is entering a new situation and is naturally somewhat uncertain and anxious. If his first two or three shots go well, he then begins to gain confidence and settle into complete, full concentration. Toward the end of the course, either or both of two things may occur. One is that he may begin to tire from the repeated effort of shooting, and concentration becomes less deep. The other, which usually occurs only during a match, is that he begins to get anxious again from the fear of "losing" a good score by firing a bad shot. This fear arises quite naturally, but it can and should be overcome. The difference between many shooters of equal ability is that this fear barely alters the performance of a shooter with strong mental discipline, while it may seriously affect a shooter with weak mental discipline. One has been disturbed by what all shooters everywhere know as "match pressure," and the other has not.

CHAPTER
3

Match Pressure

MATCH PRESSURE DEFINED

Match pressure is a state of nervous excitement. Everybody feels match pressure by the time he enters his second match, and usually when he enters his first. It is normal and natural. If uncontrolled, it can ruin a shooter's performance; if controlled, it can actually be used to increase the level of performance. Certain shooters who know how to channel it properly use it to push themselves past all previous performances they have achieved in training sessions. And that use of it can be learned by almost anyone willing to make the effort. There are no means to create instant success with regard to match pressure. However, if it can be understood and accepted, it can be controlled by the application of a proper training program. The "secret" lies in, and only in, mental discipline acquired through continued training.

Match pressure can be described as having two phases. Phase I is simply physiological fear which stimulates and excites the nervous system. This leads, among other things, to heightened sensory perception and increased awareness of the environment. Phase II begins when elements of the environment, irrelevant to the shooting process, begin to interrupt concentration. Movements outside the target area, which normally a shooter would not see, become distractions. Sounds, which normally he would not hear, interrupt concentration. He becomes aware, suddenly, of the people on the range, and may feel that they are all watching him. His sense of touch becomes more sensitive, and he becomes conscious of every move he makes, and may begin to feel awkward. The effects of Phase II can then start a heightening of Phase I—as he begins to doubt his ability to concentrate, his fear increases. As a result of increased fear, the effects are relayed back to Phase II: his awareness of the environment becomes even more heightened. A spiraling effect is thus set up, with Phase I and Phase II interacting and compounding their effects, until soon the rifleman has lost completely the ability to concentrate.

Of these two phases, the first, fear, is to some extent probably inevitable. The heightened sensory perception resulting from this excitation, however, can be used to positive advantage. The second phase, distraction by the environment, can only be harmful. It can be controlled, however, by mental discipline.

The first phase, as noted, is simple fear. Fear can be defined as a physiological reaction to a threatening situation. It is a part of our survival equipment, and was probably developed far back in time by our evolutionary ancestors. Almost all living organisms display fear. It is sometimes called the "fight-or-flight reaction." Faced with a threat, the body reacts automatically to prepare itself to cope with the threat, either by fighting it, or by fleeing from it. Either alternative will require a form of physical exertion. Consequently, the body prepares for action. The adrenal glands quickly release an increased flow of adrenalin, which speeds up certain of the bodily processes; the liver rapidly releases sugar into the blood, to supply energy; the pulse and breathing rates speed up, in anticipation of the increased supply of oxygen the body will need; the involuntary muscles of the intestinal tract slow down and become tense, releasing a larger amount of blood to flow to the voluntary muscles; the entire nervous system becomes excited, accelerating the speed of commands to the voluntary muscles, heightening the senses of sight, hearing, taste, touch, and smell, and speeding up the thought processes. As a result of increased blood flow, the armpits and the palms of the hands may begin to perspire. In extreme instances, fear can become so great that additional symptoms occur: profuse sweating over the entire body, uncontrollable tremors in the muscles, loss of control of the bowels and bladder, fainting, and, in the most severe occurrences, cardiac arrest. These extreme symptoms will normally appear, however, only in cases of the most unusual fear, and we hope that none of our readers ever experience match pressure to *that* degree!

SOME COMMON CAUSES OF MATCH PRESSURE

Because it is a built-in physiolgical response, fear occurs automatically whenever we face a threatening situation. Now, we might note that the fear-basis of match pressure can sometimes more accurately be called *anxiety.* Anxiety is generalized fear. Fear is a reaction to a specific threat; anxiety is a reaction to an unspecified, generalized threat. A person standing in the jungle looking into the eyes of a hungry lion experiences fear. A person standing in the jungle who can see no specific danger, but is afraid that *something* harmful might happen to him, experiences anxiety. Both fear and anxiety produce essentially the same physiological reactions. Match pressure with many people is probably not the fear that one specific thing threatens them, but rather that *something* may threaten performance. It is an unknown, unspecified something which may occur.

Anxiety is probably involved to some extent in everyone's experience of match pressure. But there are common sources of match pressure, whether it is experienced as fear or as anxiety. An identification of some of these sources might prove useful. For a beginner, it is usually the fear of coming in last. For the intermediate, it may be either the fear of turning in an exceptionally bad performance, or the fear of turning in an exceptionally good performance. For the advanced shooter, it may be the fear of not getting the few points that mean the difference between winning and coming in second.

The beginner is usually fearful of being disgraced before his contemporaries. No one wants to come in last, to have the lowest score. It might be helpful for a beginner to recognize, however, that only his best friends are likely to pay much attention to his score, and they will not reject him for a single poor performance. If they are beginners too, they are merely thankful that *they* didn't come in last, and are likely to let the matter drop, lest the tables be turned the next time.

The intermediate faces a somewhat different problem. He has attained a certain level of ability, and is expected to shoot a certain score. If he falls too far below that score, he is going to feel disgraced; and by the same token, if he shoots too far *above* that score, and perhaps wins, he may face a different kind of disgrace: his winning will be called luck, and he is likely to fear that he will be unable to repeat the performance, and everyone will *know* it was luck.

There are two observations to be made about this fear. First, large numbers of matches are won each year by dark horses who come out of nowhere to win. Is it entirely luck? Perhaps some luck is involved, but more than likely it is the luck of getting hot on a particular day. This happens to all shooters, with any amount of experience. On certain days, you just cannot do anything wrong. When this happens, you are performing at the peak of your ability. You have integrated every constituent of the shooting process and it is all working for you. It is luck only in the sense that you happened to get all the things working smoothly on the day of the match. But it is a performance within the limits of your ability.

The second observation is that frequently these dark horses continue to perform at the same level. Not always, of course, and maybe not for two or three, or even more, matches; but large jumps in the level of performance during a match often reveal a heretofore unrealized potential, and frequently instill the confidence and desire necessary to maintain a new, higher level of performance. If you are an intermediate in a match, and suddenly find yourself getting hot, try to realize that this new level of performance actually *is* within the limits of your ability. The experience may well be the best thing that could happen to you in terms of your future performances. This success story has happened to many others in the past; now let it happen to you.

The advanced shooter faces a different kind of fear. He probably knows the score he will need to win, and he probably knows that he can win if he just doesn't make a mistake. His is probably more anxiety than fear. He doesn't know *what* he might do wrong, he just knows that he might do *something* wrong. The danger he faces, as will be discussed below, is, more than anything else, thinking of the mistakes he *might* make. If he thinks about them enough, he's sure to make one of them.

CONTROLLING MATCH PRESSURE: MENTAL DISCIPLINE

The question now is how to control the fear and anxiety one experiences during a match. The first step is to realize that fear is a natural, involuntary reaction, and to accept its existence. Of course, this is not easy. Fear itself can be frightening. But it becomes less and less frightening the more one becomes familiar with it. For this reason, a rifleman should subject himself to match pressure as often as he reasonably can.

We say repeatedly in this book that everyone who wishes to become a champion should enter a minimum of twelve matches each year. By repeated exposure to match pressure, a shooter learns—usually at a gradual rate—to accept it, and not to be frightened by the pressure itself. And he can help himself accept it by remembering this simple fact: *everyone else is also experiencing match pressure*. If he takes a close look up and down the firing line, he'll see that no one is free from the pressure. One shooter we know begins every match by looking up and down the line and saying to himself, "Well, I'm the best here; and if I feel pressure, think what everyone else must be feeling." He's a pretty consistent winner.

The second step is to learn to use match pressure. An individual is probably going to experience it whenever he encounters real competition, and the fact is that he does not want to be without it. It is, in reality, a positive advantage. Because of the nervous excitation, he tends to focus his eyes a little more sharply; he can feel the trigger a little better; his sense of touch is more sensitive to the wind, and he is more sensitive to the state of the muscles in his body. These are all positive things that can enable him to turn out a better performance than he can in a routine training session where his senses are all slightly duller.

Now the second phase of match pressure becomes important at this point. The rifleman may say, "All right, my senses are heightened. But that will cause me to be subject to distractions. What can I do about that?" The answer is that he must exercise mental discipline. It's an answer that may not give much comfort. Mental discipline is difficult. *But there is no way to deal with match pressure except through mental discipline.* And the only way to acquire mental discipline is through training, training, training.

A person learns to exercise mental discipline by first learning to concentrate properly on fundamentals, and then by lengthening his attention span until he can concentrate throughout an entire match-length shooting course. The final stage of developing mental discipline is the utilization of matches as training vehicles. One reason for this is that anyone needs to acclimatize himself to the pressures of match conditions in order to learn to concentrate under those conditions. The only way to achieve this goal is to enter matches. He should enter an average of about one a month. He should select one match in which he intends to "shoot for record"—to go all out for the best score he can attain—and he should regard all the other matches as merely training vehicles, as learning situations in which he prepares himself for the "big one," even if the "big one" is only a small local match.

In the other matches he does not go all out to win—he may win, but that is only incidental. He is shooting the match primarily to familiarize himself with performing under match conditions. In these training matches, he should not be afraid to experiment with techniques to improve performance under pressure. He may experiment with methods of setting up and organizing equipment for better efficiency. Time thus saved is not only valuable in itself, but creates confidence in the ability to perform efficiently. He may work out a routine that enables him to develop a rhythm in his shooting. Above all, he should work on concentrating exclusively on performance when he picks up the rifle to shoot for score. He should build mental discipline by *making the effort* to concentrate under pressure. Gradually, as he shoots more and more matches, he *will* acquire the ability to discipline his mental activities. The essential ingredients are repeated exposure to pressure, repeated effort, and time. Success will not come instantly, but it will come.

One important principle is worth repeating: *Every thought and every action must be positive.* This may require considerable practice, as negative thoughts are natural under pressure. However, an entirely positive approach to shooting can be developed if it is cultivated and rehearsed until it becomes an ingrained habit of mind. The reason for a positive approach is clear: if a person is concentrating on positive control of his performance, he *is* controlling it; if he is thinking negatively about controlling his performance, he is *not* controlling it. The shooter who is concentrating on executing a smooth trigger pull is, if his concentration is deep enough, doing just that—executing a smooth trigger pull. The shooter who is thinking "I must not move my shoulder when I pull the trigger" is likely to do just that—move his shoulder. That is why an advanced shooter, experiencing anxiety over losing a point or two, must not think of the mistake he *might* make. The relationship between thought and performance might almost be stated as an equation: positive thoughts equal positive performance; negative thoughts equal negative performance.

CONTROLLING MATCH PRESSURE: SOME PRACTICAL TIPS

In the following pages we will try to pass on some bits of practical advice for coping with match pressure. These are some of the best techniques we have seen, but are by no means the only ones. They have, however, been used satisfactorily by a number of successful shooters.

Before the match: keeping occupied.

The earliest symptom of match pressure is pre-match tension—the "nerves," the "butterflies in the stomach," or the "stage fright" that anyone is likely to feel with the approach of an important match. This feeling, too, is quite normal and natural, and indeed is nothing more than anticipation of the pressure of the match itself. Some simple, practical techniques can help dispel this anticipatory tension. The most commonly used method is the ordinary device of keeping one's mind occupied with something other than the coming match. There are probably an infinite number of ways of doing this, and each person can discover a method that works well for him. Some shooters play cards or checkers or horseshoes or some other game that is not physically fatiguing. Others like to sit around and talk about topics related to the match. Still others like to shop for new equipment at the local displays. Almost anything that will keep the mind occupied will serve this function.

Some shooters have worked out routines of psychological preparation that they follow just before going onto the firing line. The most commonly used technique involves deep breathing and a conscious effort toward physical relaxation. Some like to stand, with eyes closed, and, breathing deeply and rhythmically, prepare themselves to concentrate solely on performance. Others do the same thing while sitting, or while lying stretched out prone. Some do not follow the deep-breathing routine, but simply sit or lie quietly, eyes closed, and prepare themselves to concentrate. Still others like to sit or lie still and concentrate on relaxing, in turn, every muscle in their bodies, and then, when they have achieved complete relaxation, maintain that internal state for several minutes or longer. These are simply additional ways of keeping the mind occupied with something other than the approaching match.

You may find that one of these devices will work for you—or perhaps some other technique which you develop yourself will be more satisfactory. Which technique you use is unimportant—what's important is whether the technique works for you.

There is one other technique for controlling pre-match tension that is used by a small minority of shooters. It is the technique commonly known as "going within oneself." It is usually accomplished by the individual's getting off by himself and going into a period of deep concentration. It is a technique used by athletes in a number of sports, and is not quite as unusual as it sounds. While it sometimes appears to be a form of self-hypnosis, it probably is not, at least as we normally understand the term. The individuals who practice this method apparently possess such complete control of their mental processes that they can, in their imaginations, "live through" a performance of the coming event. They are going through, in their minds, the individual steps of the performance they wish to turn in. They are, in brief, planning their performance and are totally absorbed in this imaginative process. It would seem that this technique works for only a few individuals, though no one can say with certainty that all normal people aren't capable of using it. If it does work for you, it would seem to be as good as any other technique for handling the pressure of competition that occurs prior to a match.

Some possibilities—and some reservations.

Over the centuries there have been a number of techniques developed for attaining inner calm. The best-known ones are quite old, and include Christian mysticism, Zen, and yoga. Christian spiritual exercises include those of St. John of the Cross and of St. Ignatius Loyola. These are rigorous mental and spiritual exercises designed to free the mind from worldly concerns. Zen and yoga exercises are similar in intent, but the forms of the exercises have proliferated into a number of varieties and are usually taught by individuals who have developed some variation of a basic technique. Zen would seem to be particularly adaptable to rifle shooting, for one form of it was specifically designed around exercises used in archery marksmanship.

Two things need to be emphasized here. One is that the usefulness of any of these exercises as a means of dealing with match pressure is at present unknown. The second point is that if they are useful, only a genuine, pure form of the exercises would probably be of any value. Today, there are classes on Zen and yoga being offered to the public in many major American and European cities. We are perhaps hardened cynics, but we suspect that many of the "teachers" of these subjects are self-proclaimed experts out to make a quick dollar. However, at the same time, we would not deny that the genuine forms of these spiritual or mental (and, in some cases, physical) exercises may have some value to the shooting world. At present there is little information on the subject.

Psychology, psychiatry, and psychoanalysis also offer potential help to shooters who need to develop confidence. Dramatic evidence of this possibility was found in the sudden increase in levels of performance by one shooting team in its preparation for the 1970 World Championships. From having only a small percentage of shooters placing anywhere near the top contenders, it was able to move a large number of shooters into top contention. This transformation appears to be primarily the result of the work of a psychologist who traveled with the shooters and successfully instilled in them confidence in themselves as competitors.

It is necessary to emphasize, however, that *no branch of psychological studies can impart instant confidence, nor enable a shooter to perform above the level of physical capability he has attained through training.* Neither psychologist nor psychiatrist nor psychoanalyst has any secret that will make one a better shooter. If a person lacks the confidence to perform well in a match, psychological counseling may be worthwhile. However, it is recommended only if lack of confidence is an impediment to performance at the full level of one's physical capabilities. Such help may also be useful to the person who has other emotional problems holding back his performance—an uncontrollable temper, for example, or a frustration tolerance so low that his first bad shot in a match causes him to want simply to give up. Psychological help is best sought on the advice of a competent counselor or physician.

During the match: techniques of concentration.

The way to control pressure during a match is to keep one's concentration wholly on performance. The best shooters generally follow one of two techniques to achieve this. One technique is to enter fully into concentration and stay there through the completion of a course of fire in one position. The shooters who do this enter into their concentration during the firing of sighter shots before they fire for record. From then on until the completion of the position course, they are completely sealed off in a psychological world all their own. They do not seem to hear the people near them or even to be aware of their existence. They are completely and exclusively absorbed in their own performance. Usually, though not always, these shooters do not try to maintain such a depth of concentration without a break beyond the firing of a single position course, as the mental effort required is likely to produce excessive fatigue. Between position courses, they take a break, walk around, and try to relax without letting go completely. This is the more demanding and difficult of the two methods of concentration.

Other shooters use a different technique of alternating between complete concentration and moments of diverting their attention to other things. While shooting for record, they will usually shoot two or three shots, and then, without getting out of position, turn their heads to take notice of what is going on behind the firing line. They may chat briefly with onlookers, or listen in on their conversations. When they have rested briefly, they then enter again into full concentration, and shut out of their consciousness anything but their own performance. They, too, will usually take a break between position courses, walk around, and try to relax without "letting go" psychologically.

The term "letting go" here refers to the complete *psychological* relaxation that occurs when a person feels that he is no longer required to make an effort. He "lets go" of the psychological tension necessary to make the effort. Training for a big match usually involves a long, continued effort devoted toward getting oneself physically and psychologically "up" for the big event. There is a common belief that training inevitably reaches a point of "peaking out," but the phenomenon of peaking out, at least among shooters, is most probably the result of the purely psychological experience of letting go and thereby losing the desire or will to make a further effort.

Once a shooter lets go completely, it may take him several days or weeks to get back up to a proper competitive psychological state. It is, therefore, completely to a shooter's disadvantage to allow himself to let go during a match. His concentration during the remainder of the match is very likely going to be seriously impaired. Whichever technique of concentration you use during a match—either continued concentration during a course, or concentration alternating with short periods of relaxation—it would be wise to avoid *total* relaxation. Relax *physically* by talking with bystanders or other competitors, if you desire. But don't relax psychologically. If you see another competitor who, during a break, is completely relaxed psychologically and is enjoying himself immensely by telling jokes and reliving the completed portion of his performance, be glad—you've got him beat. He's not going to be able to concentrate effectively when he starts shooting again.

The planned mental routine.   One of the best techniques to keep yourself concentrating during a match is to plan a mental routine and then follow the plan during a match come hell or high water. Actually, this is your plan of mental discipline. This mental routine, of course, should be developed and rehearsed during training sessions, where it can be modified at any time as new ideas enter your mind for improving the routine. But during the match, stay with the routine you have planned. The routine should keep your mind completely occupied, and that, of course, is one of its values, for it eliminates stray thoughts that lead to match pressure.

The routine should be based upon alternating periods of *concentration* on performance and *analysis* of performance. You concentrate on performance while actually firing each shot. You analyze each performance after the completion of each shot. The routine you develop to perform your analysis should be suited to your own needs, but it should include a complete survey of internal environment during the shot, of recoil and follow-through, and of wind conditions and their effect (if wind is a factor). Establishing and following a mental sequence of analysis after each shot helps ensure that the analysis will be complete. The analysis, of course, will help improve performance by clarifying the problems that may be holding back performance, and by finding solutions to these problems. These solutions should involve no major changes in technique—only small adjustments to the position or the equipment, and identification of new areas of the body which should be the focus of concentration. A mental routine, in short, will help both to dispel match pressure and to keep one's physical performance at the highest possible level.

Shooting one-shot matches.　　Watching a major rifle event, anyone easily discovers that one of the open secrets of champion shooters is that they do not allow themselves to be emotionally shaken by a bad shot. The champions know that anyone is likely to drop one or two bad shots in the course of a match. How do they avoid worrying about the bad shot after it has occurred? One good method is to develop the habit of thinking of the shooting course in terms of one-shot matches. Think of it not as one match of 120 shots, but rather as 120 matches of one shot each. The person who thinks in these terms is more able to work on each individual shot as a single performance. This, obviously, is necessary to full concentration. The nature of competition being what it is, it is very likely that when you shoot a particularly bad shot, you will think of your opponent and *his* possible score. The fact that this thought enters your mind does not *necessarily* mean that you have lost your mental discipline. If you can think, "All right, he beat me on that shot, but I can beat him on this next one," you have a distinct advantage over the person who thinks, "That shot may have cost me the match." Thinking of the match in terms of 120 amalgamated shots tends to make one more sensitive to match pressure in the event of a bad shot; thinking in terms of 120 matches of one shot each keeps the way open for continued victories and makes possible confidence and positive concentration.

Keeping cool and hanging on.   Two other valuable attitudes to hold are, to keep cool under all circumstances, and never to give up. These are closely related. You keep cool by allowing nothing to affect you emotionally. You do not get even the slightest bit ruffled by poor range operation, by distractions on the range, by the behavior or comments of other shooters, by changing wind conditions, by a rainstorm, or by anything else. You are totally uninvolved in these things emotionally; your whole involvement is intellectual, and it can at any moment be confined totally to your performance. This attitude is learned through training directed at developing complete self-discipline; and so is the second, which is that you never give up, no matter what happens. The operation of the range may seem designed to frustrate you, the wind and rain may seem to make shooting impossible—but you hang on and don't give up. In fact, you consider adverse conditions to be your friends—they tend to make other people want to give up; and when they do, you've got them beat. Adverse conditions affect everybody. They will naturally affect your score. But even if your score is lowered, if you try harder than everyone else, their scores will be lowered more than yours. Keep cool, and keep trying. You can win a lot of matches that way.

Facing the tough competitor.   If you are facing a particularly tough competitor in a match, it is helpful to have confidence in two objective facts. One is your own training. If you have trained yourself to shoot a winning score, you should know that that training will serve you during the match, that you *can* shoot a winning score. Second, you can realize that your tough competitor is going to be defeated sometime. It is a certain fact that someday he will be beaten; and you may as well be the person to do it. You have trained yourself to beat him, and he can be beaten. Realizing these two things will go a long way toward freeing you from match pressure and enabling you to concentrate on performance, thereby turning in the score that will win.

Enjoying the match. Finally, learn to enjoy a match, and smile. The consistent winners at big matches appear, when they are on the firing line, to be enjoying themselves. And let's face it—they *are* enjoying themselves. They are enjoying the mastery of the skills they have acquired and are now putting into use in competition. Each is proving, not so much to other people as to himself, that he is his own master—master of his body, his intellect, his emotions. His is an intensely personal satisfaction that comes not from beating others (though that is a part of it), but from having achieved a real measure of self-discipline—of having beaten the dividing forces within himself. He knows that match pressure does not come from the match itself, but from forces inside the person who faces the challenge of the match—and he has beaten those forces.

The person who smiles and appears cheerful and confident on the rifle range is likely to put himself in a much better frame of mind to win. A smile makes you appear confident. It makes the other competitors sense your own confidence, and is likely to increase the pressure they are feeling. And a smile not only makes you *appear* confident, it actually helps to *make* you confident.

Every psychologist knows that an essential ingredient to personal happiness is liking oneself. A rifleman who has trained and mastered himself to the point of becoming a winner has earned his own self-respect, and likes himself better for it. The same would be true to some degree, of course, in any area of accomplishment, but it is particularly true in the very challenging area of high-level rifle competition. Because he has proved himself, a champion shooter feels no need to be loud, bragging, or rude; rather, his behavior is usually quietly self-assured, yet he is courteous to everyone. He has proved to himself what everyone who wishes to be an adult must prove—that he can face a challenge and meet it. So if you can train yourself to meet the challenge of shooting—at any level you choose—go ahead and smile. It will express the personal confidence you feel deep down inside. It is the smile of success.

DRUGS AND MATCH PRESSURE

It's no secret that we have become a world of drug users. Drugs are available in such a bewildering variety of forms, over the counter and by prescription, are advertised so heavily, and have become so commonplace in our lives, that we have all developed the thought pattern of dealing with aches and pains and problems by "taking a pill." It is generally recognized that the situation is a largely unhealthy one that has rendered a great percentage of the world's population psychologically dependent on drugs of one variety or another. Many medicinal drugs, properly used, have been tremendously beneficial to the health and well-being of mankind. But we can say here with utter certainty that *drugs cannot and should not be used to control match pressure.* We bring up this subject because there is a widespread belief that psychoactive drugs can help control match pressure.

Generally speaking, psychoactive drugs fall into four categories. One category includes the various tranquilizers, which work upon the nervous system to produce muscular relaxation and "peace of mind." While these effects alone would be desirable under the pressure of competition, tranquilizers also cause a drop in alertness and impair the ability to concentrate— effects which cancel out the gains made by their calming effect, as sharp concentration is absolutely essential to good performance. Another category of psychoactive drugs includes all the activators, also called energizers, stimulants, or "pep pills." Activators produce the opposite effect from tranquilizers, causing a rise in alertness and short-term concentration, which is in itself desirable, but they also cause a very undesirable increase in muscular tension, some loss in fine motor coordination, and, possibly, muscle tremors.

The other two categories of psychoactive drugs are sedatives, which produce sleep, and psychotomimetic substances, which produce hallucinations and other symptoms of mental derangement. The undesirability of both of these classes of drugs on a rifle range does not need to be stated. In short, psychoactive drugs as they are now understood have no value on a rifle range, and from a practical standpoint their use would be illogical and self-defeating.

Alcohol needs specific mention because it is easily available and widely used as a means of relaxation in times of stress and tension. Its physiological and psychological effects are almost wholly detrimental to shooting performance. Alcohol speeds up the heart rate, causes deterioration in motor coordination (including the muscles which control eye movements), and seriously impairs judgment. In intoxicating quantities, alcohol taken the night before a match can cause the well-known hangover "nerves" frequently accompanied by muscle tremors. Alcohol taken just before a match, aside from its adverse effects on the shooter's physiology, can impair his judgment and coordination to the extent that his handling of a rifle can pose a dangerous threat to other people on or near the range. The best shooters in the world avoid alcohol entirely during their training for a match, or limit their consumption to very modest amounts at the end of a shooting day, but *never* drink immediately before or during a match.

Aside from the reasons already given, the use of drugs and alcohol by shooters in competition is specifically outlawed by match regulations. Even the use of non-psychoactive drugs on a shooting range is regarded as suspicious and can be grounds for disqualification. If you are required by your physician to take a course of drugs during the time of a match, be sure to ask him for an explanatory letter, addressed, if possible, to the officers of the range on which you will be firing.

In short, one simply cannot successfully deal with match pressure by the use of drugs or alcohol, both of which are wisely outlawed by shooting societies. There are no short cuts to overcoming match pressure. The only means of coping with it is to prepare oneself physically and psychologically to withstand and overcome it. This can be accomplished only by faithfully adhering to a sound training program. The challenge of shooting exists because the self-control it requires cannot be achieved through the use of drugs, but only by attaining authentic self-mastery.

CHAPTER
4

Confidence & the Will to Win

CONFIDENCE

Confidence is one of the greatest determinants of a person's ability to think positively about his performance. The person who lacks confidence is likely to think negatively; yet give that same person confidence and his approach will almost automatically become positive. It is, then, a definite asset as long as it is realistic. There is such a thing as being overconfident, which leads to a lack of carefulness, and no sport requires so much carefulness as international-style riflery. Some people seem to be born with an oversupply of confidence, and some seem to be born without enough. A shooter needs to develop a healthy degree of confidence that is, under match conditions, unshakable.

The subject of confidence seems to break naturally into two areas. These are first, overall confidence in one's self, and second, confidence in one's ability to shoot well. The first area is a broad one in which little advice can or should be given here. People who lack all confidence in themselves are likely to be quite unhappy, if for no other reason than that they are painfully inhibited by the fear that they will never succeed at anything. Several possibilities are available to the person who lacks overall confidence. One of these is to seek the help of a competent professional counselor such as a physician, pastor, or psychiatrist. Another is for the individual to choose some field of endeavor where success is very likely, and then work until success is achieved. It is a truism that nothing breeds confidence like success.

The U. S. Army's Ranger Training Program, for example, has found that men with no confidence in their ability to perform dangerous physical feats immediately gain dramatically in confidence if they can force themselves to perform *once* some dangerous feat, such as rappelling down a cliff. The conditions under which the rappelling is performed are carefully controlled so that the subject *feels* that he is entering a do-or-die situation, but actually he is in no danger. Thus, he is forced to come face-to-face with his fear and lack of confidence, and if he can successfully overcome this fear and rappel down a cliff just once, he reduces his irrational fears and gains confidence in his ability to perform other, equally challenging tasks. The same principle—called *transference*—operates in the broadest areas of experience. A person who lacks confidence in himself might learn to shoot well, for example, and find that this gives him confidence in other areas of his life.

Specifically in the area of shooting, a number of factors contribute to one's confidence. First, a shooter must have confidence in his equipment. He must know that his rifle is accurate and reliable, that it is matched with the proper ammunition, that his sights are properly attached and in good condition, that all of the accessories are properly adjusted, and, in short, that every piece of his equipment is as it should be. Confidence in equipment is easily ensured by purchasing the right equipment and consistently taking adequate care of it. Second, a rifleman must have confidence in the fundamental principles of shooting—essentially, those outlined in this book. He can acquire this through observation of the best shooters. He will see that all the good shooters do not *look* alike in every detail, but that they all observe the fundamentals without exception. He can also see that those who violate the fundamentals are consistently unable to compete with the champions. He can recognize that the fundamentals have evolved through the trial-and-error of many generations of shooters, and have been proved over and over again by experts. And not least, he should know that he *understands* all of the fundamentals. Next, he should have confidence in his ability to *execute* these fundamentals. He acquires this through training and through participation in matches. If he can execute the fundamentals properly in training, he should know that he can duplicate that performance in a match. If he can execute them properly in one match, he should know that he can duplicate or exceed his previous performance in a subsequent match. And finally, directly related to this, he should have confidence in his physical and mental condition. He acquires this through a training program that ensures sound physical and mental states. Equipment, fundamental principles, and training procedures are all discussed fully in other sections of this book.

THE WILL TO WIN

Perhaps the most elusive of all aspects of the psychology of shooting is the will to win. More than any other facet of shooting psychology, it seems to be buried in the deeper recesses of the personality. The will to win is also called motivation or competitive spirit. It is uncertain whether this spirit can be instilled, or whether one must be born with it. Probably everyone is born with a certain amount of competitiveness, which can then be heightened or suppressed by experience. For example, a person with a strong competitive spirit who is defeated time after time may finally lose the desire to compete. On the other hand, a person with a mild competitive spirit may, if he succeeds quite well, learn to relish competition.

However one acquires the will to win, it is certain to be absolutely necessary for success, and this holds true for almost any level of competition. The person who wishes to win a local club competition must have the will to win, otherwise he will not dedicate himself to the training program that will enable him to do so. The person who goes after a national championship must have the will to win that will drive him to even more effort. And the person who sets as his goal a world championship must have a powerful desire to win, and go about training himself with a thoroughgoing dedication. The shooters who compete seriously for world championships all have a burning desire to win, and because of that desire train themselves to razor-edge perfection. Anyone wishing to compete with them must train himself equally thoroughly, or better. Only a strong motivation to win can call forth such dedication. It is also true that anyone going for a world championship must go for a new record score, because the world record has a way of climbing higher each year. The person who is content to shoot last year's record score will probably lose this year. It is perhaps only by setting a definite goal that the competitive spirit or will to win can be fully developed and harnessed to produce real results.

-//-

TRAINING

When a well-known champion appears in competition, there are usually people on the range who are careful to photograph every detail of each of his positions. Many times these photographers are aspiring shooters. The most hopeful and optimistic ones believe that if they study each of the champion's positions closely enough they may discover the one detail which enables him to shoot so well. Others believe that the overall configurations of his positions are the only sound ones, and they hope to model their positions after his and become his carbon-copy "look-alikes." Sadly, in concentrating on the champion's appearance, they are deluding themselves. Appearances are the most superficial and the least meaningful part of the champion's success.

The secret of the champion's successful positions is something the photographers cannot see or photograph during a match. That secret is training—training that has taken place for two or three or more hours almost every day, day after day, week after week, month after month; training that has enabled him to develop a position that is right for him, but probably would not be right for anyone else; training that has enabled him to master motor skills, concentration, and mental discipline to a superb degree; training that has consisted of hours of thinking and planning, of keeping records and a shooting diary, of dry-firing, of position building, of analysis of performance, of physical and mental conditioning, and of shooting in matches. Much of it has been the dullest of work. But now the results of it are immensely satisfying, for he is a champion. And would-be competitors who walk up and down the line photographing him are not a threat to his retaining the championship—they are not going to be his rivals for first place, for they can't see how he got there. They are only copying the things he does on the range. They will begin to pose a threat only when they begin to copy the things he does off the range, and that is to train, train, train. It is work—hard work. It is the only way to succeed.

CHAPTER
5

The Training Program:
A Schedule of Progress

TRAINING DEFINED

Training is any activity that is designed to improve or sustain shooting performance. It is difficult to say where or when training begins. In one sense, a rifleman begins training when he first attempts to adopt the correct position, or to adjust the rifle to fit that position. In the discussions which follow, however, we will have in mind primarily the individual who is training for a specific event, for we believe that training is most effective when it is carried out with a single goal in mind. This individual could be a beginner, if he has a program extending over two or three years; but more than likely he will be someone who has already acquired basic shooting skills, and has decided that he wants to be a winner. So he chooses a specific event and sets out to win it. That event will be some time away when he begins his training program—usually a year, but perhaps even two or three years away. If it is a really challenging event such as an Olympic match, then he will have to begin his program well in advance if he wishes to win, for the other competitors are beginning theirs just as early, or earlier. The higher the level of competition, the greater the effort that must be made to win, and the longer, more thorough, and more meticulous must be the training program.

Throughout the training period, two concepts should be kept constantly in mind if the program is to be completely successful. The first concept is that the focus of training is not on score, but on performance. A good score, to be sure, is precisely what we want, but a program directed toward score tends to keep the individual's concerns focused on the target, on the placement of the holes that get shot into the bull. Such a program may keep an individual trying hard, and it may result in some improvement. But it will result in only a fraction of the improvement yielded by a program that is focused on the *performance* that puts those holes in the target. The person who trains most successfully is the one who understands that score is only an index of performance—that a match is really won not by a superior score, but by a superior performance. Clearly the focus of a successful program, then, is improved performance—improved positions, improved motor skills, and improved concentration and mental discipline.

The second concept that should be adopted by a person in training is that his program should be aimed not at defeating other competitors, but at defeating the dividing forces within himself. The famous remark made by Pogo, the cartoon character, is particularly true of competition shooting: "We have met the enemy, and he is us." A shooter is defeated not by other competitors, but by forces within himself. Again, these may be weaknesses in positions, in motor skills, in concentration, or in mental discipline. A person will train most successfully if he doesn't worry at all about other competitors, but concentrates on eliminating the weaknesses and deficiencies in his own performance. When he selects an event for which he wishes to train, he should not ask, "What score must I shoot in order to better the high score in the event last year?" He is still orienting himself toward other competitors. Rather he should ask, "If I work consistently at developing my performance, what score can I reasonably expect to shoot at the time of this event?" Now he is thinking about his own potential, his own possibilities. If the score he can predict for himself by the time of the event is well above last year's winning score, he has made a good choice of a match to try to win; and he should shoot for the score that he can potentially shoot, not just for the possibly much lower score that might win the match. If he shoots a winning score that is below his capability, he may have beaten other competitors, but he has still not met the full challenge of shooting: overcoming and controlling the forces inside himself that prevent him from realizing his full potential.

GENERAL REQUIREMENTS OF A TRAINING PROGRAM

The best training program is the one based on a comprehensive plan. This plan should actually be written out in detail, and kept available for handy reference. It may be taped to a wall or kept in the same notebook as the shooting diary, or placed on a bedside table. The exact place is not important, but the written program should be where it is a constant reminder of its own existence, and where it may easily be referred to at any time. And it should be referred to frequently—at least once a week. The program should be written out because writing it will force the shooter to formulate the plan clearly in his own mind; and once it is written, it is permanent and complete, no longer subject to the distortions and lapses of memory.

The value of a comprehensive plan is threefold. First, it establishes a clear goal: it says that the trainee wants to shoot a specific score in a specific event on a specific date. Establishing a concrete goal has the psychological value of lending force, direction, and purpose to a training program which would seem aimless if it were not designed for a particular end. Second, a comprehensive plan provides a schedule for sustained, systematic development toward that goal. Having a plan raises a person's efficiency in almost everything he undertakes. Without a plan we often flounder, wasting our time in repetitions and omissions. A training plan ensures a shooter that he will avoid wasted motion, and that he will move steadily ahead without omitting important details. Third, a plan prevents overtraining and undertraining. Without a plan that establishes reasonable gradients of progress for each month or quarter or year of the program, one is likely to rush things in the beginning, find himself fatigued and unable to perform competently, and quickly become discouraged. This is the result of overtraining, of exhausting one's reserves of psychological and physical resources. Or a shooter may find himself faced with the match he selected as a goal a year or more ago, and suddenly realize that he is not ready. He is undertrained. A detailed plan prevents both of these errors.

Once a plan is established, it should be adhered to religiously. Hence it is very important that it be workable. It should set a realistic goal, one that is actually attainable within the time of the program. For example, it would be totally unrealistic for a new shooter with three months' experience to undertake to win an Olympic competition that is only two months away. The physical and psychological conditioning necessary to win an Olympic event simply cannot be attained in five months. On the other hand, the goal should not be so easily achieved that it fails to spur one on toward realizing full potential. Not only is it extravagant to spend two years accomplishing something that could be done in six months, it is also dull and uninteresting. Anyone is likely to lose interest in, and eventually drop out of, a program that doesn't provide enough challenge to spur him on to make progress, for it is the progress we make in facing a challenge that gives us satisfaction.

Finally, the program should be workable on a day-to-day basis. Time is the resource upon which the most demands will be made. There should actually be time available for attending the matches listed in the plan, and time available for the training sessions called for in the plan. Finding the time is likely to be much easier than actually using it. Almost anyone can find an hour or two each day that is wasted or devoted to something wholly unimportant. This time could be used for training, and may be relied upon in the training plan. However, the plan should not be wholly rigid in drawing upon every available minute, for this necessitates organizing almost every minute of one's day, which for most people is a psychological strain. Moreover, there are times when a person legitimately cannot train during the hour or two set aside for that purpose. Illnesses or various other emergencies, and even weather conditions, can and will interfere with training. The training plan, then, should allow a degree of flexibility that will take these conditions into account.

In summary, one is well on the way to developing a good training program if his plan meets the following general requirements. It has a clear goal, and a systematic schedule for the attainment of that goal, with provisions to prevent overtraining and undertraining. The level of performance which constitutes the goal is realistic, neither too high so as to be discouraging, nor too low so as to be uninteresting. And the plan calls for the use of time that is actually available, but does not demand too rigid an organization of the daily and weekly schedule.

WRITING AN INDIVIDUAL TRAINING PROGRAM

The requirements outlined are general—that is, they apply to everyone. Within the framework of these general requirements, each individual will write out a set of specific requirements that apply to him alone. The individual program will include a schedule of training matches, a schedule of training sessions, and a set of training goals. The training goals will include, on the one hand, a specific match which the individual hopes to win; on the other hand, it will consist of a specific level of performance which the individual hopes to attain. We should mention here that a beginning shooter will not be concerned at all with matches, and his program will consist only of a schedule of training sessions and a goal of a specific performance level. The subject of matches is placed first in the following discussion, however, because for an experienced shooter the scheduling of matches is the first step—not in the conception or the planning—but in the *writing* of a training program.

Training matches.

The skeleton of a training program is a schedule of matches to be attended for training purposes. The dates of most events are fixed well in advance, and are published regularly in shooting magazines. Once the matches to be attended have been selected, their names and dates are written out. The simplest way of doing this is probably to enter the names in the appropriate squares of a planning calendar bought specifically for this purpose. The last event written down will be the one which has been selected as the target for the whole program. It is not a training match; it is *the* special match, the Big Apple, the objective for which all the training is conducted. Once it has been attended, the training program has been completed, and a new one will be written, aimed at another goal somewhere in the future.

The criteria for selecting training matches are convenience, timing, and level of competition. Convenience has to do with whether or not the event is within practicable travelling distance, and whether it falls on a time that is not taken up by other responsibilities. Timing has to do with the intervals between matches. A program is likely to be most successful if it schedules a minimum of twelve matches a year. If the program covers a span of one year, obviously all the training matches should not fall within the same three calendar months. Good timing means that the matches scheduled in the program are about evenly spaced. Whether a relatively long or short training interval should appear just before the program objective is something each individual must decide for himself. Some shooters like to enter a training match only a few days before this all-important event; others like to have a couple of months to devote to final training and preparation. It is also important, of course, not to schedule too many matches. If all one does is shoot in matches, no time is left for regular training sessions. Two matches a month is about the maximum anyone can comfortably handle, and may be too many for most people because such a match load takes up too much routine training time.

The level of competition likely to be encountered at each event will also have some bearing on choosing a training match. Generally speaking, matches should be such that one must make a fairly good effort in order to win. A match that provides no competition is not likely to put pressure on an individual, and one of the purposes of entering these matches is to become acclimated to match pressure. Easy matches also fail to make one try his best.

On the other hand, some of the matches should be such that one could reasonably expect to win. Another reason for entering these matches is to gain confidence and to get the feel of winning. A person who has never won an event, and suddenly finds himself out in front in an important match, is likely to get an acute case of match pressure from the totally new experience, and as a result lose the match. The experience of winning, then, should be planned as a part of the training program. As a final consideration, the level of competition should gradually rise as the program nears completion. This rise will coincide with the expected rise in the level of the trainee's performance, and will provide a desirably graduated series of experiences in which to learn mental discipline.

The purpose of entering a series of training matches is simply to get oneself prepared for the match which is the program objective. Entering matches is the only means of getting accustomed to the pressures of actual competition. But throughout the training program, the trainee never takes his eyes off the Big Apple. He never allows himself to think that any of the training matches is all-important, for not one of them is important *except* as a training vehicle. This is not to say that he doesn't try to win a training match—he does. But he keeps his mind focused *always* on the one goal he has set—to win that one big match, and for the duration of the training program, that is all that matters. The reason for this has its roots in the phenomenon of letting go, discussed earlier. If one does not keep the objective of the program in mind as most important, letting go will occur after almost every one of the training matches. Since letting go is accompanied by a deterioration of both mental and physical performance, and most people require several days at least to recover from the experience, it obviously disrupts steady progress and damages the efficiency of a training program. The most successful shooter does not let go after training matches. He knows that he can let go in style after he has won that one all-important event.

The phenomenon which we call letting go is probably more widely known as peaking out, but we have avoided that term because it already has thoroughly established connotations which we believe are misleading. Apparently, there is widespread belief that peaking out is something that happens at the point where the body and mind are in peak condition, after which a deterioration must inevitably take place. Some people believe, for example, that a shooter may peak out two weeks before a specific event. Conclusive evidence on whether or not this phenomenon actually exists is not available; however, the odds against its existence are almost overwhelming. It is true that shooters and other athletes have suffered a drop in performance a short time before a major competition, but the causes for this were probably not at all inevitable.

Possible causes could include a radical disruption in the training schedule because of travel, disconcerting situations or conditions encountered for the first time at the competition site, and vulnerability to the pressure of competition. There is no medical evidence known to us that a person cannot sustain himself at any level of physical condition, barring the effects of illness or age, for an indefinite period. It is true that what has been called peaking out is usually accompanied by a dramatic loss in motor skills, and coordination, and by other physical symptoms; but these symptoms are probably psychosomatic in origin, and related in most cases to the psychological phenomenon of letting go, or to some other psychological causes related to the situations discussed above. The best evidence for this is that shooters who have a proper mental attitude and who follow a proper training program do not experience a loss in performance either after a training match for before shooting the match which has been the objective of their programs. After this big event, as far as we can determine, they always experience it, because they then, understandably, let go. Thus, the person who looks upon each match he enters as an end in itself, requiring an all-out effort, is defeating the purpose of a training program, which is to progress steadily upward in performance without experiencing the drops and setbacks caused by letting go.

Training sessions.

Training matches are formal events, scheduled, administered, and conducted for the public by shooting organizations. Training sessions are informal events, scheduled, planned, and conducted by the individual shooter, usually on his own time, and purely for his own benefit. Training sessions are planned around the schedule of training matches, and fill out and complete a training program.

Because the specific problems dealt with in individual training sessions develop as the program progresses, nothing will be said here of the structure of these sessions, though that topic will be dealt with at length very soon. It is sufficient to say at this point that training sessions are *the* method by which an individual moves upward toward his training goal. If the schedule of training matches is the skeleton of the program, training sessions are the muscles, the heart, and the blood, for it is at these sessions that the life work of the program is accomplished. It is here that progress is made. The sessions should be planned and executed with care and respect. Individual sessions should each be written into the training calendar according to a plan, and alternate sessions planned when regular sessions cannot be met.

Sometimes it is difficult to carry through a planned training session simply because one "doesn't feel like it." On certain days it seems that we just don't have the energy or the desire to make an effort. In dealing with this state of mind, it is helpful to remember that the feeling of laziness usually passes quickly once we take the first step to get involved in some activity. The best way to overcome the temptation to miss a training session is simply to pick up one's equipment and start for the range. By the time one arrives there, the feeling has usually passed. It is important to make this effort, because one of the major keys to a successful program is that it follow faithfully a *regular* schedule of training sessions. Short sessions, observed on a regular basis, yield results far superior to a program based on long sessions at irregular intervals. It is difficult to say how many hours any one person should devote to training each week. The number would depend partly upon the time available, and partly upon the physical and psychological makeup of the individual. But assuming that the person decided to devote twelve to fifteen hours a week to training, which is probably about an average number among serious shooters, he would benefit more from five or six two- to three-hour sessions than from two six-hour sessions. Experience has shown conclusively that following a regular schedule of short sessions clearly yields more rapid improvement in performance.

Training goals.

Deciding upon which match is to be the Big Apple and which training matches are to be the stepping stones on the way to that match is simply a matter of choosing from what is available. Scheduling training sessions is also largely a problem of choosing from what times are available. But from the time at which these things are written into the training calendar, the primary focus of the program is not on winning the program objective, but rather on attaining, by the time of this match, a certain level of performance. The program objective, then, serves two functions. It provides a match which the shooter intends to win and for which he prepares himself psychologically to go all out. This is important from the standpoint of giving continuity and focus to the training program. But the objective match is also a date at which he intends to achieve a specific level of performance. This level of performance is the more important goal of the training program. If it is reached, the program has been a success, even if it did not actually win this focal match. Choosing a level of performance as a training goal is difficult, for it involves deciding both the rate at which one can progress and the limits of one's potential. And deciding either of these things is fraught with certain psychological difficulties.

In setting a training goal, a rifleman must consider realistically the rate at which he can make progress in improving his performance. Then, in planning his program, he will have to write out a schedule of progress. The difficulty is that many people doubt that progress can be scheduled. Progress, they believe, is something that develops at a rate of its own. That belief is false. The person who simply goes to the rifle range each day and shoots for an hour or two and expects the level of his performance to rise automatically as the result of some mysterious force called "progress" is going to be disappointed. Progress occurs, at least in shooting, because we make it happen. But our belief in whether or now we can make it happen is bound up in our belief in our own potential.

And here we face an extremely complex situation. Ultimate human potential is yet a mystery. As more has been learned about the vast potentials that lie hidden in almost every human being, and as world records in almost every area of human performance mount steadily higher each year, it is now widely accepted that almost none of us ever reaches the limit of his potential in any field. The greatest barriers to our seeing our true potentials in athletic events (and perhaps in all areas) appear to be psychological. Evidence for this position could be multiplied indefinitely.

First, an example from a sport other than shooting. The four-minute mile provides a good instance. Before the first official run of a four-minute mile, most track men believed it to be physically an impossibility. The human body, they believed, was simply incapable of making the exertion. Yet after the first sub-four-minute mile was run in official competition, track men everywhere were breaking the four-minute mark in a very short time. Had the human body changed, suddenly acquired a new potential? No. The same men who previously said a sub-four-minute mile was impossible were now running it themselves. Of course, they had to be physically well trained to do so. Not just anyone can get up out of his armchair and do it. But the barriers that kept the trained athletes from doing it were purely psychological. In truth, to the person who has that barrier, nothing is more real. But the point is that many of our limitations exist only in our minds. A certain amount of time and training may be required for us to reach a given level of performance; but the level of performance we are capable of reaching may be far above what we believe it to be. Who is to say—considering that we all have psychological barriers—what is possible?

An example from the shooting world will illustrate this point more to our purpose. Up until the early 1960's, many shooters believed that no one would ever shoot a score above 1150 in international style competition. Most shooters believed that 1150 was the human limit in terms of visual acuity, holding potential, and ability to withstand the pressure of competition. Then in the 1962 World Championships Gary Anderson shot an 1157 in the free-rifle event. Many applauded and believed that an unbeatable world record had been established. Very soon after this, however, other people were shooting competition scores in the 1150's. Then, in the 1964 Olympics, when Gary Anderson and Lones Wigger both fired record practice scores in the 1160's and 1170's, near-comparable scores soon began to be posted by other shooters. More recently Gary Anderson has fired competition scores in the 1180's, and Lones Wigger has fired (under the no-wind, steady-light conditions of an indoor range) a competition score above 1190. Will other people start shooting scores this high? Certainly they will. All that is required is for a champion to break through the psychological barriers, and then, once this obstacle is down, large numbers will follow.

(It should be noted here that some part of this increase in

scores probably resulted from improved equipment, particularly ammunition and shooting jackets. However, improvements in equipment cannot have accounted for more than a small percentage of the jump in scores. The rest came simply from increased performance levels based upon the same fundamental principles of shooting.)

The two major conclusions to be drawn from these facts are, of course, obvious. First, we can't be sure what are the *real* physical limitations upon shooting performance. From a purely logical standpoint it would seem that if the body is capable of shooting a string of two, three, or four 10's, it should be capable also of shooting a string of 10's throughout a complete position course (we are thinking here of no-wind, steady-light indoor conditions). Whether this abstract proposition leaves some factor unconsidered is unknown. Perhaps there is some physiological factor, such as an incidence of nerve-impulse malfunction, which would prevent the shooting of a perfect score. But we will not be able to know that until first the psychological barriers to that performance are removed. We must first have shooters who believe—really believe—that an indoor international score of 1200 is actually possible and who are willing to work for that performance level. The second conclusion is that until we do discover the physiological limit of performance, the present limits seem to be primarily psychological. It is clear that many, if not most, people tend to regard an existing record as some kind of limit. It is only the real champions who are capable of seeing the possiblities beyond this psychological barrier.

The implications and problems raised by these conclusions are vast, and the apparatus and time needed to explore the problems thus raised are unavailable. Meanwhile, the individual shooter is left with the problem of *how* to select a level of performance as his training goal. Here we can offer pieces of advice, but the final solution to the problem must be left to the individual.

First, set your goal in terms of a *minimum* level of performance. By doing this you avoid creating your own psychological barrier. For example, if you say that one year from today you will be shooting a score of 1175, you may reach that level, but chances are that you will not go much above 1175,

for psychologically this has become the limit—the veritable peak
of your expectations. However, it is *not* limiting psychologically
to say instead that one year from today you will be able to
shoot a *minimum* score of 1170. No psychological upper limit
has been established, and the way has been kept open for additional progress if your capabilities permit. A still better way of
thinking might be, "I will be shooting a score somewhere between 1170 and 1200." This would seem to add some incen-
tive to go more than just two or three points beyond a
minimum score. In deciding what the minimum score is to be,
you should take into account that what you *think* you are
capable of is likely to be somewhat below what you are *actually* capable of.

Second, select your goal on the basis of the amount of
training time available and on the gains that can be made
separately in each shooting position. This is the only basis on
which progress can be realistically predicted. Wanting or wishing to attain a level of performance will not get you there.
Only time actually spent in training will get you there. If you
accurately evaluate the state of your present performance in
each position, and the amount of time you can devote to
training in each position, you will be able to predict progress
reasonably accurately in each position; then you can more
realistically predict the gains in your aggregate score. And
third, once you have established a goal, make up your mind
that you will achieve it, and spare nothing in order to get
there. You must be absolutely determined, and dead sure,
that you will attain the goal, or there is no point in having it.
It is important to set as your minimum goal the highest level
of performance you can fully believe in.

We still have not answered the question of specifically how
much progress an individual should strive for in a training
program. Unfortunately, we cannot provide an answer. Any
two people with identical training time will make progress at
different rates. Consequently it is impossible to say how much
progress an individual *should* make unless something is known
about his average learning rate. For this reason, a beginning
shooter with little experience would be working totally in the
dark if he tried to set a rate of progress for himself too far
into the future. Beginners are advised to wait until they have

some experience on which to make judgments before establishing progress goals beyond the level of basic proficiency.

What is a level of basic proficiency? The level has risen in the last two decades, and will undoubtedly rise again. Today we would regard a performance of 350-355 in standing, 380-385 in kneeling, and 395 or above in prone as a good basic performance level. Most beginners can advance to these levels in less than a year if they are devoting twelve to fifteen hours a week to training.

But we emphasize that these scores indicate only a *basic* level of proficiency. As we have seen, matches are now being won by scores exceeding 1190. More advanced shooters will be able to make more and more accurate predictions of their progress above their present scores as they acquire experience in setting up and completing training programs for themselves. The more programs they complete, in all likelihood the more accurate will be their predictions of what they *can* achieve in a given time.

The training sequence.

Once a training goal has been established, the trainee writes into his training calendar a timetable of *minimum* performance goals he expects to attain each week, month, or quarter of the training program (whether goals are set in weekly or monthly increments is not important; the important thing is that the increments be appropriate for the amount of training time available and the rate of progress expected). The training program is now complete in basic outline, with written schedules of matches (advanced shooters), training sessions, and performance goals. To complete the writing of the program, a sequence of training events must be entered into the calendar to give a direction to the training sessions. We can now consider this sequence in detail.

Training is most effective, and progress most rapid, when progress is attempted in only one position at a time. Numerous experiments have verified this repeatedly. Attempting to develop only one position at a time definitely yields superior results to attempting to develop two or three positions at a time. The sequence for the complete training program, then, combines this principle with another important principle that should be followed across the board in shooting: priority should always be given to solving the most important problem first. Combining these principles indicates that the first phase of the sequence should be devoted to developing the standing position. Standing is the most difficult position, and it is also the most important, for the following reason. Almost all successful shooters have consistently high scores in both kneeling and prone. As a result, matches are seldom won by the scores fired from these positions; matches are usually won by the score fired in standing. Of course, matches can be *lost* by firing a poor score in any position. But generally speaking, a shooter holds his own by shooting good kneeling and prone scores; he wins the match with a superior standing score.

Following these principles throughout, the program arranges itself into four phases, either for the beginner or for the experienced shooter. For the beginner, Phase I is devoted entirely to the development of standing performance. When the shooter attains a satisfactory level, he begins Phase II, which is devoted to the development of kneeling performance (kneeling being the next most difficult position). During this phase, perhaps 10 percent of training time is allotted to standing, but no attempt is made at further development of this position; the rifleman merely attempts to maintain proficiency in standing performance. When kneeling performance is satisfactory, the shooter begins Phase III, which consists of developing performance in the prone position and merely maintaining proficiency in standing and kneeling, which each receive about 10 percent of training time. When prone performance is satisfactory, Phase IV, which might be called the consolidation phase, begins. Here the beginner attempts to consolidate and reinforce everything he has learned about the individual positions, and conditions himself to shooting the aggregate course in the sequence prescribed by match rules.

It is only after he is well into the consolidation phase that a beginner should enter competition. Generally speaking, this will be about eight to ten months after he begins training, if he is training a minimum of twelve hours a week and his progress is about average. This means that he will have spent about three months in Phase I, two to three months in Phase

II, and six to ten weeks in Phase III. Reduced training time each week, of course, will lengthen the program accordingly, or lower its standards. A new shooter should not enter competition until he has confidence enough in his positions to hold up under match pressure. On the other hand, he should not postpone competition experience so long that over-lengthy anticipation creates disproportionate match pressure. Either can be damaging to his confidence.

After the beginner has completed Phase IV (the beginner, we remember, has as the goal of his first year's program not the winning of a match, but simply the attainment of a basic level of proficiency), he may start a new program, and this time he should integrate his schedule of training and progress with a schedule of training matches, selecting a specific match to serve as the objective of the program. He goes through the same training phases, again attempting progress in only one position at a time; and again he begins with the standing position. This time, however, 10 percent of training time is devoted, from the beginning, to maintaining proficiency in the other positions. Thus we have two versions of the basic program, as follows:

For the beginner:
Phase I: progress in standing performance.
Phase II: progress in kneeling, 10% of training time devoted to maintaining proficiency in standing.
Phase III: progress in prone, 10% of training time devoted to maintaining proficiency in standing, 10% to maintaining proficiency in kneeling.
Phase IV: consolidation; generally, training time allotted is 50% to standing, 30% to kneeling, 20% to prone; OR 50% to the position that offers the most problems, 30% to the next most difficult, 20% to the remaining position.

For the experienced shooter:
Phase I: progress in standing, 10% each to maintaining proficiency in kneeling and prone.
Phase II: progress in kneeling, 10% each to maintaining proficiency in standing and prone.

Phase III: progress in prone, 10% each to maintaining proficiency in standing and kneeling.

Phase IV: consolidation; 50% to standing, 30% to kneeling, 20% to prone; OR 50% to the position that offers the most difficulty, 30% to the next most difficult, 20% to the remaining position. Matches may be entered at any time; progress schedule should be integrated with a schedule of training matches.

It should be noted that each of these phases is scheduled in the training calendar. The trainee decides in advance how many weeks to devote to Phase I, how many weeks to Phase II, and so on, and then follows the plan as it is written into his program. He does not deviate from the schedule unless there is a fully justified reason for doing so. To abandon the plan arbitrarily, without reason, is to negate the efficacy of the plan and destroy its value.

We are now ready to point out that each of the phases devoted to progress in a particular position will also have an intraphase sequence. This sequence may apply for either the beginner or the experienced shooter. These intraphase sequences will be called *steps* to distinguish them from the previously discussed *phases*. Steps cannot be scheduled quite so neatly as phases can in the training calendar. About the best one can do is to assign a limiting date and say that work in a particular step will no longer continue after that date, whether or not the goal of that step has been reached.

Sometimes it will be necessary to move ahead to the next step without having reached the goal. This is disappointing, but usually not disastrous if the overall program, and goals, are realistic. However, steps have this advantage: if the trainee meets the goal of the step ahead of schedule, he may also move on to the next step ahead of schedule. Usually a shooter will, in the series of phases, fail to complete some steps as scheduled, but will complete others ahead of schedule, thus in general keeping up with his overall plan. Therefore, when we say below that a particular step is completed when certain conditions are met, this means that the individual may move on to the next step even if he is considerably ahead of his planned schedule. On the other hand, he may have to move on to the next step without fulfilling the conditions prescribed, if the time allotted for the particular step has expired.

Step 1 consists of holding-exercises only. The emphasis falls upon the mechanical and physical aspects of position. During this step, the shooter goes through the motions of aiming and holding the rifle just as he would in shooting, but the rifle is never loaded and the trigger is never pulled. In this step three things are accomplished: the rifle is adjusted to the shooter's body; the position of the body is improved; and the muscles and other parts of the body are conditioned and strengthened for that particular position. As one progresses through this step, the duration of the holding time should be gradually increased until the rifle can be held in the shooting position for several minutes without undue fatigue. As mentioned earlier, a beginning shooter will require a minimum of several weeks to reach this level, and usually will experience sore muscles for the first week or so as the body becomes accustomed to bending to assume the position. The position should be improved with the following principles in mind: bones support the rifle, and muscles are involved only in holding the body still. Generally speaking, for a beginner this is a time of more or less free-wheeling changes in adjustment of the rifle and the body position. For an advanced shooter, changes are going to be more strictly controlled by the scientific method, for he has already established a basic position and is now working upon refinements.

Step 2 consists of dry-firing. Dry-firing means performing all the actions of shooting, including pulling the trigger, but doing so with no cartridge, or with an empty cartridge, in the chamber. By this time the position should be fairly well developed, and the individual should be capable of holding the aim inside the 8-ring. The emphasis in this step is upon perfecting hold and coordinating it with trigger pull. A technique for achieving a smooth trigger release may also need to be developed during this time.

Step 3 consists of live-firing at a blank target. This is a technique that works only if hold is fairly good. The rifleman does this repeatedly, attempting to shoot a group on the basis of feel only. This exercise has two main functions. First, it helps the shooter become more conscious of the feel of the position, and thus sharpens his ability to judge hold. Second, it gives him a means of judging the fineness of his body-sensing ability, and may indicate that this is an area that needs more work. This will be indicated by an excessively large group on the blank target. In addition, patterns in the group will sometimes indicate specific problem areas in the position to the shooter who is skillful enough to analyze the pattern.

Step 4 consists of a mixture of live- and dry-firing at a target, but without the sights zeroed on the center of the bull. It is psychologically unwise to zero the sights yet, as this would tend to take the focus off of performance and place it on score. In the beginning of this step, only the last round in ten should be live; the other nine should be dry. When the shooter can consistently place four of these live rounds in a group the size of the 8-ring or smaller, the proportion of live rounds should be doubled to two out of ten, or every fifth shot. When he can consistently place six to eight of these shots in groups the size of the 8-ring or smaller, the percentage of live rounds should be increased to fifty, or every other shot. When he can consistently fire one half or more of these shots into a group the size of the 9-ring, and none outside a group the size of the 7-ring, he moves on to the next step.

Step 5 consists of live rounds fired with the sights properly zeroed on the bull. The shooter is firing for score, though his concern remains, as always, with performance. When problems develop in this step, he should be willing to stop at any point and return to dry-firing until the problem is ironed out. During this step, the emphasis is upon overall improvement in position and performance to bring the score up to the selected level. When the selected level is reached and can be sustained for two weeks, the individual should, if he is on schedule, be ready to move on to the next phase of his program just as he had planned.

IMPLEMENTING THE TRAINING PROGRAM

When a rifleman has his training program completely written out, with a schedule of matches, training sessions, performance goals, and the training sequence all entered in his planning calendar, he is ready to implement the program. The blueprint is complete, and now the work begins. The major portion of progress, at least in terms of physical skills, will be made in training sessions. Here we will be concerned with three elements in the training sessions that are primarily responsible for steady progress: analysis of positions, the controlled experiment, and the shooter's diary.

Analyzing positions.

During the first three phases of the training cycle, changes are made in only one position at a time. In the fourth phase, changes are still made in only one position at a time, but the whole phase is not devoted to one position—the focus may fall, at one time or another, on any of the three positions. Then, sometime about two weeks before the match which is the program objective, no major changes are introduced in positions or techniques so that maximum control can be gained over them as the match approaches. Changes in position, then, occur throughout most of the training cycle. These changes are always based on an analysis of the position. The importance of this analytical process cannot be overemphasized. Progress in any position will be almost directly proportionate to how well the shooter analyzes that particular position.

Analysis of position is based upon analysis of performance, which was discussed earlier. It becomes, in turn, the basis of a controlled experiment, which will be the next topic discussed. Analysis of performance, as we remember, was based upon sensing the "interior environment" while performing the shot. It involves being aware of what one was concentrating on during the performance, and also being aware of the feel of every muscle in the body during the performance, including follow-through. Analysis of position begins when analysis of performance indicates that a weakness exists somewhere in the position. This is indicated by a recurring problem that is not caused by a weakness in concentration or motor skills, but rather by a structural weakness in the position itself. The problem may have recently appeared in the position, but it is just as likely that it existed all along, and is being noticed for the first time as a result of progressively clarifying one's understanding of the position.

Successful analysis of a position depends upon a direct, positive approach to problem solving. A widely accepted way of discussing problem solving is to say that there are four ways of dealing with a problem. Two are negative, and may be described as retreat and evasion. To retreat is to run from the problem, and to evade is to pretend that the problem isn't there. The negative approaches, in shooting or in anything else, are of little value. The positive approaches may be described as indirect and direct. The indirect approach involves attempting to get around the problem without facing it directly. For example, a person might develop difficulty in trigger pull, and know that the best way to deal with the problem is through dry-firing; yet, feeling that this is too boring or "too much trouble," he would just continue shooting live rounds, hoping the problem might disappear. The problem *might* be solved this way, but it is certainly more time-consuming and indirect than the more direct approach of resorting to dry-firing.

Examples of the direct, positive approach could be multiplied indefinitely. A brief illustration or two of how this approach may be used in position analysis will perhaps be useful. In the standing position, for example, one may discover that the shots consistently group across the target from nine o'clock to three o'clock. On the day this phenomenon is noticed, there is no wind blowing, concentration is very good, and the trigger pull is presenting no problems. Continued analysis of performance indicates that the entire body from the waist up is twisting either right or left during the moment of release and follow-through. Analysis: back bend and twist are incorrect, and some change in these features must be made. At this point, however, *no change is made.* One proceeds to shoot exactly as before, looking for other possible causes of the problem, until this diagnosis has been verified to his complete mental satsifaction. He is then ready to correct the problem by conducting a controlled experiment, which we will discuss shortly.

One more example of positive analysis might be helpful. In the kneeling position, one might find that even though everything about performance appears to be working properly, the shot group is spread out all over the bull. Closer analysis of follow-through reveals that the muzzle jump of the rifle is varying widely from shot to shot. Analysis: the elbow is not placed solidly on the knee, resulting in a constantly changing support-base for the rifle, and changes in the direction of recoil and muzzle jump. Again, no change in position is made until this diagnosis is verified by further observation. When the shooter is satisfied that this is in fact the cause of the problem, it is time to make a controlled experiment to correct the problem.

The controlled experiment.

If analysis of position is what makes possible the improvement of a position, the controlled experiment is what *makes* the improvement. Nothing is more important to the efficient, fast solution to problems. In addition, the controlled experiment is insurance against deterioration in performance. And moreover, the controlled experiment can lead to progress even where no problem is apparent. The controlled experiment is the most reliable way in which a rifleman discovers new, improved methods and techniques. The controlled experiment is the means by which entirely new knowledge is discovered and put to use. It should be one of the most important techniques in every shooter's repertory. Oddly enough, while its principles are pretty widely known, only a small number of shooters actually use the controlled experiment technique consistently. If all shooters used it faithfully, it probably would be safe to say that their individual progress, and progress in the shooting world at large, would make astonishing gains.

A controlled experiment makes use of the scientific method. It consists of verifying the effects of one, single variable in a system. In shooting, that system is particularly complex, being made up of hundreds of variables of rifle adjustment, position, motor performance, and concentration. If we wish to evaluate the effects, say, of a new adjustment in the palm-rest, it is important to keep all other variables unchanged, so that the effects of the readjusted palm-rest, and the readjusted palm-rest only, can be evaluated. If the shooter readjusted the palm-rest, changed from a post to an aperture front sight, changed the position of his feet, and put a different trigger into his rifle, he would not know the specific effects of any of these changes; he would have only the conglomerate results to go upon. His score might go up, or it might go down—but he wouldn't know specifically why. More than likely, however, it would go down with this many changes made, because a fair percentage of changes prove to be harmful rather than beneficial, and with several changes made simultaneously, the probabilities of overall harmful effects are quite high. Possibly one or two of the changes would have had beneficial effects; but the beneficial effects were canceled out altogether, and in fact reversed, by the effects of the two or three harmful changes. So not only is progress sometimes not made by changing several variables simultaneously, but the level of performance may actually be lowered.

An accurate evaluation of a change in position or technique can be made only by making one change while continuing to do everything else in exactly the same way. If one changes the adjustment of the palm-rest, no other changes are made. This way, if the change is beneficial, it can be adopted as permanent; if it is harmful, it can be discarded and the original palm-rest reassumed, thus assuring that the level of performance does not regress from the level at which the change was initiated. The experiment has then been a controlled experiment, because all the variables have been under the experimenter's direct, positive control, including the variable which was changed.

Frequently the most difficult aspect of a controlled experiment is evaluating the permanency of the effects of the change. The specific effects of a single change may often be obscured by the general effects of change itself. In certain stages of training (usually after the first year), almost any change in position or technique will appear to have a beneficial effect, usually for two or three days, and then performance will frequently fall back to its previous level, or below. At other times the opposite is true—almost any change will produce a drop in performance, which may be misleading. because two or three days later the effect might be greatly improved performance. To further complicate matters, changes that produce good effects in training sessions will sometimes not work at all under match conditions. The probabilities for this phenomenon occurring are quite low, but if it does occur the results can be disastrous.

A safe procedure to follow, therefore, in evaluating the effects of any change, is to render a judgment in two stages. First, a *provisional evaluation* is made on the basis of training sessions, but it is made only after the change has been used in a minimum of four training sessions. Six to eight training sessions would actually be better. At this point the change will be either adopted or discarded. (For a beginning shooter in the very first stages of training, this may take on the cast of a final evaluation, but, for the beginner, many things about his positions and techniques will remain provisional for an extended time.) Second, a *final evaluation* is made only after the adopted change has been tested and found to be beneficial under actual match conditions.

Probably the most obvious use of the controlled experiment is in correcting a recognized weakness in a position. In a previous section we saw how a rifleman analyzes his position to discover the cause of a basic problem. He then applies the scientific method to effect a cure for the problem. However, identical experimental methods are also applied toward correcting faulty techniques. The reader need only use common sense to see how the method may be used to evaluate a new technique of trigger pull, for example, or some other aspect of motor performance. The probable effects of the technique under consideration are thoroughly thought through, and, if they appear promising, the technique is tried out. The new technique is the only change made at the time, however, so that its effects can be accurately ascertained. If the results are beneficial, the technique is provisionally adopted until it can be tested in a match. If the effects are not beneficial, the technique is discarded and the original technique readopted.

An additional application of the controlled-experiment method is as important as its use in correcting recognized weaknesses. This is its use to discover improvements in positions or techniques which do not present any recognizable flaws. These experiments are conducted not to correct a recognized weakness, but to seek something even better than what is presently being used. Improvements, we should note, have been found in the past, and will be found in the future. Sometimes they are found purely by chance. But chance is capricious, and a man may go a whole lifetime and never stumble onto an improvement by accident. But he can actively seek new improvements through experimentation, and his chances of discovering them are vastly increased.

These experiments may be conducted at any time, but a certain amount of methodology used here will also be beneficial. First, experiments to correct a recognized problem always take priority over experiments to discover improvements. A recognized weakness is a minus factor in performance, and should be eliminated as soon as possible. An improvement is a plus factor which can be added to performance. As a minus and a plus tend to neutralize each other, the plus of an improvement will not be of full value unless the minus of an existing weakness is first eliminated. Another reason for giving first priority to eliminating weaknesses is this: an "improvement" that works before an existing weakness is removed may not work after the weakness is removed. Whenever a weakness is recognized, then, we attack it with a direct problem-solving approach. To put off or postpone attacking the problem by attempting to make an improvement first is to take a negative, evasive approach to problem solving.

A second principle of methodology is that experiments to discover new improvements work best if they are conducted with a specific purpose in mind. An experiment is an effort to verify an already-formulated hypothesis. In shooting, the hypothesis will usually be an idea about the effects of a particular change. Unless the proposed change has been thought through, and the hypothesis clearly formulated in advance, any "experimentation" is merely purposeless activity. "Trying something new" is not experimentation; it is merely random activity carried out with the hope of a chance discovery. Experimentation is planned, controlled activity directed toward a clearly defined goal.

Third, the material, or data, used for formulating a hypothesis for later testing can often be gathered on a day set aside for close analysis of a single variable in shooting. During one of these sessions, which should be scheduled no more frequently than once a week, the shooter modifies his usual training procedure and devotes his entire effort simply to understanding how a specific variable works. He may devote the entire training session to understanding how one muscle operates, for example, or to understanding the effects of cheek pressure. No changes in methods are adopted as a result of these sessions, but the sessions may *suggest* some new method which would be an improvement over the existing one. This could become the basis of a hypothesis, and the formulation of an experiment.

Sessions devoted to close analysis of single variables, or to discovering new methods, are best scheduled during the plateaus of the learning curve. As is well known, the graph of most learning curves is a series of hills and plateaus. During the hill of the curve, a shooter is usually correcting problems quickly and is already involved in making rapid progress. On the plateaus of his learning curve, however, he is more or less at a standstill, and experiments will help both to start him making progress again, and to relieve the monotony that seems to develop during these plateaus and deaden interest in shooting. Well-planned and successful experiments keep interest alive and enjoyment keen.

The shooter's diary.

Just as a scientist conducts an experiment in his laboratory, a shooter keeps a detailed written record of everything that might be of importance. A written record is permanent, and allows the scientist to record and evaluate each step of his experiment as he goes along. Imagine the absurdity of a scientist conducting a complex, two-year experiment to develop a new drug to cure cancer, and not keeping careful records. Each step of the experiment proceeds smoothly, and then at the end of the two years he attempts to put all the steps together and make the final test of his work. The experiment fails because one of the steps is not performed as it was originally. What can his only conclusion be? "Well, I must be doing something differently from the way I did it originally, but darned if I can remember what it is." Now here the scientist, on the verge of an important breakthrough, is helpless to succeed because the work of two years was unrecorded, is now lost to human memory, and is consequently utterly wasted. No scientist would dare risk the absurdity of finding himself in such a position.

A rifleman keeps a written record for similar reasons. Every shooter will have the experience of making rapid progress for a period, and then suddenly finding one day that he has difficulty keeping his shots in the black, much less in an acceptable group. This may simply be a "bad day"; but it may also be that he has developed a serious problem and is totally unable to discover the source, even after several days of working hard to find it. This is a common occurrence, and usually grows out of the fact that when we are concentrating on some particular fundamental of shooting we tend to forget others. The shooter who finds his performance suddenly and inexplicably deteriorated has nine times out of ten simply dropped something from his performance through oversight. How does he correct this oversight? If he has no diary, he may not correct it for weeks, even months. But if he does have a diary, in less than a day he can read a complete description of every aspect of position and every technique that has been part of his performance. He quickly discovers what he has been overlooking, makes the correction, and finds his performance back to normal almost at once.

In addition, a diary allows one to attempt and evaluate an experiment, and then discard the change if necessary and return to the exact position or technique used before the experiment was made. For example, looking back and discovering that his last experimental change, which was unsuccessful, involved moving the feet 3 inches closer together, he can easily move them 3 inches further apart, and *record* this change in his diary. The diary furnishes, then, a complete description of his positions and techniques. This record is indispensable to rapid progress, for it prevents a shooter from losing good features of performance that might otherwise be forgotten during the course of experimental changes.

Perhaps a more important function of the diary, however, is to increase the shooter's awareness of his training procedures. Just as talking or writing about each shot helps an individual learn awareness of and concentration on his performance, so does writing a diary about each training session (and match) help him become aware of how each training session contributes to the success of his overall program. It forces him to ask, "What did this session contribute?" and, if it contributed nothing, to ask, "How can I make the next session contribute to my progress?"

A diary does this by requiring the shooter to do two things at the end of each session. First, he must think through the completed session, evaluate it, and record his ideas in clear language. He is thus forced to think through the session more completely than he otherwise might. Second, he also writes out a plan or goal for the next training session, and this will be used to give a specific purpose to the next session. Continuity in training is thus increased, and each session is also given a specific goal or purpose. Furthermore, the goal is formulated far enough ahead so that some advance planning can be made as to *how* to accomplish the goal of the session. Once again, we will repeat that a shooter's progress is almost directly proportionate to how well he thinks. A diary is the tool which keeps his thinking clear and complete, and, by reading the diary through from time to time, he can gain an invaluable overview of his program and his progress to date.

Since a diary is, in effect, a written record of a whole training program, it should be kept in a permanent, or at least durable, form. The most widely used device is a common loose-leaf notebook of the type used by students. In this notebook may be kept the written training program as well as the diary. Entries in the diary should be kept chronologically, with every entry dated. But perhaps most important, the record and analysis of each program should be *complete and specific.*

It is totally pointless, for example, to write on the back of an old target something like, "Today I tried gripping the palm-rest tighter, and everything worked fine," and then throwing this piece of paper in a box or drawer with other similar slips of paper. Simply taking a pencil and paper and writing something down accomplishes nothing meaningful. Writing in itself has little value. It is the complete record, and the complete analysis that accompanies the writing of a good diary entry, that helps the shooter to make progress.

The writer of the above remark, for example, cannot tell on the basis of his notation when he performed this experiment, for it gives no date. He does not say what specific results came of increasing grip on the palm-rest, how it affected his physical or mental performance or his score. *How* valuable was it, or in fact was it valuable at all? There is no way of knowing.

In short, he knows no more about the experiment after writing his "entry" than he knew before the experiment was performed. A week later he will have no dependable memory or record of the experiment. Since his habits are so sloppy, it is easy to surmise that his next training session, and diary entry, will be just as unorganized and pointless as the last, for he has made no plans for the next session, nor does he have some goal to reach for except "improvement" in some vague sense. But improvement is not something vague and general—it is made up of a slight gain in some specific area here, and another slight gain in some specific there. A plan for every training session helps to make each one to yield a small improvement. And the champion knows that a gain, however small, in each training session, *is* progress. The small gains eventually add up to a gold medal.

Following are two sample pages from an imaginary diary. Notice the heading of each entry, which includes notations on place, date, time of day, weather, and mental and physical condition of the shooter. This material should always be recorded. In addition, there is a complete description and analysis of the session. You may be pleased to find that the entry in a diary does not have to be lengthy. It has merely to be accurate and *thoughtful.*

Ft. Benning: June 7, 1973. Fired from 8:30 to 11:30. Weather: light overcast, with slight gusting wind from 9 o'clock that barely stirred flags; temperature in the low 70's. Believe weather had only a slight effect on my performance. Felt physically and mentally dull throughout the session, probably because I did not get my usual amount of sleep last night.

Am continuing to focus on kneeling. Began the session by firing 20 shots quickly in the other positions: 182 standing, 195 prone. Both scores below par. Began work on kneeling by following the plan I formed yesterday: I shortened the sling by 1 notch, which has given a much tighter feel to the position. This change, I believe, has corrected the sense I've had for the past week of the rifle tending to float away from the center of the bull, seemingly of its own accord. Shot a full course, and my confidence in the change began to grow as I got used to the new feel of the position. Score: 393. Still low, but the position definitely felt better than yesterday, and I believe the position is improved more than the score suggests, especially as my overall performance seemed below average.

Tomorrow I'll continue testing the change made today.

Ft. Benning: June 8, 1973. Fired from 8:30 to 12:00. Weather: no clouds, good light conditions; temperature in the high 70's. No wind at first, but a gusting 8 mph wind was blowing from 9 o'clock by the end of the session. The flags were hanging at 45 degrees under average wind conditions. I felt in good shape today, both physically and mentally.

Continued with kneeling. Quickly fired the other positions: 186 standing, 198 prone. Performance came easily, without much effort. In kneeling the shortened sling seems to be the answer to my problems. The position now feels solid and stable, and my hold is easily inside the 10-ring. As I was having a particulary good day, however, the change must be tested another 2 or 3 days, at least. One added advantage is that in the kneeling position I now seem to be affected less by the wind. Despite a mild wind, I finished with a 396. I had to work hard for each shot, though, and waited one time at least 12 minutes for the right conditions; in fact, I had to wait quite a bit for most of the shots. I finished later than usual, and felt slightly tired, but in good spirits over the results of the experiment.

Tomorrow I'll test the shortened sling again. If performance holds up 3 more days, I'll be satisfied to keep the new sling adjustment.

A diary will become increasingly important as one progresses up the scale of performance. A beginning shooter will derive considerable value from a diary, but less value than will the advanced shooter. The person training for a world record will find a diary absolutely essential. One thing is certain: no one will be hampered by keeping a careful diary.

Summary.   If the material in this section on implementing training had to be summarized as briefly as possible, we would put it this way. Work on progressing in only one position at a time. Make and evaluate only one change at a time. Keep a complete record of everything you do.

MENTAL PRACTICE

A relatively controversial training technique involves the concept of mental practice. The same process has been variously named "conceptualization," "ideational functioning," "introspection," "imaginary practice," and "mental rehearsal." We use the term "mental practice" to refer to the process of thinking through an act of shooting without this thought process being accompanied by any overt physical activity. Thus a person could sit in a chair or lie on a bed and mentally practice shooting from the standing position. While the effectiveness of mental practice has not been unequivocally established, there is some evidence that it may be of benefit as a training vehicle among shooters if it is properly understood and properly performed. It appears in some cases to improve the motor performance involved in shooting; it seems even more beneficial in helping to develop mental discipline. The potential benefits, then, are both physiological and psychological.

The concept of mental practice is widely known among physical educators and is by no means new. But though the concept dates back to the previous century, intensive, meaningful investigation of it by physiologists and psychologists is only recently getting under way. Much remains to be learned about why and to what extent it actually works, and there is widespread disagreement about its effectiveness. To our knowledge, no experiments, other than the ones we have recently initiated, have been conducted on the subject as it relates to the peculiar motor skills involved in shooting. Thus some of what we say on the matter has to be regarded as tentative. However, preliminary experiments are encouraging enough to warrant including a discussion of the subject in this book. We feel that it is reasonable to draw upon summaries of investigations into areas other than shooting (Singer, pp. 216-218; Cratty, 1964, pp. 239-240; 1968, pp. 142-145; and

Oxendine, pp. 222-240) and apply the findings to what we have already learned in actual practice.

Common findings in research on mental practice suggest the following generalizations:

1. Acquired experience with a motor task is necessary before mental practice produces any noticeable benefits. A person who has never fired a rifle, for example, cannot practice shooting mentally with good effect because he has no experience to draw upon to enable him to participate mentally in the appropriate motor responses.

2. Mental practice should be used in combination with actual physical training, not in place of such training. There is no evidence that mental practice, used exclusively, is of any appreciable value in learning the kinds of skills involved in shooting.

3. Mental practice appears actually to aid in the improvement of previously experienced motor skills. An individual who mentally practices shooting after an actual training session, for example, might find in his next training session that the motor functions involved in hold or trigger pull have noticeably improved. This will not always be the case, it must be emphasized, but experiments suggest that it will frequently be the case.

4. Mental practice is beneficial only if the procedure being mentally rehearsed is the proper one. A shooter who mentally practices an incorrect method of trigger pull, for example, is only harming his performance.

5. Mental practice seems most effective when it is limited to sessions of no longer than five minutes. Beyond this time limit, most people are unable to concentrate effectively on this type of activity.

These general principles suggest several ways in which mental practice can be incorporated into a shooter's training program. First of all, there is the possibility of a mental practice session *immediately before* a training session. The effect of this would be to help the individual enter into proper concentration and to prepare mentally for the activity to be performed in the overt training.

A second application would be *during* a training session. Here we feel that we are on relatively sure ground, for we have employed something similar to mental practice for years with very good success. We therefore believe that this particular application can and should be used by everyone. It is described as follows. When an individual performs a shot correctly, he analyzes his performance, articulates to himself the things he did correctly, and then mentally replays the performance. The purpose is to reinforce the learning of the correct responses. If he performs a shot incorrectly, he analyzes his performance, isolates what he did wrong, and then mentally practices the performance as it *should have* been done; and he does this perhaps two or three times *before* he attempts another overt performance. In this way he "erases" the incorrect responses, and reinforces the correct responses. This is a technique not only for reinforcing motor skills, but also for reinforcing mental discipline; since the technique involves the repetition of a correct mental sequence, it obviously aids in developing the ability to repeat a successful mental performance. In this manner it helps to build positive thought processes, which are crucial to successful concentration on, and control of, performance.

A third application of mental practice would be *immediately after* a training session—that is, immediately after completion of the diary entry. The value here would be in ensuring that the motor skills learned during the session are reinforced and retained. New insights arising out of thinking about the session while preparing the diary entry might also be rehearsed at this time; this would effect retention of the insight and perhaps prepare the way for the next training session. A fourth application of mental practice would be *between* training sessions. Here the act of shooting might be rehearsed briefly several times a day. The temperament, daily circumstances, and intensity of his motivations would probably determine how frequently a given individual would work to employ mental practice in this way.

Something similar to mental practice can be used as a form of attitude training. Our own experiments suggest that this application works very well with some individuals. The technique consists of the individual mentally affirming that he *will* reach the score that he has designated as the goal of his current training program. For example, he may have determined to be able to shoot 1160 by August 1. He then establishes a routine wherein several times a day he thinks to himself, "I will shoot 1160 on August 1." Among the subjects who were instructed to use this technique, a significant percentage reported that the technique made the training goal seem much less formidable and much more obtainable; they developed a more positive attitude; and their scores improved with a noticeably increased rapidity. Some subjects even feel that it is beneficial to write the goal on a slip of paper and read it several times a day. Perhaps it would be useful to read it aloud, as acceptance of the goal would be reinforced not only by thinking, but also by involving the senses in reading, speaking, and hearing about it. You must decide for yourself whether or not this is a technique you wish to employ.

The "how" of mental practice may vary from individual to individual. As it is used in shooting, two general techniques are known, and perhaps a serious shooter should attempt to use both. Both involve closing the eyes and gathering concentration so as to exclude any unwanted thoughts from the mind. This period of preparation may vary from two or three seconds to as much as several minutes. Then, in one method, the individual, still with his eyes closed, tries to imagine that he is in the shooting position, holding the gun, releasing the shot, and following through exactly as he would like to do in overt performance. As far as possible, the thought processes should probably be unverbalized. In this technique he tries to experience mentally all of the kinesthetic, motor, and mental sensations associated with the act of shooting. A second technique is, again with the eyes closed, to try to watch himself, in his mind's eye, perform the shot as though he were outside his own body looking at himself. Again, probably, the thought processes should be largely nonverbal. In both instances, the shot is always imagined to be performed *exactly as it should be performed* to the best of the individual's knowledge.

When mental practice is used just prior to a match, it is obviously similar to the process of "going into oneself" discussed earlier. There may be a difference, however, in that going within oneself probably involves, for many people, mentally rehearsing an entire match or segment of a match, while mental practice is limited to a single performance. The processes are undeniably related, however, and those who are interested in the concept of mental rehearsal should not only use it as a means of controlling match pressure, but also as a means of supplementing overt training efforts. Since much remains to be learned about it, we do not say flatly that everyone should use it in all its forms; but if a particular application does yield good results for you, even if only part of the time, by all means take advantage of it.

CHAPTER
6

Mental & Physical Conditioning

In this chapter we will be primarily concerned with the details of physical conditioning. However, we have used the title "Mental and Physical Conditioning" to emphasize that the two kinds of conditioning are really inseparable. It is impossible, for instance, to condition the muscles to hold still beyond a certain point until the powers of concentration and will are sufficiently developed to *will* the muscles to hold still. Shooting has been called the sport of the will, and perhaps rightfully so, for in no other sport is the role of the will so important. Shooting does not require great strength or great speed. Rather it requires careful physical conditioning and a tremendous degree of physical control.

Both of these things are achieved through exercise of the will: a person must will himself to train in order to acquire a high level of physical conditioning, and, while training, must will his body to perform the tasks correctly. It is reasonably obvious that champion shooters train longer and harder than others, and they are able to do this primarily because they have strong wills. They, like anyone else, developed strength of will by exerting their wills until their willpower gradually developed to a high degree. Thus in part, they developed their willpower by forcing themselves to undergo physical training.

Mental and physical conditioning are thus complementary and, to a large extent, inseparable. In parts of this chapter, however, we will speak of them separately in order to simplify discussion.

HEALTH: THE FOUNDATION OF CONDITIONING

A shooter, just like any other athlete, must base his training program on a foundation of good health. This should include, among other things, annual medical, dental, and vision examinations, and a continuing concern in all areas of life with sound health habits. The use of tobacco is best avoided, not only because it is a risk to health, but also because of its effects upon the nerves and muscles, and the heart rate. There is some evidence that tobacco decreases the muscles' ability to hold still, and anyone addicted to cigarettes knows the nervousness and irritability that results when he needs a cigarette. When this need occurs during a match, it is not likely to help performance. Moreover, smoking appears to increase the pulse rate. Experiments conducted by one of the authors showed that stopping the use of tobacco altogether resulted in his pulse rate decreasing, in thirty days, by eight beats per minute during rest and twenty beats per minute after exercise. A slow pulse rate, of course, is a distinct advantage in shooting.

The excessive use of alcohol should be avoided. An occasional beer or before-dinner cocktail is not likely to be harmful, but alcohol should not be taken for several hours before a shooting session, or in large quantities at any time during the training program, and many good shooters prefer to avoid it altogether. Only prescription drugs, of course, should ever be taken, and these should not be taken before a match without approval from the prescribing physician. Many shooters believe that the stimulant qualities of coffee and tea produce the undesirable side effects of very small muscle tremors.

Anyone in training should have a balanced diet of food properly prepared to preserve nutritional value. Some books on nutrition and food preparation are listed in the bibliography at the end of this volume. He should also have adequate rest and sleep. Proper diet and sleep habits should be observed every single day, day in and day out. The importance of observing these practices on a steady, every-day basis cannot be overemphasized. If you are unsure of what constitutes a properly balanced diet and adequate sleep, most hospitals, public health centers, schools, and libraries have informative literature on nutrition and health, and frequently personnel who will discuss these matters with interested individuals. Your family physician is also an important source of such information.

TYPES OF CONDITIONING

On a foundation of properly maintained health, a rifleman can build a good conditioning program. This program will consist of specific conditioning for particular shooting functions, and will probably be augmented by supplemental conditioning. Specific conditioning refers to conditioning for a particular physical or mental task by actually performing that task. A shooter conditions himself to holding the rifle in the standing position by actually aiming and/or firing in the standing position. He conditions himself to the pressure of the sling in the prone position by actually getting into the prone position. He conditions himself to concentrate on hold by making the effort to concentrate while in a shooting position. Supplemental conditioning, on the other hand, is largely physical, and consists of almost any kind of nonspecific conditioning, such as jogging, swimming, isometrics, and participation in sports activities. Specific conditioning is inherent in training sessions, and is thus automatically built into a well-planned program. Supplemental conditioning must be added on if the individual chooses to include it in his schedule.

SPECIFIC PHYSICAL CONDITIONING

Specific physical conditioning has several goals. One of these is to develop the strength and endurance of the particular muscles used in shooting so the shooter can fire a 5¼-hour match without undue fatigue. Other goals include increasing the body's ability to remain reasonably comfortable in each position, sharpening the kinesthetic sense, developing the ability to hold still, and learning motor skills, including sway compensation, breath control, eye control, and trigger pull, so thoroughly as to give them characteristics of semiconditioned responses.

Developing strength and endurance.

Although when the rifle is in position it is supported primarily by bones and not by muscles, a shooter's muscles must nevertheless be conditioned in order to develop endurance. The muscles which lift the rifle into the aiming positions must be conditioned to perform their tasks repeatedly. The muscles which support or hold the body in position must be capable of enduring a complete match of 5¼ hours without becoming so fatigued that they become shaky. Merely standing upright for three hours, for a person who is not accustomed to it, can cause shakiness in the leg muscles. Muscles must be conditioned to endure any extended performance, and shooting is no exception. The usual way to develop this endurance is to begin with holding exercises. The rifle is held in the aiming position until muscles become fatigued, and the rifle is then placed in a rest position. After a brief rest by the shooter, during which time the muscles recover, the rifle is placed in the aiming position again. At first, the duration of each hold period will be relatively short, and the number of holds which can be made before the muscles become thoroughly tired will be small. Gradually, however, both the number of hold periods and their length can be increased. It is desirable to be able to hold the rifle in the aiming position comfortably for ten minutes. This will prove invaluable when shooting in adverse wind conditions. Generally speaking, a person should be capable of shooting in each position for three hours without fatigue, and for six hours in any one session without undue fatigue. The ability to shoot for three hours in any position is a great advantage if adverse conditions develop and slow down the pace of firing. The ability to shoot for six hours in a session gives one a reserve of endurance beyond the 5¼-hour match course, which provides the extra edge in confidence and strength that may mean the difference between winning and losing.

It must be emphasized that a conditioning program does *not* begin with six-hour training sessions. The length of the beginning sessions is based sensibly on how long the individual can perform before fatigue sets in. This time will vary widely among individuals, depending on each one's physical condition at the start. A good rule to follow is to continue training for only about ten shots after fatigue noticeably begins to affect performance. For beginners, this time will probably be somewhere between thirty and sixty minutes in each position, and one to two hours a session; experienced shooters will be able to shoot for three or four hours in each position, and six hours or more each session. To reach the point where one's endurance will last for six or more hours, one devises a conditioning plan that becomes part of the training program. The plan will call for a *gradual* increase in the length of training sessions until the desired duration of sessions is reached. From one to three months may be required to build up to the desired duration; it is unusual for the process to take longer than three months.

Of course most people will not be able to train six hours every day, and in fact this is neither necessary nor desirable. For one thing, building overall endurance and stamina can be accomplished in large part by a good supplemental conditioning program. For another, training for six hours every day would very likely turn most people stale in a very short while. If an individual had unlimited time at his disposal, we would favor training sessions of two to four hours a day, conducted four to six days a week. These should be complemented by a supplemental program, and, for two or so weeks before an important match, training sessions of six hours duration. For example, one might schedule sessions for two hours on Monday, Tuesday, and Wednesday, three hours on Thursday, and four hours on Saturday, with a four-hour session every alternate Sunday. During this time, the four-hour session could occasionally be expanded to six. About two weeks before an important match, the schedule might be changed to five-hour sessions on Tuesday and Thursday, and regular six-hour sessions on Saturday and Sunday. Not everyone, of course, will be able to devote this much time to training. The figures presented here are intended to indicate *maximum* training hours in a program designed to being a shooter to maturity as quickly as possible.

Perhaps the most important requirements of a conditioning

program are that it be systematic and regular. A plan for systematic progress in building endurance and stamina should be formulated carefully and followed just as carefully. And above all, training should be on a regular basis. As we mentioned earlier, it is much better to train two or three hours a day five days a week than to train seven hours a day two days a week. Long, widely spaced training sessions usually result in one's shooting while overly fatigued, and thereby developing motor habits that are positively damaging to performance, for concentration will inevitably deteriorate before the end of sessions conducted on such a basis. Shorter sessions every day lead to the development of good habits, for both the body and the mind are sharp throughout the entire session.

Achieving reasonable comfort.

Specific conditioning is also aimed at increasing the body's ability to remain reasonably comfortable in a position. Reasonable comfort while shooting is desirable, for pain hastens the fatigue of both mind and body. Now no one would claim that shooting positions are completely comfortable; one doesn't normally assume a shooting position when he wants to relax. It is partly because the body is unaccustomed to the positions that they are uncomfortable, particularly at first.

Anyone who has trained in the standing position using the back-bend-and-body-twist knows that the lower back muscles become almost painfully sore for a week or so, until they become accustomed to the position. The kneeling position forces the ankle over the kneeling-roll to bend in an unusual way and receive an unaccustomed amount of body weight— hence it must be conditioned to accept this bend and weight. The prone position places unaccustomed pressure on the arms, and is therefore uncomfortable at first. And in both kneeling and prone, the upper arm must be conditioned to accepting the pressure of the sling, both to achieve reasonable comfort and to minimize the pulse beat that will at first be transmitted directly to the sling. These shooting positions never become completely comfortable. But with specific conditioning, they can become reasonably comfortable, and this is one training goal.

Developing the kinesthetic sense.

Another goal is to develop the kinesthetic sense. Kinesthesia is the "feel" that everyone has of his body and the positions of its various parts in relation to one another. Kinesthesia is recognized by most physiologists as a true sixth sense. It is what enables you to close your eyes and with any finger you choose touch any part of your body you could touch with your eyes open. You may not be able to do this at first, but with practice you can, for you can learn to feel the positions of the parts of your body. This rather astounding capability plays two major roles in shooting. First, it enables a shooter to memorize the feel of a position; this is valuable in aiding him to assume the same position each time he shoots or begins a new session. Second, kinesthesia enables a shooter to feel the condition of each muscle in his body. This ability, too, is developed with training. With a little practice, a rifleman will be able to sense within very narrow ranges how much tension is present in each muscle, and also whether the degree of tension is stable. It is this ability to judge the stability of muscle tension that will enable him to anticipate unwanted muscle movements. This anticipation of movements is the key to judging the durability of a hold, and its importance is obviously paramount.

Developing muscle tone.

Muscle tone is closely related to kinesthesia, and also to hold. Tone is the amount of tension in a muscle when the individual has otherwise relaxed the muscle. People who are sedentary and in poor physical condition have soft, flabby muscles, or very little tone. People who are athletic and in good physical condition have firm, tough muscles, or a good deal of tone. The presence of good tone is a sign of a strong, well-conditioned muscle. Generally, good muscle tone improves both the kinesthetic sense and the ability to control the muscles and produce a good hold. Apparently a healthy level of tone sharpens both feedback from the sensory nerves in the muscle, and the muscle's response to input from the motor nerves which control its movements. There is no scientific evidence for this statement, but a large number of good shooters unquestionably accept the value of tone as an aid to good performance. This implies that a program of supplemental physical conditioning, as well as specific conditioning, might be beneficial, especially for the person whose body muscles generally lack tone. It should be noted here, however, that efforts to increase tone beyond a certain level are likely to interfere with or direct attention away from regular training sessions. Beyond a certain level, tone can be further increased only by such training efforts as heavy weightlifting. These efforts are incompatible with good specific conditioning, as we shall later see. The goal is not to create as much muscle tone as possible, but only to have a degree of tone which provides good kinesthetic feedback and quick, accurate motor responses.

Using muscle tension.

A further aid to good kinesthetic and motor function is a slight degree of deliberately created tension in the muscles during the process of aiming and releasing the shot. Tone is the degree of tension in a muscle when it is otherwise relaxed. The kind of tension we are talking about now is added on to normal tone. Almost all shooters use this technique, though many do so unconsciously. Describing their interior environments in the standing position, for example, most riflemen will say that they are slightly tensing almost all body muscles. This seems to be part of a seemingly intuitive approach to creating a stable hold. The amount of tension created varies among individuals, with the descriptions ranging from "almost imperceptible" to "obvious, but mild." Of course, this tension should not be too great, or it will quickly cause fatigue. Some shooting experience may be necessary to recognize, and perhaps to create and use, this tension. However, it seems to become a part of everybody's technique naturally, and reasonably soon after training begins.

Developing hold.

Hold appears to depend in part upon both kinesthesia and muscle tone and tension. Hold is the ability to control the muscles and keep them still. Most people take this ability for granted, believing that anyone can hold still in any natural position. Actually, anyone may be able to maintain a given position for a time, but to hold *still* in any position requires considerable training. The ability to hold still is largely a product of concentration and will, but it is also a product of specific conditioning. The muscles themselves must be conditioned to hold still in each of the different shooting positions. A good hold in standing, for example, does not ensure a good hold in kneeling. A considerable portion of training is devoted to developing hold, even among champion shooters, for the process of refining hold is never-ending. Hold is a product of training the muscles to *enable* them to hold still, and also of learning to concentrate sufficiently to more or less *make* them hold still.

Developing semi-conditioned motor responses.

Motor learning, or learning to perform with the muscles, frequently involves two stages. The first stage, during which learning is taking place, may be called the period of *controlled response.* During this stage, the individual must concentrate on and consciously direct the responses of the muscles involved in the performance. The second stage coincides with the completion of learning, and the motor responses involved in performance may be accomplished with the individual aware of what he is doing, but not concentrating on the responses themselves. This, as we have seen, may be called the *semi-conditioned response,* since the individual has learned the motor skills so thoroughly that he responds more or less automatically in a certain way to a certain situation. We earlier cited as an example of semiconditioned responses the act of driving an automobile. Let's now look at this example in more detail. We can all remember the awkwardness and difficulty of using our hands and feet the right way when we were learning to drive. The task required considerable concentration and mental effort. After learning to drive, however, most people can handle a car without any apparent mental effort, and are able to drive while thinking or talking about something entirely different. They are aware of what they are doing, of course, but only peripherally; they are actually concentrating on something else. Other familiar semiconditioned responses include walking, swimming, bicycle riding, and just about any other physical activity that can be routinely performed without concentration.

The psycho-physiological mechanisms involved in semi-conditioned motor responses are not clear, and possible theoretical explanations need not concern us here. It will be useful, however, to understand three characteristics of semi-conditioned responses. One is that an individual may at any time turn his full concentration to the performance of the particular motor response. Put another way, the response may move out of the area of peripheral awareness into the center of consciousness. Thus an individual may at any time concentrate on the movements involved in driving or swimming, for example.

The second characteristic of semiconditioned responses is that they may be superseded by other semiconditioned responses. One semiconditioned response to a situation may be replaced by another semiconditioned response to the same situation. For example, the individual who learns to drive a car with a manual gearshift becomes conditioned to apply both the brake and clutch pedals in the situation involving an approach to a stop sign. If he switches to a car with an automatic gearshift, he will, unless he consciously directs himself not to, automatically respond to a stop sign by pushing down the brake pedal and the nonexistent clutch pedal. With a little effort, he will soon respond automatically to a stop sign by pushing down the brake pedal only. The clutch-and-brake response has been superseded by the brake-only response. If he then drives a car with a manual gearshift, he will have to make a conscious effort to depress the clutch pedal in response to a stop sign until this response is again thoroughly learned and reconditioned. In shooting, the fact that semiconditioned responses can be superseded is both an advantage and a disadvantage. It is an advantage because it enables one to make progress by learning ever-better responses. It is a disadvantage because some of the semiconditioned responses are superseded when we don't want them to be—bad habits creep into our performance. When this happens, conscious attention must be turned to the motor function involved. The unwanted semiconditioned response must be eliminated and replaced by a desired response.

A third characteristic of semiconditioned behavior is that, in an advanced stage of learning, an individual may learn two or three different semiconditioned responses, and be able effortlessly to choose the appropriate one to make. For example, an individual may learn to make both a brake-and-clutch and a brake-only response at a semiconditioned level, and automatically make the right one depending on whether he is driving a car with a manual or an automatic gearshift. In the same way, some advanced shooters, for example, have acquired three separate semiconditioned trigger-pull responses, each one being especially adapted to one of the three shooting positions. These shooters can effortlessly, and perhaps unconsciously, make the right response in the appropriate situations.

There are probably many semiconditioned responses involved in the shooting process, but four in particular stand out. They are, roughly in order of increasing difficulty, sway-compensation, breath control, eye control, and trigger pull.

Sway-compensation.   For most people, sway-compensation is perhaps the most easily developed motor skill in shooting. In fact, it is so inherently easy that it may be closely related to the reflex ability of the eye to remain focused on a fixed point even though the head is turning or swaying. If so, it is thus closely allied to one kind of true reflex behavior, and in fact there is some question as to whether it is a natural or a learned response. Specifically, sway compensation is the response of correcting for the effects of body sway on the aim of the rifle in the standing (and possibly the kneeling) position. As mentioned earlier, a certain amount of body sway is unavoidable in the standing position, and yet most people are capable of compensating for this sway and holding the aim of the rifle in the bull without any conscious effort. There are, of course, limiting conditions under which this response can occur: if the sway if too fast, or exceeds certain maximum tolerances, the compensation response ceases to be automatic, or attainable even by conscious effort.

You can test this response by a very simple experiment. Assume the standing position in front of a mirror (rifle unloaded, of course!) and take aim at the front sight reflected in the mirror. Then consciously cause your body to sway gently

from side to side. Most people say that the rifle seems to remain aimed at the reflected front sight almost as if by magic. But it is not magic—it is the phenomenon of sway-compensation, and whether a reflex or a semiconditioned response, it is involved every time you aim in the standing position, and possibly in the kneeling position as well.

Breath control. Proper breath control is clearly a learned response in shooting, and one of the goals of specific training is to make breath control a fully developed semiconditioned response that needs no concentration or mental effort. Fortunately the goal is very easily attained, and most people are effortlessly using proper breath control in a relatively short training time. The technique for learning it is simply to concentrate on doing it properly—to rehearse it as a controlled response until, after a sufficient number of repetitions, breath control will become a semiconditioned response and you will be able to shift concentration elsewhere. You will be aware that you are using techniques of breath control, but the real focus of your attention will be on more important things.

Proper breath control depends in part upon the shooting position being correctly adjusted to the height of the target. The explanation of the technique itself will make the reasons clear. The usual shooting sequence is as follows: the rifle is placed in position, the aim is allowed to settle on the target, and the shooter then takes a deep breath; this deep inhalation usually causes the muzzle to elevate in the standing position, and to depress in the kneeling and prone positions. To some extent the position is correctly adjusted to the height of the target if, when the shooter begins to exhale, the muzzle begins to move toward the center of the bull (this movement will be downward in standing, upward in kneeling and prone). When the vertical movement of the muzzle brings the sights into correct relation with the bull, the shooter cuts off the flow of air from his lungs. With breathing fully suspended, the sights should rest in the center of the 10-ring. At this time, a normal, comfortable amount of air should remain in the lungs. If this is not the case, the position is not satisfactorily adjusted to the height of the target. Broad, general changes in the vertical adjustment of the muzzle are made by adjusting the position and the rifle accessories; only very fine vertical adjustments are made through control of the breathing, and the position is correct only when breath-controlled vertical adjustments result in a comfortable amount of air in the lungs.

As the shooting sequence continues, the shooter holds his breath while he evaluates his sight picture and hold, and while he releases the shot. If, however, this sequence is slow and the individual becomes conscious of a need for air as a result of holding his breath too long, the shooting process should be halted; without removing the rifle from position, he breathes normally until his need for oxygen is satisfied, takes another deep breath, and exhales slowly until the vertical alignment of the sights is correct, and once again begins holding his breath. He continues holding his breath until the shot is released, or until the entire cycle is repeated.

There is no correct amount of air that should be held in the lungs. The right amount is what feels comfortable for you. Some shooters like to have relatively full lungs during their hold; most prefer the amount that remains at the end of a normal exhalation; a very few like to force as much air from the lungs as they can. Only you can say what technique is best for you. Once the most successful technique has been established, it should be learned as a semiconditioned response.

Eye control.   Another goal of specific training is to make eye control a semiconditioned response. As explained in a later section titled "the eye and the sight system," the eye should not be allowed to focus on one point of the sight picture for more than two or three seconds. The proper technique is to change the point of focus at brief intervals, darting the eye from one point to another around the center of the sight picture. Many shooters feel that they make these darting movements at a more-or-less regular cadence, but not all agree on this point. Whether these movements are made in time to a cadence is probably immaterial—the important thing is that they be made with reasonable frequency. Initially a shooter will have to consciously direct these movements in the controlled response stage, but later they will take on the characteristics of semiconditioned responses. However, this is one semiconditioned response that appears to be quite unstable, and the habit of staring at a fixed point in the sight picture seems to appear easily and frequently in most people's performance.

It is probably a good idea to devise some systematic way of checking at various intervals in your training sessions to determine if your eye control is taking proper care of itself. If not, the response must be relearned and reconditioned, and this is perhaps best accomplished through simple holding exercises, where no attempt is made to pull the trigger. A simple device for reminding yourself to check your eye control habits is to make advance queries in your diary, making notations on pages well ahead in the notebook.

Trigger pull. Probably the most vexing task in specific training is to maintain proper trigger pull as a semiconditioned response. Conditioning trigger pull is complicated by the fact that the proper technique is difficult to learn in the first place. A shooter first learns to pull the trigger as a controlled response to a specific situation: a 10-ring hold. After a while this becomes a semiconditioned response, and the trigger finger moves automatically under the stimulus of a perfect sight picture. At these times it seems that the proper function of concentration is to *inhibit* the movement of the trigger finger until the hold is judged acceptable. During these periods, if conscious inhibition is not applied, the trigger finger may release the shot unexpectedly, when the rifle drifts into the 10-ring. Properly, when the hold is judged acceptable, the inhibition is withdrawn, and the trigger finger is simply allowed to move as if of its own will. When the process operates this way, trigger pull is at its best. However, one hour later, the efficacy of the semiconditioned trigger pull may deteriorate to zero.

Shoulder jerks, eye blinks, flinches of other types, delayed reactions, and false starts can all appear in the trigger-pull sequence. Next to recoil, it is the part of shooting most susceptible to Murphy's Law which states, "Anything that can happen, will." How or why problems appear in the trigger-pull response is not always certain. But when they do, trigger-pull techniques usually must be relearned from the beginning. This conditioning process is best accomplished by dry-firing, which is probably fifty to a hundred times faster than any other method.

Trigger pull appears to be specific for each position. A loss of good control in standing, for instance, is not necessarily accompanied by a loss of control in kneeling. Moreover, many successful shooters believe that the relationship between concentration and trigger pull is different in each position, as well as the *method* of trigger pull being different in each position. Consequently any generalizations are likely to be controversial, but we will risk the following ones, hoping that they will prove right in perhaps a majority of cases.

In the standing position, trigger pull at its best has all the characteristics of a semiconditioned response. Concentration during performance tends to center on hold, and the movement of the trigger finger is only in the periphery of awareness.

In the prone position, trigger control is often slow and deliberate, and tends to be in or near the center of concentration. Here the movement of the trigger finger resembles a controlled response more than a conditioned response.

In the kneeling position, trigger pull at its best frequently appears to occupy an indeterminate position, neither in the center nor on the periphery of concentration. With some successful shooters it tends to be closer to a conditioned response, with others it tends to be closer to a controlled response. With only a few shooters does it take on the extreme characteristics of these responses found in standing and prone.

There are three general techniques of trigger pull, any one of which is adaptable to one or more shooting positions. These are, first, a fairly rapid, straight pull; second, a slow, steady pull described as a careful squeeze; and third, a pull which may be described as a squeeze in stages, in which a small amount of pressure is applied and held for a period, then more pressure applied and held, and so on until a tiny increase in pressure sets off the shot. (Some shooters tend to finger the trigger, or touch it lightly on and off before attacking, but as this is seldom related to the actual pull, it may be regarded as merely an adjunct to one of the above techniques, and not a technique in itself.) Some shooters develop techniques which are intermediate between, or variations of, these more standard techniques.

Most shooters have a natural preference for one or another of the techniques in each position, so that choosing a technique is little or no problem. Many find, however, that their preference changes from time to time in some positions. But technique is much less of a problem than maintaining a smooth pull unaccompanied by other muscle movements. These undesired movements can occur, and frequently do, without the shooter's being aware of what has happened to his performance. Next to hold, trigger control probably requires more concentration than any other factor involved in shooting.

SPECIFIC MENTAL CONDITIONING

We touch once more on the subject of specific mental conditioning, which was discussed at length in the psychology section. In this chapter we have discussed physical conditioning with the understanding that mental conditioning plays an integral part in such an effort. But it is worth repeating at this point that the role of mental conditioning is central to a successful program of specific conditioning. Consider the role the mind actually plays in reaching all of the goals discussed above. As mentioned, the will is involved in what after all amounts to *forcing* oneself into a program to develop physical endurance, and to conditioning oneself to the initial discomforts of shooting positions.

Of equal, or perhaps greater, importance is the role of concentration. As none of the shooting positions is ever completely comfortable, concentration must be developed to the point of being unaffected by the discomforts experienced. Concentration is even more deeply involved in kinesthesia and hold, for in the one it is sensing the state of the entire body, and in the other it is controlling the entire body by willing it to hold in a given position, despite the minute changes in the center of gravity that occur constantly throughout the body. Concentration is in fact the necessary condition under which kinesthesia and hold can be developed.

The same can be said of the conditioned motor responses. Sway-compensation seems fairly easy to attain, but as one progresses through breath control, eye control, and trigger pull, the mind plays an increasingly central role in learning these functions, in detecting problems with them, and in relearning them when problems develop. It is only by continued effort that the mind can be conditioned to concentrate deeply on all of the things involved in shooting. Throughout the specific conditioning program, precise physical goals will remain clearly in mind; but mental conditioning will remain more in the center of attention.

It should be emphasized that none of the goals of specific conditioning can be attained by any other method than shooting. The best way to train for shooting is to train *by* shooting. (The sole exception to this principle was discussed in the earlier section on mental practice.)

SUPPLEMENTAL CONDITIONING

Through a supplemental conditioning program, the body can be raised to a level of general fitness unattainable through shooting alone. This can be a great advantage, physically and psychologically. The possibilities for attaining improved general fitness are so broad as to be difficult to describe; they are even more difficult to prescribe. The supplementary program that works for some shooters simply will not work for others. Some shooters, in fact, claim to have no supplementary program at all. However, in our observations, these individuals, while they perhaps do not have a *program* of activities, are in fact physically very active, participating in a variety of team sports and other activities which keep them physically fit. Perhaps they are capable of performing these physically beneficial activities while thinking of them as recreation instead of training. This is a neat and satisfactory trick, fully desirable if one can pull it off.

Many other successful shooters, however, are the type who like to plan and schedule supplementary activities as a part of their programs. There is no way to say what activities are best. The precise exercises or activities performed are unimportant; what is important is whether the particular training effort works for the individual. If it does, it is right for him. Later we will describe what we believe is a very good supplementary program; but it is by no means the only one. First, we will look in a very general way at the kinds of activities that can be included in a program.

Two of the most important goals of supplementary conditioning are increased endurance, or stamina, and decreased pulse rate. Endurance allows one to perform physical activities without fatigue. The value of this, particularly in international-style competition, needs no explanation. A decreased pulse rate is also a great advantage, because the proper shooting technique in the kneeling and prone positions is to release the shot during the interval between pulse beats. If the pulse rate is lowered, which lengthens the intervals between beats, the shooter has gained a distinct advantage, both psychological and physical.

The types of exercises which increase endurance and lower heart rate (after a period of rest) are those which require long, continuous effort. Two of the best exercises for these purposes are distance jogging and swimming. A surprisingly large number of successful shooters jog on a regular basis. Swimming is also good, and is occasionally useful to provide variation or to replace jogging on a hot day, but facilities for swimming are not always available. Facilities for jogging are almost always available, however, and in inclement weather one can keep up a jogging program by running in place indoors, which may be boring, but which should still be bearable if it occurs but infrequently.

There would seem to be an almost unlimited number of other activities that contribute to these goals and to general physical fitness. Following is a list of a few such activities, but everyone could probably think of others. These are listed because they have been used frequently by shooters: volleyball, basketball, softball, touch football, tennis, golf, walking combined with hunting or fishing, bicycle riding, skiing, horseback riding, backpacking, numerous forms of calisthenics, and isometrics. There has long been a belief that weightlifting is detrimental to shooting because it produces muscle tremors; however, this belief is based on only a partial truth. *Any* full muscular exertion will produce muscle tremors or shakiness for a short period until the muscles rest enough to recover from the resulting fatigue.

Many standard weightlifting body-building programs are designed to add bulk to the body muscles by working them to a state of fatigue, allowing them only just enough time to recover completely—usually forty-eight hours—and then working them to a state of fatigue again. The body reacts to this by building more muscle tissue to enable it to cope with the exertion without fatigue. Weightlifting programs take advantage of the body's response by raising the poundage of the weights, or increasing the number of repetitions of the exercise, as the body builds more muscle tissue. By thus recurrently fatiguing the muscles, the process of building bulk goes on continuously. This type of body-building program requires heavy weightlifting sessions about three times a week. Obviously, this type of weightlifting program is not compatible with a training schedule which calls for shooting sessions four or more times a week. On at least some of those days the muscles will not have recovered from weightlifting and will be subject to tremors. However, this does not mean that *all* weightlifting is detrimental to shooting.

A lighter program, designed merely to exercise systematically all the muscle groups and maintain them at a given level of strength and tone, but *not* to add bulk by completely fatiguing the muscles, would have no ill effects on shooting, provided the lifting were done about twenty-four hours before a shooting session. Such a program, if based on a thorough understanding of weightlifting principles and very carefully scheduled so as not to interfere with shooting, may in fact be beneficial, as weightlifting contributes somewhat to the kinesthetic sense and helps develop control of particular muscle groups. (No one, incidentally, should attempt weightlifting without first consulting an experienced instructor, lifter, or a good manual on the methods and principles of this very special sport.)

Any heavy exercises which produce fatigue shortly before a shooting session will cause muscle tremors and interfere with performance. It is therefore advisable to schedule athletic activities immediately *after* a training session. This allows the body about twenty-four hours to recover fully from fatigue, and muscle tremors will not be present during the next shooting session. If tremors are present—if the individual still feels shaky from the exercise—then the supplemental program is too rigorous, and should be reduced and then built up in gradual stages, if this is desired.

Whether a rifleman looks upon supplemental conditioning as part of his program or as recreation, sufficient physical activity should be included in the day-to-day routine to ensure a good level of physical fitness. No one can shoot well who is easily fatigued, weak, and generally in poor physical condition. Some excellent shooters are trying always to improve their physical condition throughout each training program. For example, when they begin a training program, they may be capable of jogging a certain distance in a certain time; throughout the program, they continue to increase the distance they run, and also their sustained speed.

A surprising number of joggers also combine mental conditioning with running and will force themselves to sprint the final distance, as an exercise in self-control and willpower. Other shooters use this technique also, but make no effort to increase their level of fitness through a program; they try, rather, only to maintain a given level of fitness. They usually begin with a good level of fitness, however. People who lead physically active lives may sustain a satisfactory level of fitness without a formalized supplemental program. Others who lead sedentary lives may need a rather complete supplemental program.

All shooters, whether they feel best maintaining a level of fitness, or gaining in fitness, or whether they work at a formalized supplemental program or not, benefit by their fitness in other ways: they gain added confidence in themselves. The person who is well trained, and *knows* he is well trained, goes to the firing line with an added degree of confidence in his ability to perform, and that confidence may be the decisive factor in winning or losing.

A SUGGESTED SUPPLEMENTAL CONDITIONING PROGRAM

Variations of the following program have been used for years by a large number of successful shooters, and an outline of the basic program is therefore offered as a suggested supplemental routine. It is *not* a necessary part of a training program, nor is it the only routine which may be followed. Each individual must discover whether he needs a supplemental routine or not by determining what works best for him. Anything that increases performance is desired; anything that is detrimental to performance should be avoided. What works for one person probably will not work for another, and each individual will eventually custom-design a training program that is best for him and works only for him, and it may or may not include a daily routine of supplemental physical conditioning.

Before shooting.

Isometric exercises are best. These produce the following advantages: they warm up the muscles in preparation for shooting; over the course of time they somewhat increase strength and improve muscle tone; they sharpen the kinesthetic sense; they increase control of individual muscle groups and therefore aid in developing hold; they require a relatively small expenditure of energy and therefore do not fatigue the muscles prior to shooting. Isometric exercises are based upon the principle of pitting a muscle against an immovable object. The immovable object may be a wall or exercise rack, or it may be another body muscle. The muscle is pitted against the immovable object with maximum effort, which is continued for a period of about ten seconds, and then gradually released. The following exercises constitute a fairly complete isometric course. See the accompanying illustrations for clarification of the proper body positions during performance of the exercises.

Exercise 1.   Place your palms together in front of your throat, forearms horizontal, fingers pointing up, the tips of the fingers about level with the chin. Press the palms together as hard as possible for about ten seconds, then slowly release. (Hold all exercises ten seconds.)

Exercise 2.   Grip hands together in front of your waist. Press the palms together as hard as possible, using all the force in the arm and chest muscles.

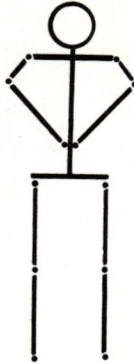

Exercise 3.   Beginning with the arms down at the sides, palms front, make a fist with each hand and then slowly, over the ten-second period, bring the fists up toward the shoulders. Concentrate on tensing the muscles of the upper arm, especially the biceps.

Exercise 4.   With your hands just slightly above shoulder level, extend the arms to the rear as far as possible, while also bending the torso back as far as possible.

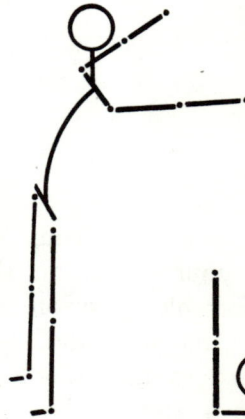

Exercise 5.   Raise your arms straight overhead and extend them upward as far as possible.

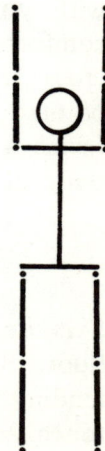

Exercise 6.   Place your arms straight in front of your body, and extend them forward as far as possible.

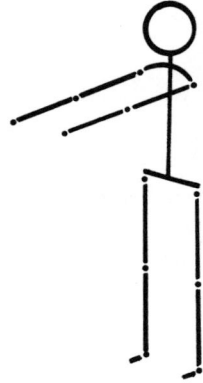

Exercise 7.   With the feet shoulder-width apart, place your hands on your hips and tense arm, abdomen, and leg muscles.

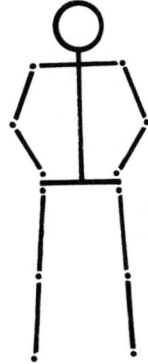

Exercise 8.   Sitting on the floor with your hands on the floor in a comfortable position at the sides, cross the legs and, with the toes pointed so that the top of the foot forms a straight line with the shin, tense all of the leg muscles.

Exercise 9.   Lie face down on the floor. By arching the back and extending the arms backwards, try to touch your heels with your fingertips.

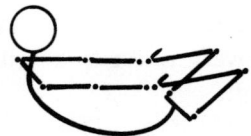

Exercise 10. Stand with your right side next to a wall, arms down. Push against the wall with the back of your hand as though trying to push the hand through it. Use all the force of the arm and shoulder muscles. Turn your left side to the wall and repeat.

Exercise 11. Standing with your back to a wall, place fingertips on the collarbone and push the chin forward as far as possible, holding the shoulders back against the wall.

Exercise 12. Standing with your back about 18 inches from a wall, place one hand on the wall; then, keeping the knees straight, curl the toes up as far as possible and touch the floor with the free hand.

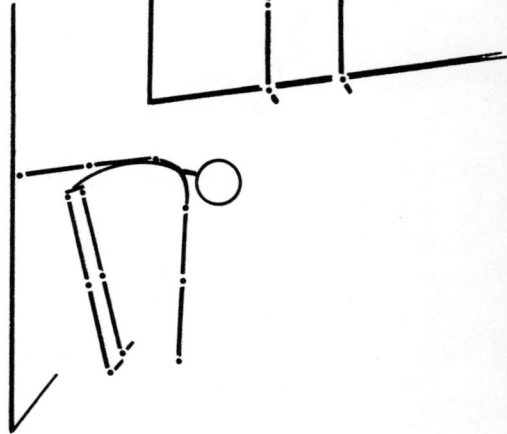

After shooting.

Perhaps the most popular after-shooting exercise is jogging. Jogging has these advantages: it increases endurance; over a course of time it somewhat strengthens all the body muscles; it trains the body to utilize oxygen more efficiently and therefore lowers the breathing rate; it strengthens the circulatory system and therefore reduces the pulse rate; it especially strengthens leg muscles, which are so important to the kneeling and standing positions. Most shooters jog between 1 and 2 miles daily, but some prefer to jog 3 miles or more. Jogging is usually done every day, including non-shooting days.

Additional.

In conjunction with jogging, one may also do calisthenics, which are also performed daily. Or, as an alternative, a program of *light* weightlifting may be followed every alternate day. Care must be taken that the poundage or the number of repetitions used in weightlifting exercises is not too great. As an alternative to either calisthenics or weightlifting, other sports activities may be substituted.

FINAL TRAINING IN PREPARATION FOR A MATCH

In the last two to four weeks of your program, you begin making final preparations for the event which has been the objective of your entire program—the event we have called the Big Apple. During this time your training methods will undergo some significant changes. Some of these may be summarized as follows:

1. You will no longer have progress as a primary goal. This, remember, is the final stage of the consolidation phase. Your purpose now is to put together all you have learned in a series of dress rehearsals for the match. If you find a sure improvement at this point, go ahead and adopt it; but remember that there is not much time left to test new methods, and if there is any doubt about a proposed change, save it until after the match.

2. As many as possible of your training sessions are now six hours long. Naturally you will be tired at the end of each of these sessions. But by now you should be well conditioned, and should be able to perform without losing proficiency as a result of fatigue. These training sessions help condition you to the mental and physical demands of the actual match, and help you become familiar with the mental and physical sensations produced by such a course.

3. Each full training session is a dress rehearsal of the match itself. Each time you shoot a six-hour session, you rehearse and become more proficient in the exact routine you expect to follow in the match. You set up your equipment

the same way, you begin shooting at the same time of day that you will begin the match, you eat lunch at the same time, you shoot the same number of sighter shots, you take the cartridges out of your ammunition box in the same order, you take the same number of breaks, you wear the same clothes—in short, you follow *exactly* the same physical routine you expect to follow in the match, and rehearse it until you can do it without thinking about it. More important, you rehearse and refine the *mental* routine you expect to follow. You concentrate fully on each shot; you analyze your performance, including follow-through, after each shot; you focus constantly on your own performance, perhaps upon weather conditions, and you put other competitors completely out of your mind; you forget about score and concentrate instead on performance, so that an occasional wide shot is forgotten and creates no psychological pressure; you shoot 120 one-shot matches; you learn to relax physically during breaks, but not to let go psychologically; you rehearse being cool, so that mishaps and foul-ups leave you completely unruffled. In short, you rehearse the mental discipline you must use in the match, and rehearse it until it becomes so automatic and natural that you can do it, too, without thinking about it.

4. You follow the same daily routine that you plan to follow during the match. Your supplemental conditioning program levels off, and you no longer strive for gains if you have been working on them all along. If you jog, you now jog the same distance you plan to jog during the days of the match. You eat meals at the same time and get up at the same time; you go to bed one-half hour earlier (or, during the match, you will stay up one-half hour later, in order to be sure of falling asleep without difficulty). Your use or non-use of tobacco, alcohol, coffee, tea, and prescription drugs is the same as it will be during the match. In short, you are rehearsing the day-to-day life you will lead during the match.

5. None of the above should seem unusual, or in any way produce tension. This final stage of preparation is not a drastic change in your program; it is merely a leveling off. After all, you have been working toward this stage for several months or more, and if your program has been well planned, all of these things will fall into place with no feeling on your

part of a break in continuity. All the various parts of your training program have been leading to this consolidation period for a long time; you have achieved the level of performance you aimed for; your training is now thorough and complete. You feel strong and confident. You eagerly look forward to the match. You are ready, and you know it, and this match is the perfect chance to prove it to the world. This period of final preparation is, if anything, the most pleasant part of your entire program. Prior to this stage you have been struggling to improve; now you are simply maintaining proficiency. Moreover, now is the time when you are reaping the rewards of all of those days and weeks and months of training and travelling to matches. You have climbed the ladder of performance, and now you are ready to reach out and pluck the Big Apple. It is there. And it can be yours.

—III—

SPECIAL PROBLEMS

Most of the problems that arise in shooting are connected in one way or another with psychology, training, or equipment and positions, the subjects of the other sections of this book. The problems discussed in this section are, too; however, they are so common, so complex, and frequently so severe that they seem to stand out as special problems, and deserve separate treatment. They are, in the order in which they will be treated, the eye and the sight system, recoil and muzzle jump, and adverse weather conditions.

The Eye & the Sight System

Though the following discussion of vision will seem quite lengthy to some, it actually treats only a small part of the data available on the structure and function of the human eye. Readers who wish to familiarize themselves more thoroughly with the technical aspects of vision may consult two sources which are relatively comprehensive and contain detailed bibliographical references to additional information. These are *Vision and Visual Perception*, edited by Clarence H. Graham (New York, 1966), and Chapters 6 and 7 of Clifford T. Morgan's *Physiological Psychology*, Third Edition (New York, 1965). These sources are technical and presuppose some scientific and physiological background on the part of the reader, but learning the material would undoubtely be of some benefit to any shooter. Much of what we have to say in the following discussions will be drawn from these sources.

THE EYE

Visual acuity.

Good visual acuity is absolutely essential to precision shooting. Visual acuity is the capacity to discriminate details of objects in the field of view. Good visual acuity is the ability to discriminate fine details; poor visual acuity is the ability to see only gross features. Unless fine details of the sight picture can be seen, the best shooting position and the best equipment will be of only limited value. For a rifleman, visual acuity depends primarily upon the eye itself; secondly, it depends upon the selection of a proper sight system; and thirdly, it depends upon the proper use of the sight system. Each of these factors will be discussed in turn.

Eye health. As a part of the entire physiological system, the eye is dependent for its health upon the health of the rest of the body. Illness anywhere in the body, including the teeth, can change visual acuity. Maintaining good overall health for the sake of good vision is only one of the reasons why a shooter should keep himself physically fit. But the eyes also constitute a separate system of the body, and are therefore subject to specific health problems. Certain eye diseases are of an extremely serious nature, even though in the early stages they are not troublesome or even very noticeable. If undetected and untreated, however, they can result in rapid and irreversible damage to the eye. Everyone, therefore, whether he is a shooter or not, should have a thorough eye examination by a qualified specialist at least once a year. Regular eye examinations are important to a shooter for additional reasons, both allied with performance. First, slow changes in the eye may result in a slight loss of visual acuity, which, though undetectable, can nevertheless affect scores. Second, having confidence in one's vision is part of confidence in one's overall ability. Have your eyes checked regularly, know that your vision is good, and then you will no longer wonder or worry about vision. You can concentrate properly on performance.

Shooting glasses. If there is one cardinal rule about the eyes, it is this: *Always wear shooting glasses while firing a rifle.* The purpose of the glasses is to protect the eye from wind-drying, from wind-blown particles, and, most importantly, from the extremely dangerous effects of blowback. Blowback consists of burning power, hot gases, and even small particles of metal that are propelled back through the bolt of the rifle as a result of a cartridge case rupturing during fire.

This gas and the small debris it carries can reach very high temperatures and velocities, and if allowed to strike against the eye can do irreparable damage, resulting even in complete loss of vision. The dangers are extreme with center-fire rifles, and these guns should *never* be fired unless the shooter is wearing not only glasses, but glasses with lenses made of high-impact, tempered glass.

Choose all shooting glasses, whether they have corrective lenses or not, for protective quality, for overall sturdiness, and for comfort. It is of great importance that the frame surrounding the lenses be designed so that it does not obstruct the field of view through the sights when the head is placed in the sighting position. Either adjustable frames, or large lenses, are helpful in avoiding this problem. Whenever you buy new glasses, get to know them before you go into competition. Uncomfortable, unfamiliar glasses can be a distraction and impair performance. If necessary, use paddding to make the contacts with the nose and ears more comfortable, and wear the glasses enough so they feel natural. In addition, learn to protect them and care for them properly. When they are not in use, keep them in sturdy, protective cases in your equipment box. Keep them free from scratches and cracks. Learn the conditions of temperature and humidity that may cause them to cloud or fog with moisture, and keep cleaning materials at hand. An anti-fog cleaning cloth, or a tube of anti-fogging chemical, is a good investment. Three types of glasses are desirable: a clear pair, a green or smoke pair, and an amber pair. Each is helpful under a different light condition, and the specific usefulness of each will be discussed below.

Corrective glasses.

Many people believe that a person who must wear corrective lenses cannot see well enough to be a champion shooter. That belief is simply false. If a person's eyesight can be corrected to 20/20 vision, visual acuity is not likely to be a limiting factor in his performance. The standard figure, 20/20, means simply that a person can perceive some critical aspect of a test object that subtends an angle of one minute of arc at a viewing distance of 20 feet. The ability to discriminate within one minute of arc is considered "normal" vision and is usually sufficient for competitive shooting performance, whether or not it is achieved by corrective lenses. Some people, of course, have better than normal vision, and cases are known of people who can discriminate details within one half minute of arc. Many shooters have better than normal acuity. But it is also true that a sizable proportion of world-championship-caliber shooters wear corrective lenses. Corrected vision means that any weakness or imperfection in the eye has been eliminated by the correcting medium (the lens of the glass), and normal acuity is attained.

As a general rule, corrective glasses should be made especially for shooting. In addition to being formed of high-impact glass, the lenses should be ground to accommodate the eye as it looks through the lens when the shooter is in a shooting position. Corrective lenses are normally ground to correct the eye deficiency when the axis of vision is straight forward through the center of the lens. In the standing and kneeling positions, the head may be placed so that the axis of vision moves to an area of the lens slightly nearer the bridge of the nose; in the prone position, the axis of vision will almost certainly be moved to an area near the top of the lens. These factors will be given more consideration in the later discussion of head position.

The point is that lenses that correct certain defects—particularly astigmatism—must be especially ground to accommodate the displacement of the eye from its central axis during shooting. These are highly individual problems, and are not always present in corrected vision. The safest thing to do is to discuss the problem with your eye specialist, making sure that he understands all of your requirements, and then have him prescribe shooting glasses. In some cases, one set of glasses will do for both the standing and kneeling positions because of the similar head positions, and a separate pair will be needed for the prone position. It is possible that vision in some cases may be satisfactorily corrected for shooting by contact lenses, and the eye can then be protected with non-prescription shooting glasses, in which case the problem of specially ground shooting glasses is eliminated.

THE SIGHT SYSTEM

The metallic sight system consists of a front sight mounted near the muzzle of the barrel, and a rear sight mounted over the receiver. In production models the mounts are usually placed accurately by automated equipment. With custom-built guns, or rebarreled guns, the placement of mounts is frequently done by hand. If you are having such a gun made up, it is important to insist that the mounts be placed with absolute precision, otherwise you may end up with an unusable rifle. Have the work done by an experienced gunsmith with proper equipment. The slight additional cost is cheap insurance against the headaches that could result from a damaged gun.

The condition of the mounts is critical. Both front and rear sights usually slide into grooves on the mounts and are affixed there by the tightening of screws. If the mounts themselves are loose, or if they are chipped, worn, dented, improperly shaped, or the wrong size, the results can be an improperly aligned or otherwise undependable sight system. The same results can come from worn or damaged sights. Frequent inspection, and proper care, of mounts and sights is a simple matter and can contribute to your confidence in your equipment.

A very small percentage of shooters require an offset system to achieve proper alignment of the sights with the eye. Offset systems mount the same way as regular systems, but both front and rear sights are extended 1 or 2 inches to either the right or left of the bore. These systems are commercially available from several manufacturers. Obviously, the front and rear sights should be matched, and the safest way to ensure proper matching is to purchase a complete, matched set. Offset systems are more subject to damage for several reasons, and their use is recommended only when body conformation prevents the use of a normal system. There is no evidence that they will improve the scores of most shooters, but they are clearly more fragile, more troublesome, and more expensive.

The front sight.

The front sight consists normally of a short, tubelike hood

in which interchangeable inserts can be affixed. (The length and size of the hood and hood extensions are regulated by match rules that are subject to change. The legality of a hood should be confirmed by consulting the current rule book.) The inserts are normally either post or aperture types. The posts usually come in varying widths, and the apertures in various diameters. Transparent plastic discs of differing colors are also available for use in the front sight, and are used successfully by a few shooters.

The post sight.   With a post insert, the width of the top of the post should appear equal to the diameter of the bull; that is, blade and bull should appear to be of equal width. The blade should approach the bull from six o'clock (if the rifle is canted, the insert should be modified to achieve a six o'clock approach). Two methods of patterning are used. First, the post appears to touch the bottom of the bull. It should in no case move into the bull, for judgments of vertical alignment then become almost impossible. A second method is to pattern so that the bull seems to float above the top of the post, with a thin line of white preserved between them. Whichever method is used, the post must pattern with the bull consistently on each shot.

The aperture sight.   The aperture sight is the most widely used, and about the only way to pattern with it is to form a concentric circle around the bull, with a uniform line of white existing at all points between the inside of the aperture and the outer edge of the bull. As a rule of thumb, the aperture should appear to be about 1.5 times the diameter of the bull. However, this rule is subject to modification under varying light conditions. One aperture size will yield a clear image under some light conditions, but other light conditions will call for a different aperture size. (This subject is discussed at length below.) With standard equipment, aperture sizes are altered by changing inserts. However, a variable front aperture is now available commercially; it is undoubtedly a good investment for many people, though not everyone changes front aperture sizes enough to warrant the expense.

Post or aperture?   One question in the mind of every beginning shooter is whether to use a post or aperture front sight. There is no simple answer to this question. People possessed of unusually high levels of visual acuity seem to be able to use either type effectively, and for them it is clearly a matter of preference. For most people whose vision is closer to average, however, an aperture is usually best. We say *usually*, because some people with average vision cannot get good results with an aperture. The reason is not known, but it is probably psychological rather than physical. However, a post clearly places a greater burden upon the eye because it demands a higher resolution acuity. Resolution is the eye's ability to perceive the separation between two elements of a pattern. The smaller the elements of the pattern, the more difficult becomes the task of resolution. Extensive research has demonstrated that the task of resolution is in fact the most difficult aspect of visual acuity (Graham, p. 362).

A post thus places greater demands upon the eye's resolving power for this reason: the pattern consists of the bull (element 1) and the top line of the post blade (element 2) with a size equal to the diameter of the bull. With an aperture, the bull (element 1) is the same, of course, but the circumferential interior line of the aperture (element 2) is over three times the size of the top line of the post blade (circumference = 3.17 X diameter). The aperture obviously supplies larger elements and thus reduces the task of resolution, probably not by a ratio of 3:1, but certainly to some degree. However, if you possess the high level of acuity that enables you to attain good resolution with a post sight, there is no reason why you should not use one if it feels more comfortable.

The same demand for high resolution acuity is made by a small front aperture that allows only a narrow ring of white to surround the bull. The task of resolving the fine line around the circumference of the bull becomes extremely difficult. The aperture should be large enough to allow for easy and clear resolution. However, it should not be so large that patterning is made difficult. Within these two limits—which vary extensively among individuals—there is considerable leeway. If light conditions do not seem to affect the pattern definition regardless of the aperture size, then the choice of aperture size is largely a matter of preference. Some good shooters occasionally alternate aperture sizes from month to month, or season to season, as their preferences change. The rule is simply to choose the size that works best for you.

The rear sight.

In position shooting the rear sight almost universally used is an aperture drilled in a disc that is adjustable both horizontally and vertically along the sight frame. The rear sight should be of good quality and in good condition, of course, and should be capable of fine gradations of adjustment. The usual gradations are one-quarter, one-sixth, or one-eighth-minute-of-angle per click of adjustment. The adjustment mechanism should be absolutely reliable and consistent. If the click mechanism is worn or broken, erratic adjustments will result, with a consequent loss in scores. To keep wear of the adjustment mechanism to a minimum, many shooters buy a separate sight for each shooting position. This eliminates the necessity of making large-scale adjustments between shooting positions, and ensures longer life and greater reliability in the adjustment mechanism. If this procedure is used, each sight should be kept in a secure box that is clearly labeled to indicate for which position it is to be used.

The size of the rear aperture, as we shall see below, is truly critical. Most commercial rear sights are supplied with a series of interchangeable discs with apertures of different sizes. The size of the aperture is changed by screwing a different disc into the sight housing. A complete series of these interchangeable discs is the minimum most shooters can own if they want good scores. But interchangeable discs are time consuming and troublesome to keep and use. By far the best solution to the problem is the use of a variable iris-type rear aperture. These are commercially available, relatively inexpensive, and can be fitted to almost any commercial competition sight. They allow aperture size to be controlled quickly and accurately with only a twist of the fingers. Such an aperture is recommended as essential to attaining maximum efficiency in performance.

Eye relief.

Eye relief refers to the distance between the eye and the

rear sight aperture. Eye relief will of necessity change from position to position. In prone, a relatively short eye relief will be used; in kneeling and standing a relatively longer eye relief is used. These differences in relief depend in part upon the changing position of the head and the mechanical limitations posed by the rear sight mount. If the mount does not allow for the adequate adjustment of the sight forward and backward in relation to the eye, it should be changed, or replaced by one that does.

Generally, eye relief should be somewhere between 2 and 6 inches. This does not mean that 1 inch or 7 inches of relief is incorrect—it means only that 2 to 6 inches is the eye relief used by most good shooters. But there are very strong practical reasons why relief should not vary too far from these figures. If the rear sight is too close to the eye, recoil will cause it to slam into the eye or eyebrow. Conceivably some tissue damage could result to the eye or face, but the greatest danger is in setting up a startle or fear reflex that will, on subsequent shots, cause the eye to blink or the head to jerk away in anticipation of recoil, thereby upsetting hold and follow-through. On the other hand, if the rear sight is too far away from the eye, the rear aperture will necessarily be so large that its effective optical value will be lost, as we shall soon see.

Sight alignment.

Sight alignment refers to the pattern made by the front sight cover and the field of view circumscribed by the rear sight aperture. The front sight cover should be centered perfectly in the field of view. If it is not, the axis of the rifle is not aligned with the center of the bull, even though the bull may be centered perfectly in the front sight. Most shooters prefer a rear aperture that allows a field of view about 1.5 times the diameter of the front sight hood. This size makes for easy and almost automatic sight alignment by providing an easily discernible pattern. The task of sight alignment seems especially easy if an aperture front sight is used, because the pattern becomes a series of concentric circles consisting of the bull, front aperture, front sight hood, and field of view circumscribed by the rear aperture.

PROPER USE OF THE SIGHT SYSTEM

We have seen above that the eye should be in good health, that corrective glasses should be used when necessary, and protective glasses should be worn always while shooting. We have discussed the front sight and sight picture, the rear sight and sight alignment, and, to some extent, aperture sizes. For the remainder of this discussion we will assume that your vision is normal and that you have an adequate sight system and understand basically how it functions.

We will now discuss how to make the best use of the sight system. It should be made clear that each individual has eyes that are at least as unique as his own hands or face. No two people have eyes exactly alike, and therefore no precise laws can be laid down about aperture sizes, or eye relief, or tinted shooting glasses, that will pertain to all people. What we will now discuss are general observations that will apply, perhaps with slight modifications, to most people. There may be people who are exceptions to these observations. If your own vision fails to fit the patterns described below and is suspected as the source of some problem in your shooting, the best advice is to consult an eye specialist and discuss the problem in detail with him.

The role of light.

In very simple terms, the eye "sees" only the light that enters it. Vision depends upon a light source being present. If there is no light source, as in the total darkness found in a deep underground cave, we can see nothing but blackness. If a light source is present, however, most objects reflect some of the light which strikes them, and the reflected light then enters the eye and the object is "seen." The object's color is determined by the wave length of the light it reflects. Under white light, if the object appears blue, it absorbs most wave lengths of light and reflects primarily the wave length we perceive as blue. If it appears red, it absorbs other wave lengths and reflects the wave length we see as red. If it reflects all wave lengths and absorbs almost none, it appears white, for white light is a mixture of all wave lengths. If it absorbs all wave lengths and reflects almost none, it appears black, for black is an absence of light.

"Graying out" of the bull.   One of the factors affecting perception in shooting is brightness contrast. Brightness contrast refers to the relation between varying regions of a visual field which are differently illuminated, or which reflect different amounts of light. One of the best possible examples is the contrast between a black bull's-eye, which reflects almost none of the light striking it, and the white field on which it is placed, which reflects most of the light striking it. The result is a high level of brightness contrast between the black and white areas. Under most light conditions, brightness contrast makes for clear perception: the black bull is clearly visible upon the white field. But under certain ratios of brightness contrast, a reversal effect takes place which causes the bull to appear a dull gray. The range of brightness contrast at which this occurs varies widely from individual to individual.

This effect has been called variously "enhancement," "assimilation," and "equalization" (Graham, p. 229), though shooters usually call it "graying out." The causes of this phenomenon are not clearly understood, but it seems to have to do with the ratio of the contrast in relation to the amount of light entering the eye. Experience in shooting bears out the fact that the ratio can be controlled by manipulating aperture sizes, which control the total amount of light entering the eye, thus affecting the ratio of contrast brightness. This is possible at both the front and rear sights. Sometimes graying out can be controlled simply by varying the size of the rear aperture. Since, with a variable aperture, this is a very simple operation that does not involve disturbing the shooting position, it should always be the first line of defense against graying out. If it does not work satisfactorily, then the front aperture size may be changed. A smaller front aperture allows less white to show around the bull, reducing the ratio of brightness contrast by allowing less total light to enter the eye; a larger aperture raises the ratio. Either way, the limited range at which enhancement or graying out occurs may be avoided, thus clarifying the sight picture.

The range at which graying out occurs, of course, will change as the general level of illumination changes, as when the sun goes behind a cloud. An aperture that provided a clear contrast under strong sunlight may not do so under shadow. You will have to discover by experience what front aperture size works best for you under a given light condition. You should also work out a simple rule for yourself which will save time during a match. The rule should be something like this: when graying out results from a change from bright to dim light, change to a larger (or smaller) aperture; when it results from a change from dim to bright light, change to a larger (or smaller) aperture. The effectiveness of changing to a smaller or larger aperture varies greatly among individuals. You should discover which is the most effective for you, and then *memorize* the rule for match use. This will save much time and anguish during the pressure of competition.

One other possibility needs mention here. An alternate method of changing the brightness contrast ratios when graying out occurs is to change shooting glasses. Changing from clear to amber or green, or vice versa, may sufficiently change the amount of light entering the eye to escape the graying-out range of brightness contrast. Changing glasses is usually quicker and easier than changing a front sight aperture, and if it is successful, it accomplishes the same end.

If you have never experienced the phenomenon of graying out, don't be disturbed; be glad. Some shooters never experience it once they have found a satisfactory aperture size for both front and rear sights, no matter how much the general level of illumination varies between normal extremes. The reason probably has to do with the structure and physiology of their eyes. We know one world champion who chooses aperture sizes solely on the basis of the formula of 1.5 times the diameter of the bull (front aperture), and 1.5 times the diameter of the front sight hood (rear aperture). Normal variations in levels of illumination then have no effect upon his ability to see the entire sight picture with clear definition.

"Flattening" of the bull: Most shooters experience at some time the phenomenon of the bull, and possibly the central elements of the front sight, appearing to flatten on one side. This distortion may have several causes, some of which are unknown. One very likely cause, however, is misalignment between the rear aperture and the pupil of the eye. The center of the rear aperture should be exactly aligned with the center of the pupil. When the aperture and pupil are not

centrally aligned, sufficient light enters the eye to stimulate what *appears* to be normal vision; but this apparently normal vision conceals deficiencies in acuity resulting from the fact that most of the light entering the eye is now entering through the *edge* of the pupil rather than its center.

Because the light rays coming through the edge of the pupil must be more sharply bent, or refracted, in order to be brought into focus on the back of the eye, those light waves have reduced capacity to stimulate vision. This phenomenon is called the Stiles-Crawford effect, after its discoverers. They found that light rays passing directly through the center of the pupil and striking directly upon the light-sensitive cells at the back of the eye are the most effective stimulants of vision. Light waves passing through the edges of the pupil must be bent, and therefore strike the cells in the back of the eye at an angle; these light rays are reduced in effectiveness as stimulants of vision in proportion to the angle at which they strike the cells (Graham, p. 328). Thus, when the rear aperture is aligned with the edge of the pupil, a major portion of the light entering the eye is restricted to the edge of the pupil and is consequently bent at an angle. The most highly bent rays, which enter the extreme edge of the pupil, simply fail to stimulate vision, and the side of the bull from which they reflect appears to flatten out. Actually, it simply disappears, because the light fails to stimulate vision.

This can be verified by a simple experiment. Look through the sights and move the eye as far to the right of the rear aperture as possible, consistent with being able to see through the sights. The left side of the bull will flatten, or fade out, because the light rays from the left side of the bull are entering the left margin of the pupil, are bent at a greater angle. and hence fail to stimulate vision. If the eye is moved up in relation to the rear aperture, the bottom of the bull appears to flatten; if it is moved down, the top appears to flatten; and so on as the eye is moved around the rear sight. If this is the cause of a distorted bull, the rule for correcting it is simple: adjust your position so that the eye is moved in relation to the rear sight toward the flat side of the bull. This should bring the center of the rear aperture and the center of the pupil into alignment, and the aberration will probably disappear. Other factors, as we shall see, may be responsible for the aberration, in which case different measures must be taken.

Eye movement and after-image. Something similar to graying out and flattening of the bull can result from the phenomenon known as *after-image.* All features of after-image are not fully understood, but in theory it is linked to one of a series of events that make possible our seeing. Light enters the eye and on passing through the lens is brought into focus on the back of the eye, or retina. The retina is covered with a mosaic of cells which contain light-sensitive chemicals. When light strikes the cells, a chemical change takes place, and the cells respond to this change by sending nerve impulses to the brain. The brain synthesizes these impulses in some unknown way so that we see the object from which the light originates. After-image is believed to be caused by a residue of chemical change that remains in the retinal cells after we have stared fixedly at a single point in the field of view. After-image and its effects on shooting are perhaps best explained by using the accompanying diagram for an experiment. On the left is a model sight picture. Stare at the center of the bull for a minimum of ten seconds, then shift your vision to the black dot on the right. In a moment, a white "ghost" ring should appear around the dot. The ring is an occurrence of negative after-image (there are several kinds of after-images, but we are concerned not with the types, only with the phenomenon itself). If you look at the edge of the black dot, you will see a ghost dot, also white, seeming to float over or behind the black dot. This ghost dot could possibly account for some occurrences of either graying out or flattening of the bull. Whether it does or not is problematical.

One thing is certain, however, and that is that after-image should be avoided, because the strange effects and illusions it creates are obviously a hindrance to clear vision. After-image is easily avoided if the eye is not allowed to focus on a fixed point for more than two or three seconds. While looking through your sights, then, keep moving your point of focus around the central elements of the sight picture. Avoid staring fixedly at any point such as the center of the bull or a portion of the front sight, and you will not be bothered by after-image.

Depth of field: the rear aperture as artificial pupil.

The rear aperture has potentially great optical value as an artificial pupil. A rear aperture that is small enough will have the effect of blocking rays that would ordinarily enter the eye through the marginal areas of the pupil. As a result of this, two effects are obtained: visual acuity is increased and depth of field is increased. These effects, which can be of tremendous advantage to a shooter, are worth discussing separately in detail.

Visual acuity is dependent upon so many factors that any discussion of it is likely to be controversial, at least as far as eye specialists are concerned. However, most shooters believe that a small rear aperture enables them to see the target with slightly better acuity. The best explanation has to do with the Stiles-Crawford effect: light entering the eye only through the center of the pupil is the more effective stimulus of vision. A small rear aperture, if aligned with the center of the natural pupil, acts as a small artificial pupil, restricts the light entering the eye to the center of the natural pupil, and this ensures a high level of acuity. Whether the Stiles-Crawford effect actually is responsible, or some other factor is involved, or whether the apparent increase in acuity is purely psychological, is unknown. Whatever the cause, however, most shooters are agreed that acuity appears to be increased by the use of a small rear aperture.

The apparent increase in acuity could also be explained as the result of increased depth of field. Increased depth of field is perhaps the most valuable advantage to be derived from a small rear aperture. Depth of field refers to the distance between the farthest and closest points at which objects are clearly visible when the eye is focused on a given point. For example, if the eye is focused on a point 24 inches away and can see clearly any object between 28 and 20 inches away, the depth of field is 8 inches $(28 - 20 = 8)$. The further away the point of focus of the eye, the greater the depth of field. For instance, focusing on a near object, as cited above, yields a short depth of focus of about 8 inches; but focusing on a point 6 feet away, the eye might see clearly all objects between 5 and 7 feet, thus having a depth of field of 2 feet, or 24 inches. At some point of focus, usually about 20 feet away, most people achieve a depth of field of infinity beyond 20 feet. In other words, the focus of the eye does not change in seeing clearly objects beyond a distance of 20 feet. The depth of focus may then be expressed as infinity with a nearness limit of 20 feet.

The depth of field can be increased by a reduction in pupil size. Under the right conditions, for example, the depth of field can be increased by a small rear aperture so that the nearness limit in infinity focus is reduced from 20 feet to a point near the front sight. As a result, the front sight and the bull can be brought into focus simultaneously if the eye is used correctly. The reasons for the increase in depth of field are too complex and technical for full discussion here, but the phenomenon is easily illustrated by a simple experiment.

On a piece of paper, make a small mark half the size of a .22 caliber bullet hole. Then place yourself 5 to 7 feet away from the mark. Hold up a finger 12 to 15 inches in front of your face, and, with one eye shut, line up the finger on the spot as you would line up a post front sight on a bull's eye. (The spot, of course, will appear much smaller than a bull's-eye would be, and your finger much broader than the front sight would be.) If you focus on your finger, the spot will blur and become indistinct. But, if you look through a pinhole punched in a piece of cardboard, you will find that both the spot and the finger can be brought into focus, or at least into much better focus, at the same time. This is because the pinhole acts as a small artificial pupil. The rear aperture of your rifle will act in the same way, bringing both bull and front sight into focus, or at least improved focus, simultaneously.

There is some disagreement among shooters about exactly where their point of focus is under these conditions. Some believe they focus on the front sight, some believe they focus on the bull, and others believe they focus on a point somewhere between the two. It is probably impossible to determine exactly their point of focus under these circumstances.

But in practice it makes little difference, so long as the depth of field is deep enough to include both bull and front sight.

A rear aperture larger than the pupil of the eye does not increase the depth of field because it does not artificially reduce pupil size. Large rear apertures are necessary on hunting and military rifles because the targets are often moving objects which must be located quickly in the sight picture. A large field of view is thus desirable. With these rifles, the point of focus should properly be the front sight. This is necessary to maintain proper sight alignment. The target will thus have to be somewhat blurred. But in competition shooting at a stationary target, a small rear aperture gives three extremely valuable advantages: the problem of sight alignment is reduced to a minimum; visual acuity is (or appears to be) increased; and both the front sight and the target are brought more clearly into focus simultaneously. This might seem to suggest that the smaller the rear aperture, the better, with no limit attached. But such is not the case. If the aperture is too small, not enough light passes through it to stimulate clear vision. Experimentation will quickly show you the lower limit of rear aperture size that is consistent with clear perception of the target.

Apparent aperture size is of course determined by the distance of the aperture from the eye. At several inches, the aperture will have to be enlarged to allow for a large enough field of view, and will lose its optical value. Hence the guideline that eye relief should not exceed 6 inches. Some experimentation will quickly show the best eye relief and aperture size for you.

Tinted shooting glasses.

Tinted shooting glasses, if they are of good quality, will have the effect of narrowing the spectrum of light waves that enter the eye. A green lens, for example, will tend to filter out some of all wave lengths except green; a yellow lens will filter out some of all wave lengths except yellow. Tinted lenses can be used to advantage under certain conditions. Green lenses are best used under conditions of bright light and glare. They usually reduce appreciably the amount of light entering the eye and soften glare, thus making the eye somewhat more comfortable. They should not be used, of course, under conditions of poor light where they filter out so much light that perception is impaired. Yellow or amber lenses are best used under conditions of haze where the level of illumination is moderate or slightly low. Yellow lenses should not be used in very low levels of illumination, as they filter out some of the limited number of rays entering the eye and may thereby impair perception. Yellow lenses do *not* gather light and increase the number of light rays entering the eye, as some people believe. Clear glasses are useful for any light condition where they are comfortable.

There is some evidence that tinted lenses give a slight advantage because they tend to relay only monochromatic light (light of the same wave length) to the eye. Experiments have shown that monochromatic light from the middle of the spectrum yields acuity scores slightly higher than either white light or monochromatic light from either end of the spectrum. Briefly, these experiments show that green light and yellow light are best for visual acuity, but only slightly better than white light. Red light yields lower acuity scores, and blue light the poorest scores of all (Graham, p. 331). Blue light is particularly susceptible to scattering. The light from a clear sky appears blue because it consists primarily of scattered blue light that is being bounced back and forth by the dust and molecules of gas in the air; because it travels downward in extreme zigzag patterns, it enters the eye from all directions, and the entire sky thus appears blue. Because of its scattering propensities, it is also readily scattered by the clear solids and liquids that make up the lens and interior of the eye. Monochromatic blue shooting glasses would therefore be undesirable from an optical standpoint. The value of yellow glasses under conditions of fog or haze is perhaps that they most effectively filter out the blue light that is scattered by low-lying moisture in the atmosphere and is somehow interfering with visual acuity. It should be emphasized that the increase in visual acuity produced by monochromatic light is very small. The *primary* value of tinted shooting glasses is that they ease the strain placed upon the eyes by various light conditions. Their use is desirable, but not urgent.

CHAPTER
8

Recoil, Muzzle Jump, & Zero Sight Setting

Recoil is the familiar "kick" that accompanies the firing of a gun. It is an example of Newton's third law of motion, which states that the action of every force is accompanied by an equal reaction in the opposite direction. More specifically, when the powder inside a cartridge ignites upon firing, the expanding gas that results drives the bullet forward and the rifle backward with equal force. The greater weight of the rifle, of course, prevents its travelling the same speed and distance as the bullet. The force of recoil can be described mathematically (see *The American Rifleman*, June, 1971). However, our concern is not with the force of recoil, but with its effects upon marksmanship. Those effects can be explained in terms of another of Newton's laws, the so-called first law of motion. The first law of motion states that a body at rest remains at rest, and a body in motion remains in motion with a constant speed along a straight line, unless some outside force changes that motion. This law also is involved in recoil and in the firing of a bullet from a rifle. The bullet and rifle remain at rest, in relation to each other, until the force of expanding gas becomes great enough to overcome their inertia. Since the bullet is much lighter than the rifle, it begins moving first; but the rapidly expanding gas quickly generates enough force to overcome the inertia of the rifle and put it into motion also. With almost any competition shoulder rifle, it is safe to say that recoil begins after the bullet has begun to move down the bore, but before it has cleared the muzzle. It is here that the second principle in the last-stated of Newton's laws comes into play.

The force of recoil is exerted along a straight line in the opposite direction from the bullet, and continues in that line *unless some outside force changes that motion.* There are several factors which change that motion, and the most obvious is the design of the stock. The butt of the stock drops below the axis of the bore, and the buttplate is the part of the rifle that encounters the most direct resistance during recoil. Assuming that the buttplate is directly below the axis of the bore, the buttplate is then directly below the line of force of the recoil, and thus acts as a hub or pivot, which, instead of directly opposing recoil, deflects it upward, causing the muzzle of the rifle to jump upward. This upward jump is not, as some people think, simply a movement away from gravity; it is a result purely of the deflective force exerted by shoulder resistance transmitted through the stock. Now, as at least part of this upward jump occurs while the bullet is still in the bore, it obviously has an effect upon the initial point of the bullet's trajectory, and hence upon its point of impact. If the rifle does not recoil the same way each time, the point of impact will not be the same each time, even though the shots are released under identical sight pictures. When this happens, we say that a change in zero has occurred. The term *zero* is a shortened form for *zero sight setting,* which means that the sights are set exactly on the point of impact on a target at a given distance under given wind conditions.

Any number of forces can change the direction or extent of muzzle jump during recoil, and hence change the zero sight setting. If, for example, the shoulder is placed high on the buttplate, the deflective force of the stock is reduced, and the muzzle jump is less. If the shoulder is placed low on the buttplate, the deflective force of the stock is in effect strengthened, and the muzzle jump is increased. If the rifle is canted to the left, the drop in the stock causes the buttplate to lie to the right of the bore; the deflective force of the stock then causes the muzzle to jump to the left, as well as up, during recoil. But not only the position of the buttplate is involved in determining the direction and extent of muzzle jump. Other forces that can affect recoil come from the placement of the palm-rest, the fore-end stop, the placement and tension of the forward hand in relation to these, placement of the sling on the arm, tension in the sling, placement and tension in the trigger hand, direction of trigger pull, placement and pressure of the cheek against the stock, and overall body resistance to recoil. In addition, there are probably numerous other forces that may affect recoil and hence point of impact of the bullet.

How does one avoid inadvertently changing recoil from shot to shot, and hence losing points due to a change in zero? The answer is easy, though the achievement of it is not. The answer is that a shooter attempts to keep exactly the same forces acting on the rifle each time he shoots in any one position. He tries to keep exactly the same points of contact between himself and the gun, and exactly the same pressure in each of those contacts. This is achieved, however, only by the utmost care, and it seems that Murphy's Law is particularly applicable to changes in muzzle jump. We have already encountered Murphy's Law in a simple form; a fuller statement is, "If a thing can happen, it probably will; the greater the inconvenience potential, the higher the probability." It seems that almost anything that can change zero will happen if it is at all possible. The most minute details can effect these changes. One of our acquaintances who used to accurize rifles would test them in an underground tunnel. He would sit in a chair and shoot the rifle from a bench-rest device attached to a massive oak table which appeared completely solid and stable. He swore that even if he tried to keep every element of his firing unchanged, but simply moved the position of his feet under the table by only a few inches, the muzzle jump would change enough to change the zero of the rifle. If such a minor adjustment could affect his shooting from a bench rest, a shooter firing from an unsupported position must be particularly conscious of, and careful about, forces that might change muzzle jump, and hence his zero.

It is because recoil and muzzle jump are crucial in determining point of impact that mental follow-through is so important. One who mentally follows through to the completion of recoil will be able to detect changes in muzzle jump and will be able to adjust his position to eliminate the changes. Muzzle jump has more effect in smallbore rifles than in center-fire rifles, generally, because of the slower barrel time of the smallbore cartridge. For this reason, follow-through plays a particularly important role in smallbore shooting.

The effects on zero by changes in a position are so pronounced that a shooter should never attempt to zero his rifle in one position and then use the same sight setting in another position. A zero sight setting for prone, for example, will usually be completely wide of the mark in standing. The chances of the two coinciding are highly improbable. It is also highly improbable that a zero sight setting obtained from a cradle or bench rest would remain a zero setting in an actual shooting position. A rifleman should find his zero in each position by firing the gun from that position. The changes in sight setting from one position to another should be memorized, or a different rear sight used for each position. All the factors involved in the change of zero from position to position are perhaps indeterminable, but surely one of them has to do with the forces that affect recoil and muzzle jump.

Adverse Weather Conditions

Less is known about the effects of weather than perhaps any other factor in shooting. There are scores of ideas and theories that one hears about the best ways of dealing with wind and light conditions, and the best that can be said is that *some* of them work *some* of the time. For the most part, however, they are based entirely on observations of a single variable. The truth is that no one formula or statement can predict with any useful degree of accuracy the effects of weather upon shooting.

We are all aware that weather is an exceedingly complex phenomenon, and it is probably even more complex than we know. It is for this reason that weather forecasters, using a vast, worldwide system to collect data, and using as well sophisticated sensing instruments in orbiting satellites, and the most elaborate computer systems to process the data thus gathered, are able to predict weather with only about 70 percent accuracy. The effect of each variable involved in creating weather forces is at present incalcuable. Even in our rather simple discussion, we will be concerned with the as yet indeterminable relationships between wind speed, wind direction, air density, sectional variance in air density, temperature, humidity, air pressure, topographical effects upon wind direction and velocity, the effects of range design upon air currents, heat reflection/absorption ratios between different range areas, and the refraction of light by air temperature variations. These factors are not always mentioned by name, but they will be implicit in the following discussion. These, we feel, are factors which have a direct bearing upon shooting, and we also strongly believe that there are additional factors which we do not know about. It can be seen that the possibility of putting all these variables into a mathematical formula to predict weather effects upon shooting could be accomplished realistically only by a computer with instantaneous sensing devices set up along the whole trajectory on each individual firing point, and then the shooter would have a difficult time synchronizing his performance with the computer's rapid readout. The possibilities of such a situation becoming a reality are remote, to say the least.

If science is predicting future events on the basis of known variables, the number and complexity of variables involved in weather preclude a shooter's analysis of it from being a science. "Doping" the weather as yet remains an art, not a science. Therefore, we do not offer a single formula or even a series of formulas for predicting weather effects upon shooting. We offer some mathematical guidelines upon occasion, but it must be borne in mind that these are given not as complete, foolproof means of gauging weather effects, but as only one means which must be used in conjunction with several others. In effect, formulas based upon "half-value wind," "full-value wind," etc., are more or less useless in international style competition, where it is far easier and more accurate to take one or two sighter shots and determine weather effects directly. For the same reason, it is pointless to investigate the masses of evidence on ballistics and wind effects, as they have no real working value for the person actually shooting a match and wondering how many clicks of sight adjustment will put him into the 10-ring. Experience with the wind is the best way of learning how to dope the wind. And we repeat here the axiom which underlies everything said in this book: it is not how much experience you have that counts, but how much you gain from it.

The following discussion will be divided into three sections devoted to wind, mirage, and precipitation. The separation of the first two is obviously artificial, and is done only to facilitate discussion. It will be seen that the effects of wind and mirage are intimately interrelated.

WIND

The two major forces which change the course of a bullet's trajectory after it leaves the barrel are gravity and wind. Gravity begins effectively to change the path of the bullet the instant it leaves the barrel. Thus a bullet fired on an initial path parallel to the earth's surface will, from the instant it leaves the barrel, fall to the ground at exactly the same speed and in the same amount of time as a bullet simply dropped to the ground from the same height. As far as we are concerned in a practical way, gravity itself is always constant and always pulls the bullet downward in a vertical direction. As this force is constant and predictable, a shooter never worries about gravity-caused changes in his sight zero. Wind, on the other hand, is neither constant nor predictable, and most shooters worry about it a great deal.

Wind, working with gravity, is capable of causing purely vertical changes in sight setting. If a bullet is travelling directly into a headwind, it is slowed down, gravity has more time to pull it downward, and its point of impact on the target will be lowered. If a bullet is travelling with a direct tailwind, its velocity is increased, gravity has less time to pull it downward on its flight to the target, and the point of impact is raised (assuming it has passed the high point of its trajectory). But absolutely direct headwinds and tailwinds seem seldom if ever to exist on rifle ranges. Usually, wind blows across a range and by means familiar to everyone changes the path of the bullet. The most obvious effect of a crosswind is horizontal—the bullet is moved either to the left or to the right during its course of flight. But some of the effect is also vertical, depending upon the spin of the bullet and the direction of the wind. (The spin of a bullet probably has a lot more effect on its trajectory, by virtue of its creating vacuums and pressures, than we realize. After all, these same spin-created vacuums and pressures are responsible for the curves and other changes of direction of a baseball thrown by a good pitcher.)

The inconstancy of wind is doubly perverse—it is not only inconstant across time, but also across space. When you have the opportunity to watch a lake or pond under a moderate wind, study the effects of the wind on its surface. At almost any given time, parts of the surface will be glassy-smooth, while other parts will be ruffled by wind. Moreover, at times the wind will be blowing in one direction in one area, and in a different direction in another area. In addition, these areas will be constantly shifting their sizes and shapes. Translate the space over the pond into a firing range, and you can get some idea of the capricious and sometimes contradictory wind forces operating on the relatively low trajectory of the prone position.

To get some idea of the action of wind some distance off the ground, watch sometime the edge of an advancing fog or low-lying cloud. Several feet above the ground, the fog will move in totally irregular patterns, advancing, retreating, rising, falling, and swirling as it rides the slow wind currents, which flow and eddy in no two places in the same way. Winds moving at moderate to high speeds also seem to be characterized by these irregular movements, as our sense of touch reveals when we stand in a wind. The trick a shooter must accomplish is to get a bullet to travel the distance between muzzle and target and be only minimally affected by the wind. Let's look at some of the means at his disposal.

Equipment.

As strange and as controversial as it may seem, each rifle appears to have its own particular capability to buck the wind. Some rifles send out a bullet that seems very little affected by the wind; others fire bullets that are blown several minutes of angle off course. How is this possible? We have some theories, but none of them will be offered here, simply because we have no evidence to prove them. But leaving the how's aside, years of coaching and looking through spotting scopes from behind firing lines has provided enough personal experience to convince us of this fact: there is such a thing as a "wind rifle" that is minimally affected by wind. This idea, of course, is not entirely new, and some people have been working on developing such a gun for years now, but with no reliable or complete success as yet that we know of. Some have approached the problem from the standpoint of materials used in the barrel; others have approached it from the standpoint of design. Undoubtedly, the discovery of the principles behind a good wind gun is not far off. In fact, one gunsmith in South Africa whom we know claims recently to have found the key, and reliable reports suggest that he has; but his method remains secret, and as yet none of his guns have been made available to us for testing and evaluation.

Evidence that some guns possess superior wind-bucking capability is obtainable through a relatively simple experiment, which we have performed and you may duplicate. Two shooters of about equal ability are placed side by side, with rifles of matched accuracy as determined in zero wind conditions, identical sight radii, and identical sights. It will be seen that the number of clicks of sight correction for the same changes in wind conditions will be different for the two rifles, even though the sights are known to be identically calibrated; and this will be true regardless of which shooter is firing the gun, or from which firing point. Now the experiment will not always yield this result, of course, because a majority of rifles fall into a general range where individual guns are more or less comparable. But occasionally, among otherwise equally accurate rifles, certain ones will stand out as possessing exceptionally poor, or exceptionally good, wind-bucking capabilities.

Most good wind guns are exceptionally accurate to begin with. High accuracy under zero wind conditions, however, does not ensure that a gun will possess this wind-bucking capability. Almost all good wind guns are unusually accurate, but not all unusually accurate rifles have wind-bucking capability. If one has not had the good fortune to acquire a good wind gun, though, the next best line of defense against wind is plain old accuracy as determined under zero wind conditions. This means, simply, acquiring the most accurate gun available and mating it with ammunition that yields superior performance. In smallbore ammunition, one has no choice except to buy the best brand, and the best lot number of that brand (as assigned by the manufacturer), for the particular rifle.

In bigbore ammunition, more options are available. In addition to changing brands and lot numbers, one can also change bullet weight, shape, sectional density, and velocity, all of which affect wind-bucking capabilities. It is important to remember that the usefulness of the velocity factor resides in *remaining* velocity as the bullet approaches the target, and not in muzzle velocity alone. While it is generally true that increasing velocity and/or weight increases wind-bucking capability, these changes may be more than offset by increased group sizes and an overall loss in accuracy. Stated another way, a heavier, faster bullet may be less affected by wind, but that is of little value if these bullets will not fire a satisfactorily small group to begin with. A lighter, slower ammunition may be more affected by the wind, but because it yields a small, tight group when wind effects are discounted, it still yields a superior score even under heavy wind conditions if the rifleman performs correctly. This assumes, of course, that the bullet in question is not abnormally susceptible to wind deflection. The chances of a particular bullet design, weight, and velocity being accurate and also abnormally susceptible to wind are probably quite small. It should be mentioned that changes in center-fire ammunition components—such as changing bullet weight or design—may require changes in barrel design if maximum benefits are to be derived from the new ammunition.

Wind-doping techniques.

As wind-doping is not a science but an art, there is no one factor or distinct combination of factors that can be used with complete success. It is generally true that each range has its own peculiar wind conditions and wind indicators. It is also generally true that conditions vary from firing point to firing point on each range, depending upon wind direction, velocity, range design, and perhaps other factors. Therefore, a person who sets out to dope the wind must perform his evaluation from day to day, and from hour to hour. To do this successfully, he will need to study every possible indicator at the particular range he is working on. These indicators will include not only wind flags set up on the range, but also the movement of grass, tree leaves, dust, clouds, mirage, and anything else that might indicate wind activities. All of these indicators must be studied in connection with the effects of wind upon bullets, either as fired by himself, or as fired by other people whom he is watching through a scope. With experience he learns to "read" various of these indicators in order to dope the wind accurately. What are the most important indicators? It is impossible to say precisely, for they vary widely from one site to another. As mentioned, the movements of things above the surface of the ground, such as tall grass, bushes, and tree leaves, are among the more reliable indicators if they are present in the right places. If they are not present, then things actually on the surface of the ground, such as dust, fallen leaves, and other debris, are probably the next best indicators. In direct sunlight, mirage is also quite useful, for it is usually the first indicator of a change in wind direction (see the section entitled "mirages" for a fuller discussion). Wind flags, of course, are almost always available, but they are seldom consistent from one range to another, and give widely varying readings according to the moisture they have absorbed from or lost to the atmosphere.

Whatever indicators are used, it can be stated with certainty that the most important wind conditions are those on the nearest one-third of the firing range. This was established in a test conducted in facilities where wind conditions could be mechanically controlled. Smallbore rifles were test fired from a cradle at 50 meters under zero wind conditions and a control group established for each rifle and lot of ammunition. The firing was then repeated in identical fashion, with wind machines blowing across the range from the left, at 50 kilometers per hour, on the last 18 meters of the range (from 32 to 50 meters). The firing was then repeated in identical fashion, except that this time the wind machines were blowing across the first one-third of the range (from 0 to 18 meters).

The results were conclusive. The effects of wind on the far third of the range were almost negligible; the effects of wind on the near third of the range were major. Wind near the targets moved the groups only a small amount, while wind near the rifle moved the groups several inches. The important conclusion is this: when doping the wind, the most important area to watch is the first one-third of the range. The indicators there are the ones to concentrate on, as the wind in that area is the wind that will have the more pronounced effect on the bullet's trajectory. Usually there are flags in this area. However, if possible, watch other indicators as well. Several flags are a better indicator than one flag; and so is a flag in combination with leaves, grass, or other indicators, better than a single flag.

Techniques for shooting in the wind.

Wind has surprising effects. One of these is that the best outdoor scores are usually fired under conditions of a 2- to 3-mile-an-hour wind that is fairly constant. Under conditions of no detectable air movement, scores invariably fall well below average. Probably the no-wind factor in itself is not responsible, because the absence of wind certainly does not adversely affect indoor scores. Possibly the cause is related to some factor accompanying the no-wind condition, such as barometric pressure, but that factor has not yet been positively identified. However, everybody knows what wind can do to a shooter's scores when it is present in strength.

A successful shooter learns methods to counteract the effects of wind. Basically there are three techniques for shooting in the wind. One is to find a zero sight setting for a particular wind condition and then "chase" each shot with another shot delivered as quickly as possible. The idea is to get as many shots down-range as can be done before wind conditions change. This is the least desirable method, because performance is rushed and hence becomes unreliable. The second method is to shoot at normal intervals, making sight changes based on estimates of wind changes between shots. This is a tricky business, however, and demands more wind-doping ability than any human can consistently muster. The third, and most desirable, technique is to hold the rifle in the aiming position and "wait out" the wind, firing only during periods when wind conditions are identical. This is unquestionably the best technique in international style shooting, where sufficient time is allowed to make such a performance possible. It does require, however, that the shooter be physically conditioned to hold the rifle in position for periods of up to ten minutes while he waits out the wind, but the effort is well worthwhile.

To use this technique, one must establish a zero sight setting. This is *not* a sight setting for zero wind conditions; rather, it is a sight setting for the *prevailing* conditions of that particular day. If, for example, the wind is blowing from the right and is worth five clicks of correction from the no-wind setting, the zero sight setting for that time is five clicks right of no-wind zero. This setting should be recorded, either by writing it down or by making a mark on the sight calibrations, so that adjustments can be made to keep up with changes when this becomes necessary, but the zero sight setting can readily be found whenever prevailing conditions recur. This will save a lot of effort spent in hunting out a lost zero setting.

Using the technique of waiting out the wind, one attempts to shoot only when the wind conditions are right for the sight setting. Ideally, one shoots the entire course without ever changing the sight setting, even though wind conditions may be varying—one simply shoots only when the wind conditions correspond to the zero setting. However, in most cases, prevailing conditions during one part of the day will not be prevailing conditions during another part. In this case the zero sight setting should be changed to fit the new prevailing conditions, and again the sight setting recorded. If the wind is switching rapidly back and forth from left to right, possibly a no-wind setting would be the best one to use.

One must be careful in making horizontal sight changes to accommodate wind changes, for clicks left or right are usually accompanied by elevation changes in the bullet trajectory. Shot groups fired in heavy, varying wind conditions usually have a marked tendency to spread out on a line drawn across the bull from ten o'clock to four o'clock. This is easily understood if one recognizes that the right-hand spin of the bullet, in conjunction with a wind from the right, creates a vacuum in the ten-o'clock area of the axis of the bullet, and the bullet tends to move into the vacuum. Similarly, a wind from the left causes a vacuum in the four-o'clock area. The simplest way to remember how to make vertical changes for wind differences is this: increases in wind velocity increase the vertical ten-to-four-o'clock spread; decreases in wind velocity decrease the vertical spread. Thus, if you click right to accommodate for an *increased wind from the right*, you will probably also need to click down, because the increased wind velocity has increased the tendency of the bullet to rise toward ten o'clock. But if you click right to accommodate for a *decreased wind from the left,* you will probably need to click up, for the decreased wind velocity has decreased the bullet's tendency to move down toward four o'clock. The characteristics of each gun and sight system are different, but as a general rule, three clicks of windage adjustment require one click of elevation adjustment in order to obtain a zero sight setting.

For minor wind changes, a very few shooters use the technique of canting the rifle to achieve a proper zero. The effective limits for this technique are about three clicks right or left of the zero setting. This technique is used almost exclusively in prone, for the effects of changing cant in the kneeling or standing positions are too unpredictable, and errors are compounded by a changed hand position. This technique is learned by using a front sight-bubble, and first learning the amount of cant necessary to effect the equivalent of each one click of change. The bubble thus provides a guide by which to duplicate that degree of cant until the "feel" of the cant is thoroughly memorized. It is a difficult technique, with inherent risks; if you must use it, use it carefully.

Under very severe wind conditions, just about all shooters will be forced to modify their positions in order to achieve any stability at all. The usual modification is to "tighten up" the position. This is accomplished by two means: an increase in overall muscle tension, and adjusting the position and the rifle in order to achieve more stress or tightness in the position. Needless to say, even if the waiting technique is employed with patience under such circumstances, scores will be lower than normal, as the position will necessarily be less reliable. If the adverse conditions persist throughout the match, however, all the competitors are in the same boat.

One of the more damaging things that happens to many

shooters is that when shooting in a wind they forget about concentration and hold. When a lull occurs, they attempt to get off as many shots as possible, and usually this results in wildly erratic performance. When a lull occurs, the shooter may choose to fire rapidly, but only as rapidly as he can without losing concentration on, and control of, hold. Also, even *during* a wind, concentration on hold will generally produce superior results.

The ability to hold the rifle in position for ten minutes, required sometimes by the technique of waiting out the wind, must be accompanied by a good deal of patience and persistence. Observation of champion shooters will show that every one possesses an unusual degree of patience. They have the patience to perfect techniques and to train thoroughly, and that same patience comes to the surface when they must shoot under adverse weather conditions. They are all capable of using the full time allowed for the match in order to gain every possible point that can be acquired by waiting. This characteristic might also be called persistence. The champion never gives up. He always tries as hard as possible to win. He looks upon the wind as his friend, because it blows upon his competitors, discourages or frustrates them, and causes them to give up. The champion knows that when all others have given up, he has won the match.

MIRAGE

The word "mirage" is popularly used in two ways. Off the rifle range, a mirage is something that appears to exist in a certain place but actually does not. On the rifle range, mirage means visible waves of heat in the atmosphere. In both cases, mirage is caused by refraction, and so the two are closely related. First, we will deal with the false appearance of objects—the common meaning—as this will provide a useful background for discussing mirage in the shooting sense.

As discussed in the section on the human eye, light is bent, or refracted, when it passes through substances of differing density. In that discussion we have already seen how light rays are refracted when passing from air through the denser medium of the lens of the eye. In this discussion, however, we will be concerned with refraction only as it takes place outside the eye.

Refraction can be illustrated by putting a pencil in a glass half-filled with water. Part of the pencil appears to be broken or out of place where it enters the water, but of course it is not; it *appears* out of place because we "see" light rays entering our eyes at a different angle. Those passing through the water are bent differently by this watery medium which is more dense than the air through which the other rays pass.

Media of differing density need not be different substances. The same substances at different temperatures possess differing densities. Water, for example, is most dense at about 34° F., is somewhat less dense at lower temperatures where it becomes solid ice, and is least dense at very high temperatures where it becomes a gaseous steam. Air, like water, possesses different densities at different temperatures, though air would have to be cooled to extremely low temperatures to reach liquid or solid states. However, for our purposes, when on a sunlit day air comes into contact with the soil or other dark surface which absorbs heat from sunlight, some of the heat transfers to the air, which expands in volume and loses density. It consequently becomes lighter, and rises; cooler, heavier air then moves to the spot where it too will become heated and rise. This heated air, being less dense than the unheated air elsewhere, refracts or bends light passing through it to a different degree than does the cooler, denser air.

The degree of refraction can be slight or extreme, depending on the temperature (and density) variation. An example of extreme refraction is the phenomenon we frequently experience when driving an automobile down a highway under a hot, bright sun. Sometimes part of the road at a distance will appear to be wet, or to resemble a pool or lake. When we arrive at the spot, however, it is only a perfectly dry road. The appearance of wetness, or of a lake, is due to our actually seeing the sky on a portion of the road. The light rays coming down from the sky meet the hot air above the surface of the road and are bent at such extreme angles that they enter our line of vision when our eyes are directed to the road. Similar instances of extreme refraction, involving a double bending up and down of light rays by alternating layers of hot and cold air, are responsible for the famous mirages of lakes on desert sand, or cities floating on the surface of the sea.

The rising hot air on a highway or a rifle range can sometimes be seen with the naked eye as rising waves or ripples of heat. These visible, rising waves of heat are what shooters call *the* mirage. The most useful way of seeing the mirage on a rifle range is through a spotting scope. It is most clearly seen by focusing the scope on the target, and then moving the focus back toward the telescope until the target begins to blur. So focused, the scope will reveal, under conditions of direct sunlight, waves of rising hot air. The waves are visible because of their refractive power. If no wind is blowing, or if the wind is directly toward or away from the observer, these waves will rise straight upward and appear to boil. If the wind is blowing from either side, the waves will appear to run in the same direction as the wind, for the rising hot air is in fact moving with these air currents.

In considering the effects of these moving heat waves, it is necessary to take into account the effects of both wind and refraction. First, however, it will be useful to deal with refraction in isolation. For reasons which are not necessary to explain here in detail, when the waves of the mirage are rising or "boiling" upward, they bend the light up, and then down, in such a way that the target *appears* to be higher than it actually is. Thus a shot aimed at the center of the *apparent* bull will be high in relation to the actual bull. If there is a wind from the right, and the waves of the mirage seem to move from right to left, the light is refracted in such a manner that the bull appears to be left of its actual position, and a shot aimed at the center of the *apparent* bull will be left of the actual bull. If the waves move from left to right, a shot aimed at the apparent bull will be right of the actual bull, for the same reason. Now, the mirage, in and of itself, does *not* change the path of the bullet. In the no-wind conditions of a boiling mirage, the mirage does not push the bullet upward to any appreciable extent; it merely makes the target *appear* higher than it really is, and in reality we aim at a point above the actual bull.

The refractive power of the mirage can be illustrated by a

simple experiment using a scope equipped with cross-hairs. The scope should be locked into an unmoveable position in the early morning, before the sun begins to warm the earth enough to create mirage, and the cross-hairs centered on a target or some other stationary object of known dimensions. Care should be taken that neither the scope nor the cross-hairs are moved during the course of the experiment. As the sun rises and creates sufficient heat along the surface of the soil, mirage waves will begin to appear. If these waves rise, the target will appear to rise along the vertical cross-hair of the scope. If the mirage is running from right to left, the target will appear to move to the left along the horizontal cross-hair, and perhaps slightly upward as well; if the mirage is running from left to right, the target will appear to move to the right along the horizontal cross-hair, and perhaps rise slightly. Our own experiment of this type was run with scopes focused on regulation target frames at distances of 600 and 1000 yards. At various times, the bull *seemed* to move as much as 4 feet at 600 yards, and more than 6 feet at 1000 yards. In actuality, however, the target frames did not move at all, and neither did the scopes. The frames appeared to move because of refraction. Under these conditions, a shot aimed at the mirage-displaced bull's-eye would have been completely off the frame of the target.

In reality, the perverse effects of mirage are aided and abetted by wind. When the mirage appears to run from left to right, or right to left, the visible heat waves are really being pushed in those directions by the wind. Thus, under usual circumstances, the mirage running from left to right not only makes the bull appear to be to the right of its actual position, but the accompanying wind will also move the trajectory of the bullet to the right. The effects are thus compound, consisting of the effect of refraction plus the effect of wind. It would be foolish to say how much each factor is responsible for changing zero sight setting, because the ratios may vary widely under different climatic or weather conditions. In one of our experiments, it was determined that refraction was responsible for about 60 percent of the effects, and wind about 40 percent. These ratios may vary widely, however, depending upon both topographic and climatic situations. Shooters might find it useful to experiment with these factors, using a stationary rifle scope as a means of judging refraction, and flags or other means of determining the effects of wind upon bullet trajectory.

It is obvious that the combined effects of refraction and wind are greater as the distance between shooter and target increases. Mirage is much more apparent, for example, at 300 meters than at 50. Some shooters, in fact, discount the value of mirage altogether at 50 meters, though some watch the mirage carefully at this distance. However, at any distance the techniques for shooting through mirage are much the same as for shooting through the wind. One focuses a spotting scope to make the mirage visible, establishes a zero sight setting for a prevailing mirage condition, and then waits out changes in the mirage, shooting only under the condition preselected for zero sight setting. The other techniques, as used in shooting through the wind, can be used with mirage also, but are less desirable.

Still another possibility suggests itself, though it would be expensive, and perhaps require equipment too heavy for practical use in competition. This would be to obtain a spotting scope with a cross-hair, which could be focused on the center of the bull to establish a norm for judging mirage. Great care would have to be exercised to ensure the absolute stability of the spotting scope, and probably a mount or stand of considerable weight would be required to attain the needed stability. Then, using the norm established in the scope as a guide for zero sight setting, click adjustments could be made to account for refraction as the bull *appeared* to move on the cross-hairs of the spotting scope. In computing click adjustments on the sights, the wind factor would also have to be accounted for. Though it would require special equipment, such a technique might prove worthwhile to anyone who could find a way to make it workable.

When we consider the full implications of the refraction phenomenon involved in mirage, the problems raised by it seem exceedingly difficult. For example, we use the spotting scope to see the mirage, or heat waves, at a distance very near the target. But the section of air embraced by the depth of field of the spotting scope is only a fraction of the air that actually exists between the shooter and the target. What about the refraction potential of the rest of that air? It too contains rising heat waves, the amount determined by the angle of the soil surface in relation to the sun, and the color of the surface, among other things. These heat waves are subject to other wind currents (or lack of them) and are also bending the light rays.

In addition, not only heat waves change the density of air. A high humidity, for example, has the effect of making air more dense. So does a high barometric pressure, and certain conditions created by winds. These factors may vary from place to place along the length of a rifle range. Yet these sections of air and the refraction potentials they contain are invisible to the shooter whose scope is focused on or near the target, and who can see only heat waves.

How does the individual cope with these complex problems? The answer is that probably he cannot. He can consider wind indicators, but aside from visible mirage he has no indicators of refraction. The only consoling fact is that the other shooters have no advantage over him, because they also are unable to perceive refraction.

PRECIPITATION

Light or moderate rain can actually be an advantage, for three reasons: clouds and rain diminish or altogether neutralize the effects of mirage, rain is a reasonably good wind indicator, and rain helps defeat your competition by making them want to give up. Snow is unusual during a match, and is not likely to have any real effect except for the accompanying cold. Sleet and hail usually result in a match being called off or postponed, as does a heavy rain that seriously reduces visibility. But light-to-moderate rains are tolerable, and about the only real effect of moderate rain is a small amount of discomfort to the shooter.

Proper rain gear helps to reduce or avoid the discomfort. A poncho or some form of rain suit, with a stiff-brimmed hat that can be kept from falling down over the eyes, will keep one reasonably dry. An anti-fog treatment applied to shooting glasses and spotting scope is extremely useful under conditions of high humidity. With these aids, and, again, a measure of patience and persistence, a shooter can turn in a good performance despite the weather. This persistent effort will be doubly valuable, as most other competitors will be hurrying to finish and get into a dry place, or becoming irritated with the dampness, or otherwise letting up on their effort. If you keep trying, your chances of winning are increased; the number of real competitors is reduced to those few who are, like yourself, still performing at the peak of their ability.

Proper care should be given to equipment in foul weather to prevent water damage, or interference with mechanical function. A shield improvised out of cartridge boxes and held in place with rubber bands can be fitted over iron sights or telescope lenses to keep them dry. Sights and other parts of the rifle, including the critical fore-end of the stock, can be kept dry also by means of inexpensive plastic sheets held in place by tape or rubber bands. Great care should be taken to prevent the rifle stock from absorbing water and swelling or warping; the effect will almost certainly be a drastic loss of accuracy, which could be permanent. Shooting boxes can easily be kept closed, and all ammunition should be kept as dry as possible. Again, inexpensive plastic sheets will serve this function nicely, and liberal quantities should be a part of every shooter's emergency supplies. With these items handy, you can begin to look upon a normal rain as your friend.

— IV —

EQUIPMENT & POSITIONS

Equipment and positions make up the material, physical side of shooting. Equipment consists of a whole range of items, each of which is highly specialized and designed for a particular kind of match. Equipment that is legal in one kind of match may not be legal in another. The shooting positions themselves are highly specialized, and are used almost exclusively in competition; they would hardly be suitable, say, for use in hunting. In the following chapters we attempt to discuss the specialized features of equipment and positions in detail.

The discussions are organized around international-style matches, for reasons explained at the beginning of this book. Official shooting organizations in many nations have different styles of matches, or have modified somewhat the standard international regulations. Generally speaking, these matches have less restrictive regulations regarding both equipment and positions. If you intend to participate in matches other than standard international ones, contact the official shooting organization in your country for a rulebook on the course of fire and the equipment, positions, and techniques that can be legally used.

CHAPTER
10

Equipment

TYPES OF MATCHES AND TYPES OF RIFLES

At present there are six international-style rifle matches: smallbore English match—60 shots prone, 50 meters; smallbore free-rifle—40 shots each, prone, kneeling, standing, 50 meters; smallbore standard rifle—20 shots each, prone, kneeling, standing, 50 meters; air rifle—40 (or 60) shots standing, 10 meters; bigbore free-rifle—40 shots each, prone, kneeling, standing, 300 meters; and army rifle—20 shots each, prone, kneeling, standing, 300 meters. Generally, the only differences between the smallbore and bigbore free-rifle events is the caliber of the rifle used and the distance of the target; otherwise they conform in all respects. Also, as we shall see, there are similarities between the smallbore standard rifle event and the army rifle event.

An individual *could* purchase seven different rifles for use in these events—a smallbore prone rifle, a smallbore free rifle, a smallbore standard rifle, an air rifle, a bigbore prone rifle, a bigbore free rifle, and an army rifle (an "army" rifle in name only—not really an issue military gun). Most people, however, find it more convenient to limit the number of rifles they use, and many restrict the number of events they will enter so they can compete with only two or three rifles, and frequently with only one. An individual can compete in some form of international style competition with just as many, or just as few, rifles as he wants.

Basically, all the rifles mentioned above fall into two broad categories: "free" rifles which are free to assume any number of configurations through adjustments to the palm-rest, butt plate, and butt-hook; and "straight" rifles which are severely restricted in configuration and do not have a palm-rest in the usual sense of the word, and have no butt-hook at all, though some of these rifles do have adjustable butt plates. These latter rifles are used by many shooters in the prone portions of free-rifle events, and they are used in standard, army, and air-rifle events. The free rifles are used by most shooters in the kneeling and standing positions of free-rifle events, and by many in the prone position and in English matches as well.

With regard to shooting positions, the basic difference between these categories of rifles is simply this: a free rifle allows an individual a broad latitude in designing a shooting position, for the changeable configuration of the stock allows him to fit the rifle to the position; a straight rifle restricts this latitude somewhat, for the position must be designed to fit the configuration of the stock. Even with a straight rifle one is not overly restricted, however, and as these guns are available in different stock dimensions, and, within limitations, with different degrees of drop, offset, weight distribution, etc. But, whichever type of rifle is used, the same principles of positions, and position building, apply. About the only really different principle is that in the standing position a straight rifle, because it lacks a butt-hook, requires the use of muscle support to hold the rifle against the shoulder. Otherwise, the basic position principles remain identical.

The ensuing discussion of equipment and positions will be oriented primarily to the smallbore free-rifle event, for reasons already explained. Readers can take most of the material and, with the aid of common sense, apply it to the equipment and positions of most other kinds of rifle events.

OFFICIAL REGULATIONS

Before discussing equipment and positions in more detail, it is necessary to state this most important piece of advice. All items of equipment, and all aspects of positions, are subject to regulations established by the governing body of international shooting, the International Shooting Union (ISU). These regulations are subject to change at any time, and changes do come at any time. Therefore, when you are choosing equipment and building positions, and before you enter a match, *check with the current ISU rules to make sure that all aspects of your equipment and positions are legal.* What was legal last year is not necessarily legal this year. It is a disheartening and frustrating experience to attend a match and be disqualified or at least harassed because some minor detail renders a piece of equipment illegal. Don't take chances—check on the legality of *everything* you use, from rifle to shoelaces. This advice is given on the basis of long experience, and we consider it valuable advice indeed. The same advice applies to the rules of national and local organizations.

BUYING EQUIPMENT

From the very first, buy the best equipment you can find. The most frequent mistake made by beginning shooters is to decide, "Well, I'll buy some cheap equipment first, to see if I like shooting; if I do like it, I can get some good equipment later." But in the long run there is no such thing as cheap equipment. If you buy a substandard gun and accessories, the chances are very good that you are going to be stuck with them whether you move on to better equipment or not, because to sell at second hand a piece of equipment that was shoddy to begin with is almost impossible. Moreover, substandard equipment, because it doesn't work well, often creates so many problems, or is so inaccurate, that it takes all the pleasure out of trying to shoot well, or actually prevents one from shooting well. A far wiser and more economical procedure is to buy good equipment. Good equipment is a pleasure to use and makes good shooting possible. If, later on, it is no longer wanted, the chances of selling it at second hand are far above those of selling a shoddy rifle and accessories.

How does one recognize good equipment? Probably the best recommendation for a brand name is that it is used by the world-champion shooters. A reliable, experienced friend may also be a good source of recommendation, but use care in taking his advice because if he is not a champion, perhaps it's because his ideas about equipment are wrong. Many of the champions are offered equipment for test and evaluation purposes by the major arms manufacturers, and thus they are able to pick and choose very carefully. They are going to know, and use, the best equipment available. Find out what several of the top contenders use, and then follow their example. Shop around at various stores, get to know the dealers somewhat, and compare prices. Sometimes amazing amounts of money can be saved on identical items simply by comparison shopping. If possible, buy from a well-stocked dealer who is likely to keep spare parts on hand, and preferably from one with a good gunsmith on the premises. Incidentally, really good gunsmiths who understand the requirements of international style shooting are more rare than whooping cranes. If you are lucky enough to find one, spare nothing to stay in his good graces.

NECESSARY EQUIPMENT

The following items are basic. You could not satisfactorily shoot a match without them, and you could do a good job with these alone. These and all other items you use should be expressly suited for international-style competition and should be legal according to *current* ISU rules.

1. *Rulebook.* Must be current. It governs everything you use and everything you do. Also has valuable information on match procedure. Get to know it thoroughly.

2. *Rifle.* Should be a precision instrument, superbly accurate, the best (not necessarily the most expensive) money can buy.

3. *Sights*, front and rear. Many successful shooters stay with sights supplied by the rifle manufacturer, though others will seek out a different brand name. Should be absolutely reliable and accurate. It's a good idea to have three rear sights, one each for prone, kneeling, and standing.

4. *Palm-rest.* Few shooters use the factory item in its original form. Most retain the mechanical skeleton and attach a grip of some original design that suits their own imagination.

5. *Butt-hook.* Some years ago, custom-made (i.e., home-

made) butt-hooks were widely preferred. Today the factory-supplied hook is more widely used.

6. *Sling.* This is an extremely important piece of equipment. It can possess no cuff, must be narrow enough to meet ISU specifications, and should be of top-grade leather. Web slings are almost useless because they stretch. Leather slings will also stretch, but over a period of weeks or months instead of minutes. Because of this stretch, sling adjustment will need correcting from time to time.

7. *Glove.* A good leather shooting glove is the best bet. A thick padding in the glove may disqualify it under ISU regulations.

8. *Coat.* A leather coat specifically designed for ISU competition, and tailor-made for the individual, is recommended, but the rules change fast on these. As this is an expensive item, make sure the salesman and the manufacturer know what they're doing, and get the measurements accurately.

9. *Sweatshirt.* Should have cushioning qualities so as to dampen pulse beat. Strict rules govern these, also.

10. *Pants.* Almost any everyday kind of slacks or jeans will do. Should be durable. Some shooters prefer a tight fit for support, others a loose fit for comfort.

11. *Shoes.* Some years ago, combat boots or ski boots were preferred; today many good shooters have gone to low-quarter canvas tennis shoes. Whatever type of shoe is used, some training time is necessary for the individual to get used to the feel of the shoe.

12. *Shooting glasses.* High-impact glass, comfortable frames, and proper fit to allow for unobstructed vision while shooting are essential. At least one pair is mandatory, and if only one pair is owned, the lenses should be clear glass. Two additional pairs are desirable, but not urgent: green or gray, and yellow.

13. *Spotting scope.* An important item that should be chosen carefully. Durability, clarity, and variable range focus are essential features. The scope should be in the 20-25-times power range. The mount should be heavy and stable, and you definitely need enough extension rods to bring the scope up to shoulder level in the standing position.

14. *Shooting mat.* The ISU specifies an allowable thickness.

Should be durable, comfortable, legal, and easy to transport. Generally, however, the mat is provided at ISU matches.

15. *Kneeling roll.* Choose this for size and its ability either to retain or to lose its shape under pressure, whichever you want. It shouldn't leak sawdust or other stuffing all over your car and shooting equipment.

16. *Hat.* Definitely a fun item, as well as a useful one. Should protect you from sun (including sideglare) and rain, but should express your personality, too. Use your imagination on this one.

17. *Diary and pen.* A small, loose-leaf notebook is excellent. The pen should contain waterproof ink.

18. *Masking tape.* Usefulness limited only by one's imagination.

19. *Maintenance equipment.* Maintenance equipment will include an assortment of screwdrivers, a cleaning rod, wooden cleaning rod guide, metal and nylon bore brushes, cloth bore patches, bore cleaning fluid, an anti-oxidant lubricant, oil, and cleaning cloth. An old toothbrush is useful for cleaning the chamber and bolt. A preservative wood treatment for the stock should also be included, as recommended by the manufacturer.

Additional items that may be useful in inclement weather include plastic sheets, rubber bands, and an anti-fog gel or spray for use on glasses and telescopes. A liberal supply of absorbent cloth, such as old diapers or terrycloth towels, is useful in any kind of weather.

SELECTION AND CARE OF AMMUNITION

All ammunition carrying the same brand name is not the same. Ammunition is manufactured in batches, or lots, containing individual production runs of cartridge cases, bullets, powder, primers, and other components, if any. Each of these lots is assigned a number by the manufacturer. The number should be printed or stamped on both the case and individual box containers. Just as different brands of ammunition will perform differently in any given gun, so will different lots of the same brand. Lots which perform very well in one rifle may not perform at all well in another. The difference in scores produced by different lots can often be astounding. Always use the brand of ammunition that performs best in your particular rifle. In addition, always train with a lot number that rates good in terms of accuracy, and preferably with one that rates superior. When you run across a lot number that has truly exceptional accuracy in your gun, save it for use in matches. Many bigbore shooters obtain superior ammunition by fireforming brass to a particular chamber and then hand-loading to the specifications they have determined to be the best for that rifle.

Ammunition must receive proper care if it is to maintain its accuracy. Generally, the best procedure is to protect it from jolts and bumps and any pressures that might bend or dent the bullet or case. In addition, it should be kept dry and under even, moderate temperatures. Extremes of moisture, or extremes of temperature, can drastically alter the characteristics of ammunition. A lot that is matched to a rifle, and then placed in the high temperature of the trunk of an automobile that is being driven under a hot sun for two or three days, may no longer give satisfactory performance. Unpressurized cargo compartments in airplanes also drastically affect ammunition. We once carried exceptionally accurate smallbore ammunition in an unpressurized cargo compartment on a transatlantic flight. On arrival, the ammunition that had once been exceptionally accurate would shoot groups larger than 6 inches at 50 meters, and this in the rifles with which it had been matched! When you travel with ammunition, protect it carefully from being jarred or crushed, and from extremes of temperature, humidity, and air pressure. It will then be the same as when you tested it.

OPTIONAL EQUIPMENT

The following items of equipment are not essential, but they aid one way or another in training, performing, or in caring for your other items.

1. *Equipment box.* A strong, light, easily carried box for loose equipment and small items is a great help. Some shooters have found an old suitcase satisfactory; others use large metal tool boxes. Prevents loss of individual items, keeps equipment clean, and protects it from damage and weather.

2. *Gun case and gun box.* One each for every rifle. Some shooters would consider this essential rather than optional. The case keeps the rifle dry and clean and protects it when not in use. The metal box provides a more sturdy form of protection during travel. Your rifle is a precision instrument, and you should if anything be overprotective of it. It should never be bumped or jarred, and neither metal nor wood parts should ever be bent or placed under stress, as the accuracy can thus be permanently impaired.

3. *Ammunition box.* Usually a wood block with a hinged cover, with drilled holes for each individual round. These help to keep ammo clean and dry, but their greatest value is in providing a means of knowing exactly how many rounds you have fired, how many sighter shots, and how many record shots. This knowledge is a comfort to you during a match, and if targets should get mixed or mislaid (which sometimes happens), it can be invaluable information. Some ammo now comes commercially packaged in plastic containers with individual holes for each round; these containers can serve the same purpose as a wooden box.

4. *Special trigger.* Although most smallbore shooters use the trigger that comes supplied by the rifle manufacturer, a few smallbore shooters, and a larger percentage of bigbore shooters, use triggers of some other design or manufacture. These are customarily marketed under the name of the designer. The most important characteristic of a trigger is consistency. It should pull in the same stages and at the same weight each time, its break should feel the same each time, and its operation speed should be the same each time. The exact type and feel of a trigger is relatively unimportant if it suits the individual and he is accustomed to it. The trigger will create problems, however, if it feels mushy one time and grating the next, or if its operation speed varies by as little as a few milliseconds from one pull to another. Several years ago the preferred trigger was a double-stage set trigger adjusted to an extremely light pull. Most successful shooters today, however, get better results with a trigger pull of between 3 and 8 ounces. If a separate prone rifle is used, the trigger there is usually heavier, about 1 to 1½ pounds. Both double-stage and single-stage triggers are widely used. Undoubtedly the preferred trigger of the future will be

electric, for it allows any desired feel to be built into the pull, while the break remains consistent within degrees unobtainable in mechanical triggers.

5. *Custom stock.* Most people can use production model stocks with no problem. A few people, however, because of body conformation, benefit from a stock with a special drop (distance of butt plate below the axis of the bore) or cast (distance of butt plate to left or right of the axis of the bore). Some prefer other special features as well. Stocks of special dimensions can sometimes be ordered from the manufacturer of the rifle, or ordered from equipment houses, or made at home by the skilled hobbyist.

Care must be taken that the stock is fitted precisely to the action, or the accuracy of the rifle will suffer severely. An alteration often made to ensure this fit, even with factory models, is to have the action "bedded" in fiberglass or some similar material. This operation requires some skill, and should be performed by a competent gunsmith. Perhaps the most common and easiest modification of stocks is the application of a homemade cheek piece. Sometimes interchangeable ones are used, one for kneeling and one for prone. These range from cardboard held in place with masking tape to sophisticated wood or fiberglass inlays. In designing one of these, care should be taken not to destroy the sturdiness of the stock.

6. *Rifle scope.* A scope on the rifle is a good means of checking rifle and ammunition accuracy, and of getting a good clear view of the limits of your hold. Is it confined to the 10-ring, or does it wander outside? The extent of these movements will probably be startling to you the first time you see them through a glass, even if they are confined to the 10-ring. With most guns, mounts will have to be attached to accommodate the scope. Have this done by a *reliable* gunsmith. The scope must also be focused for *your* eye, and adjustments must include parallax as well as distance and cross-hair focus. Consult the manual that comes with the scope. Also, in some countries, there are "any-sight" matches in which telescopic sights may be used during competition.

7. *Stopwatch.* Helps you keep track of elapsed time and time remaining with much greater ease than is possible with an ordinary watch. A great comfort on the firing line.

8. *Ear protectors.* Not necessary for smallbore firing, but make the transition from smallbore to bigbore much more tolerable, and provide comfort, as well as valuable protection to hearing. Recently discovered evidence reveals that the decibel level of bigbore rifle noise can permanently destroy the ability to hear high-frequency sound. For bigbore shooters, then, ear protectors are an especially good investment.

ADJUSTMENT OF EQUIPMENT

Whenever possible, equipment should be adjusted to fit the individual shooter's position. With a free rifle this usually means making adjustments in the palm-rest and butt-hook or plate. A beginner should work only with these adjustments, and usually they will be all that is necessary to make the rifle conform to his position. A few individuals, however, with either a free rifle or a straight rifle, will need to have adjustments made in the dimensions of the stock itself. It will take most people about a year or more of shooting experience to know if a change of this nature is required, and exactly what the change must be. If it is necessary, it should be made. As early as possible in a shooter's career, his equipment should be made to fit his position as accurately and comfortably as possible within legal limits. Then he can forget about equipment and place his attention where it properly belongs—on performance.

One of the most common errors in adjusting equipment other than the rifle involves management of the spotting scope. The scope should *not* be set up and focused, and then a position assumed that allows access to the scope. Rather, the shooting position should be assumed, and then the scope set up and adjusted in such as way that the individual can see clearly through the scope without disturbing his position. The head movement required to see through the viewfinder should be minimal—no more than 3 or 4 inches. (Incidentally, it has been determined that it makes no difference whether or not the eye used for sighting is used to look through the scope. The after-effects on vision are inconsequential.) Care must be taken in the placement of the scope, so that no contact is made with any part of the scope or mount by the shooter's body or clothing. Any such contact can be declared artificial support and result in the offender's disqualification.

The adjustment of many pieces of equipment can be recorded so that accidental changes in adjustment are avoided. The simplest way to do this is to place strips of ordinary masking tape along the fore-end rail, the butt-plate assembly, the sight mount rails, and the edge of the sling. Then pen or pencil marks and notations can record the position of the palm-rest, fore-end stop, butt-hook or plate, sight mount, and sling buckle, as they are applicable in each position. This makes possible speedy assembly of equipment and also ensures that the equipment will be adjusted consistently from session to session.

Beginners may also use a similar method of recording the positions of their support areas in the standing and kneeling positions. Bits of tape, chalk marks, or pencil marks on a floor, shooting mat, or a large piece of heavy paper, can be useful in helping a new shooter assume the same position with his feet (and his knee, in the kneeling position) each time he trains in a position. After the position is well learned, of course, these aids are unnecessary.

CHAPTER
11

Positions

A useful prelude to a detailed examination of the three basic positions will be a general survey of position theory. A full statement of the theory will provide a basis for understanding the why's and wherefore's of all positions. As this preliminary survey will, in effect, attempt to state in general terms what the sections on each position say in specific terms, there will consequently be some overlap and repetition. This repetition is, on the one hand, undesirable; but on the other hand, as noted earlier, this arrangement allows for the section on each position to be a self-contained unit, with reference to theory where useful, but with primary focus on the actual physical details of the position.

We remind you here that the sections on positions deal only with physical structure. The functional elements in the shooting process—activities such as eye use, breath control, trigger pull, etc.—are discussed in other portions of this book. We hope that this system of presentation has merit in that it clearly separates structural principles from functional principles, and thus lends simplicity and clarity to the descriptions which follow.

THEORY OF POSITIONS

The theory of positions may be outlined as follows. With the aid of palm-rest, butt-hook, and/or sling, the body is positioned so that the weight of the rifle is placed upon the skeletal system; muscles are employed only to hold the skeletal system stationary. Stated another way, the weight of the rifle is supported by a system of bone-to-bone contacts that are uninterrupted by muscular effort; that is, when the rifle is placed in the firing position, no bone-to-bone contacts that can be used to support the rifle are prevented by muscular effort. The elbow of the forward arm, for example, is not prevented from contacting the bones of the rib cage or hip bone in the standing position, nor prevented from contacting the knee joint in the kneeling position. *Direct* contact between the bones of the elbow and rib cage, or elbow and knee, is of course prevented by flesh and clothing, but not by muscular effort.

Thus muscles are not used to hold the rifle in position; they are used only to hold the skeletal system in position. This does not mean, of course, that muscles are not involved in an important way in aiming the rifle. They are. In the standing and kneeling positions particularly, if a shooter were to relax completely all of his muscles, he would collapse to the ground. Many, if not most, of the muscles of the legs and trunk are involved in supporting the skeletal system in these positions. The muscles of the legs and trunk constitute by far the major portion of the muscles of the body. And it is precisely this fact that the great advantage is gained by using the technique of bone support: the weight of the rifle is shifted off the muscles of the shoulders and arms, which, if they bore the weight directly, would quickly fatigue, develop tremors, and become subject to spasms, jerks, and cramps. By utilizing bone support, a rifleman removes the necessity for support of the rifle by the muscles of the arms and shoulders, and creates a situation in which the burden is shifted to the great muscle systems of the legs and trunk, which support the skeletal system directly, and the rifle indirectly. These muscle systems, because of their great bulk, reserves of strength, and efficiency in supporting the skeleton, can endure the rigors of a match without fatiguing to the point of impairing the rifleman's holding ability.

As mentioned, the use of bone support is achieved with the help of mechanical aids. In the standing position the principal aid is the butt-hook, which holds the stock in position against the shoulder, thus freeing the trigger hand and arm of all support function. Another mechanical aid is the palm-rest, which extends the forward forearm and raises the aim of the rifle up to target level when the elbow is placed against the rib cage or hip. (A straight rifle without a butt-hook requires that the trigger hand and arm use some muscle power to hold the rifle in position by pulling the stock back against the shoulder. Otherwise, the same use is made of bone support. Compared to the body configuration used with a free rifle, the angles of the bone structure and the total configuration may be slightly different, but with the exception of the muscle support just mentioned, the principles used with both rifles are exactly the same.)

In the kneeling and prone positions, the chief mechanical aid to bone structure is the sling. The sling forms the base of an inverted triangle whose sides are formed by the upper arm and the forearm. The sling is positioned so as to prevent the forearm from falling forward, and transmits the weight of the rifle back to the upper arm. The triangle thus created supports the weight of the rifle without employing muscular effort.

In the standing and kneeling positions, maximum use of bone support is also achieved by placing the body and rifle in a state of equilibrium, or balance, which minimizes muscle use while achieving a high degree of body stability. In the standing position, equilibrium is attained by bending the torso to the right and back of the feet to balance the weight of the rifle to the front and left of the feet (right-handed shooters). When the center of gravity of the body-rifle structure is directly over the center of the support area provided by the feet, a state of equilibrium is achieved. In the kneeling position, equilibrium is usually more easily attained, as the support area is much larger. Three basic variations of the kneeling position are used: the high position, with the torso almost upright and the major portion of the body weight placed on the heel above the kneeling roll; the low variation, with the torso moderately erect and the major portion of the body weight placed on the side of the foot, which is placed beneath the buttocks (in this variation, the knee touching the floor and the forward foot also bear some body weight); and the forward variation, in which the body is bent well forward and weight is distributed more or less evenly among the three supports provided by the feet and knee. In all of these variations, a state of equilibrium can be found which minimizes the work of muscles in supporting the body and rifle.

Head position is extremely important in attaining equilibrium, and also in assuring proper use of the eyes. In the kneeling and standing positions, the head should be held upright, just as it is while one is standing at attention. This means that in the standing position, the neck will have to be bent forward and twisted somewhat to the left to offset the backward bend and twist to the right of the torso. In kneeling, the neck will be bent toward the back, though in a very upright high kneeling position the neck will not be bent at all; in most kneeling positions, a slight twist of the neck to the left will usually be necessary to bring the face in line with the sights. An upright head position prevents the reflexive swaying movements that occur whenever the head is bent to one side. The vestibular apparatus, the organ of balance in the inner ear, is involved in initiating this swaying motion when the head is bent, but the vestibular apparatus will remain inactive and will not set off reflexive body movements if the head is upright. Holding the head upright thus helps minimize body sway in the kneeling and standing positions.

Holding the head upright also makes possible the most efficient use of the eyes. With the head upright and facing the target as much as possible, the eyes are allowed to retain their normal position, looking directly out of the sockets. Fatigue of the eye muscles is prevented, and vision is not obstructed by the bridge of the nose or the eyebrows, as it is when the eyes are focused on a point to the front of the shooter but the head is twisted or tilted to one side. In the prone position, the sway reflex is nonexistent, but head position is still important to allow for proper vision. The neck will have to be bent back and twisted to position the eye to see through the sights. However, this bend and twist should not be so severe that the neck feels strained or cramped; it *should* be sufficient to allow the eye to look through the sights without vision being obstructed by the bridge of the nose or by the eyebrow.

Some experimentation with the "high" and "low" variations of the prone position will help to establish a configuration that allows for a suitable head position. If a proper head position cannot be obtained in any one of the positions, either a redesigned stock, offset sights, a cant to the rifle, or some combination of these should be employed to achieve proper head position, as it is one of the more crucial elements in all shooting positions.

In its most concise form, the theory of positions is that maximum use is made of bone support and equilibrium so that muscles may be used primarily to maintain hold. This means that the exact body configuration which fulfills these conditions will be different for any two shooters who differ in body proportions. As almost no two people have the same proportions, probably no two people will fulfill these principles with exactly the same configurations. It is foolish for a rifleman to try to copy someone else, for what works for one person will not necessarily work for another.

Therefore, as you read the following descriptions of each of the shooting positions, keep in mind that what is being described is a basic—or what might also be called a "classic"—configuration. The description of each position is based upon what approximates an average body conformation. For most people, assuming the position exactly as it is described is a good place to start the process of building a personalized position. A few people will find that, because of their body structure, the classic configuration is exactly right for them. Most will find, however, that *slight* changes will be necessary to achieve the configuration that takes maximum advantage of the theoretical principles outlined above. Any dramatic change from the positions as described will almost certainly violate these principles; but slight changes may be necessary to achieve them. Remember, the basic requirements of a position are that it be legal, reasonably comfortable, and capable of producing a good hold. Any change you make from the basic configuration is right for you if it achieves these ends.

A NOTE ON THE PHOTOGRAPHS

Successful shooters make use of the principles stated in the preceding theory of positions, yet look different from one another because they in fact have made individual adaptations of body placement in order to achieve those principles. To illustrate this fact, we are complementing the descriptions of each position with photographs of various successful shooters.

By studying them carefully, you will see that the shooters' positions differ from one another probably in direct ratio to the differences in their physical proportions. It is therefore probably most helpful to study the positions of the shooter whose physical proportions most resemble your own. Remember, however, that his proportions will not be *exactly* like your own, and you should attempt to build your own position on the correct principles, not on the appearance of someone else, no matter how much he resembles you. You may get useful ideas or suggestions from the positions of any of these shooters.

The positions are described step by step, with the various points taken in the order they are encountered as one gets into the position. The descriptions are not only of the positions, then, but also of the process of assuming them. All the descriptions are for right-handed shooters.

PRONE

For obvious reasons, prone is the most stable of the three positions. The center of gravity is quite low and the support area, or area of contact between the body and the shooting mat, is relatively large. The great size of the support area gives special characteristics to the position: the large number of contact points between the body and external objects gives the position a more definite feel, making it possible to learn the position more quickly and re-establish it more easily than the other positions; and the great stability of the position combined with this clearly defined feel makes it possible for an individual easily to develop variations from the basic position and be more aware of these variations than he might be in other positions. Consequently, most prone shooters develop very definite ideas about what is right or wrong in this position as they discover things that work for them.

The sensations of the position are so strong and clearly defined in the consciousness that a particular variation, when it leads to success, creates a psychological situation in which it is difficult not to assume that this is *the* variation that should work for everybody. Yet the widely differing ideas among different shooters about the details of the position are not incorrect, for there are a great many real experts on the prone position, capable of shooting English match scores of 600. All of them use the same basic position; but all have highly individualized variations of the basic position.

What this illustrates quite nicely is that the so-called basic or classic manifestations of all three positions are suitable for the individual who exists more frequently as a statistical average than as a real person. Some variation upon each of the three classic positions will probably be right for any given individual; the variations are more difficult to perceive clearly in kneeling and standing because the feel of these positions is less clearly defined as a result of fewer contact points between the body and external objects. But variations in these positions are just as important as personalized variations in the prone position. The classic position illustrates the correct principles to be used; the variations adapt the individuality of different physical dimensions to conform to these principles.

A good prone position should provide a true natural point of aim. Less stable positions yield only a natural area of aim, and in them the rifle must be *held* still on a given point. But in prone the aim of the rifle should rest naturally, without any effort on the shooter's part, on a single point, without any movement except for a slight and probably unavoidable pulse beat. This pulse beat is not always detectable with iron sights on the rifle, but a rifle scope will give a clear picture of its extent. In a good position, the pulse beat does not cause the cross-hairs of the scope to move far beyond the limits of a .22 caliber bullet hole as seen at 50 meters distance. The correct technique, with scope or iron sights, is to shoot between pulse beats when the rifle is motionless. Shooting when the rifle is moving up or down in the pulse beat can throw the shot more than a scoring ring off call, because the movement of the rifle during the pulse beat combines with the forces or recoil to produce highly unpredictable variations in muzzle jump that are much more extensive than the pulse-beat movement itself.

As the basic position is assumed, the shooter encounters the major points of the position as follows.

Positioning the sling.

The sling is usually attached to the rifle and arm before the shooter lies down prone. It is easily accomplished if the shooter kneels and places the butt of the rifle on the mat. Some shooters will have masking tape on the stock rails marked to show where to place the fore-end stop, and the position of the sling buckle will be similarly marked. A beginner might use this guide: If the rifle stock fits him reasonably well, he can determine the generally correct placement of the fore-end stop by measuring the distance between the center of the trigger guard and the end of the butt plate; the same distance forward from the center of the trigger guard will be the point to place the stop. Fine adjustments should then be made.

The length of the sling should be such that it comfortably supports the weight of the rifle once the shooter is in position. The left hand should be snug against the fore-end stop, but not tight enough to produce pain or to cut off blood circulation. The sling should pass flat over the outside of the wrist, without twisting. (A wristwatch, incidentally, will usually cause discomfort if it lies beneath the sling.) On the upper arm, the sling should be buckled tight enough to keep it from sliding down the arm, but loose enough to allow for free circulation of blood. Most important, the sling should be placed either high or low on the upper arm. If it is placed in the middle, the sling is directly over the brachial artery which passes through the triceps muscle near the surface, and will thus pick up an emphatic pulse beat. Generally, the sling should be high on the arm if the shooter has a high prone position, and low, almost near the elbow, if he has a low prone position. It should not be too low, however, to lose its support function for the weight of the rifle. Even when placed either high or low on the arm, the sling will pick up some pulse beat, though far less than if it were over the triceps. This pulse will be quite strong among beginning shooters, but will diminish somewhat as the upper arm is conditioned to the sling. A sweatshirt with good cushioning qualities is helpful in diminishing the effects of pulse beat, but the most important factor is correct positioning of the sling.

Orienting the position.

With the sling properly positioned, the individual places himself prone on the shooting mat. His *back muscles* should be completely relaxed, and his *spine* should not be twisted, but perfectly straight, and headed somewhere between 5 and 15 degrees to the right of the target. The *left leg* should be parallel to the spine, with the toe of the left foot pointed in. Pointing the toe out is uncomfortable and creates no advantages, and has the disadvantage of placing too much weight on the right elbow. The left leg and foot should feel natural and comfortable. The *right leg* is angled out from the spine at approximately 45 degrees, more or less, depending on individual body conformation, with the knee bent, so that the lower leg is roughly parallel to the spine. The toe of the right foot is pointing out, so the toes of both feet are pointing to the shooter's right. The right leg is angled out and bent to locate the right shoulder closer to the center of the position, and to facilitate easier breathing, which will also help to reduce pulse beat. Both of these ends are most completely accomplished if the right leg is brought up to angle away from the body at something less than 90 degrees. To avoid placing an unbearable strain on the left elbow, each individual must find a position for the right leg that works most satisfactorily for him. Among prone shooters, there is probably more variation in the placement of the right leg than in any other feature of the position.

The *left arm* is then placed in a position slightly to the left of the rifle, at a comfortable distance which supports the rifle but avoids strain. Some years ago it was fashionable to place the left elbow completely under the rifle, but this has been shown to produce no advantage, and to have the disadvantage of being painful after a short time. The left hand and wrist should be straight, and the left hand should *not* grasp the rifle. If the wrist or the hand is bent, a springing action occurs which causes unpredictable muzzle jump. Grasping the stock similarly causes change in muzzle jump, and contacting the barrel in any way changes the normal barrel distortion that occurs during passage of the bullet and can affect the point of impact. The stock should rest on the heel of the left hand, not the fingers. This part of the hand contains a source of pulse beat, but with some experimentation with different ways of placing the hand against the stock, this source of pulse can be avoided. By ISU rules, the left hand must be 15 centimeters (approx. 6 inches) above the ground. If the rifle stock fits properly, and the length of the sling and the position of the fore-end stop are properly adjusted, the left hand should be a legal distance from the ground.

The spotting scope is then placed in position. Using the right hand, the scope is placed so the target is brought into focus and, with only a minimal movement of the head, the eye can be positioned to see clearly through it. Care should be taken that the scope nowhere makes contact with body, clothing, or rifle.

The butt of the rifle is placed against the shoulder. Some shooters use the butt-hook in this position, which may be a good idea as it aids in getting a consistent placement of the stock each time the position is assumed. Its use is not urgent, however, and is largely a matter of individual preference. Using an adjustable butt-plate, every effort should be made to get the maximum area of contact between the butt-plate and the shoulder. This maximum contact helps to ensure consistent recoil and muzzle jump. Of course, great care should be taken to position the butt-plate against the shoulder in exactly the same way each time the position is assumed, and to maintain that placement throughout the string of fire. Ideally, the butt-plate, once in a satisfactory position, should be left against the shoulder throughout a string of fire, and not taken from the shoulder for reloading.

The right arm or elbow is placed at a comfortable distance from the body; if it is too close, the right shoulder will be too high, uncomfortable, and unstable; if it is too distant, it will not support the body. The right arm has two functions that are almost unrelated. The function of the portion of the arm between the shoulder and the elbow is to support the weight of the body. The *only* function of the portion between the elbow and hand during the hold is to place the hand up near the trigger. The thumb may rest along the side of the stock or through the thumbhole. The hand is positioned on the stock and grips it with a pressure that is comfortable and allows for the best control of the trigger finger. Some shooters prefer a tight grip, others a loose one. It makes no difference how much grip is used so long as it facilitates proper trigger pull and so long as the grip is consistent each and every time the rifle is fired in that string of shots. Any change in the position of the hand, or the pressure of the hand, will possibly affect muzzle jump. The right hand does *not* guide the rifle into the 10-ring. This is accomplished by other means. The trigger finger may be positioned on the trigger at any place between the extreme tip of the finger and the first joint back from the tip. The exact placement, again, depends upon what allows the individual's particular bone and muscle structure to function with the greatest degree of control.

Undoubtedly the most difficult factor in prone is in maintaining consistency in the placement of the stock against the right shoulder and consistency in the functioning of the right hand and arm. Particular care must be taken while looking through the spotting scope and while loading the rifle to see that no part of the position is disturbed. The head should move only slightly for use of the scope; and the right hand, without disturbing the placement of the elbow, should perform the work of loading and then return to exactly the same placement on the stock for the next shot.

The head is placed naturally, without straining the neck or shoulder, in a position to see through the sights. If the rear sight is properly placed, eye relief should be somewhere between 2 and 6 inches. If the stock of the rifle and the configuration of the body are well designed, the right eye should look out the central axis of the socket, not across the bridge of the nose. The eye will necessarily be turned up toward the eyebrow, but not so far that the eyebrow interferes with vision, or that the muscles which control eye orientation become fatigued. There should be contact between the cheek and the stock, but no excess pressure. If contact cannot be made, the cheekpiece should be built up until contact is achieved. Generally, the cheekpiece in prone is about level with the axis of the bore. As this might be too high for use in the other positions, many shooters have adjustable cheekpieces for prone and kneeling. Consistent cheek pressure on each and every shot is extremely critical. A change in cheek pressure affects not only recoil and muzzle jump, but also eye-sight alignment. The importance of consistent cheek pressure cannot be overemphasized.

Final orientation of the position now takes place, so the natural point of aim is horizontally centered on the bull, using bones only and no muscles to support the rifle. This adjustment is made by shifting the entire body around the fixed placement of the left elbow, which rotates on the mat, but otherwise does not move. The configuration of the position should be maintained in entirety, so the effect is as if the shooting mat had been revolved without disturbing the shooter. Large vertical changes are made by digging in the toes and shifting the entire body forward or backward, again maintaining the fixed position of the left elbow. Small vertical changes are made by controlling the amount of air in the lungs. If a multiple-bull target is used, final orientation should be made each time the aim is moved from one bull to another. Only bones should be involved in aim; muscles are never used to push or guide the rifle into the 10-ring. After each such reorientation, the spotting scope may need slight repositioning. In regulation ISU matches, single-bull targets are used throughout, and one orientation of the position should normally prove to be adequate for the entire prone course.

On the left, a classic position. Note that the left leg is approximately parallel to the spine. The right leg is thrown out at a moderate angle and has a moderate bend at the knee. On the right, a frequently seen variation. The right leg is thrown farther out with the knee more sharply bent, rolling the position to the left side. The advantage here is that the rifle is placed nearer to the center of the position.

Refining the position.

Once a good prone position is found, and well learned, the position will usually not require much training time to sustain performance at a very high level. This does not mean, however, that the position has reached perfection. In all positions, the process of refining and improving goes on continually throughout a shooter's career, which may be a lifetime. These improvements are made by means of improved concentration and analysis of performance, which make possible analysis of the position. Unless concentration is complete, and accompanied by keen awareness and analysis, improvements will be haphazard and faltering. Within the bounds of legality, a shooter must constantly seek ways of refining the position to produce increased comfort and holding ability. His progress will depend primarily upon how well he thinks about the position.

More variations. In the widely used variation on the left, the right leg is thrown out moderately far, but the knee is only slightly bent, if at all. The left leg in this position is not exactly parallel to the spine, but angled slightly toward the right leg. In the variation on the right, the right foot is underneath the left ankle. Note that in other respects this is a classic position.

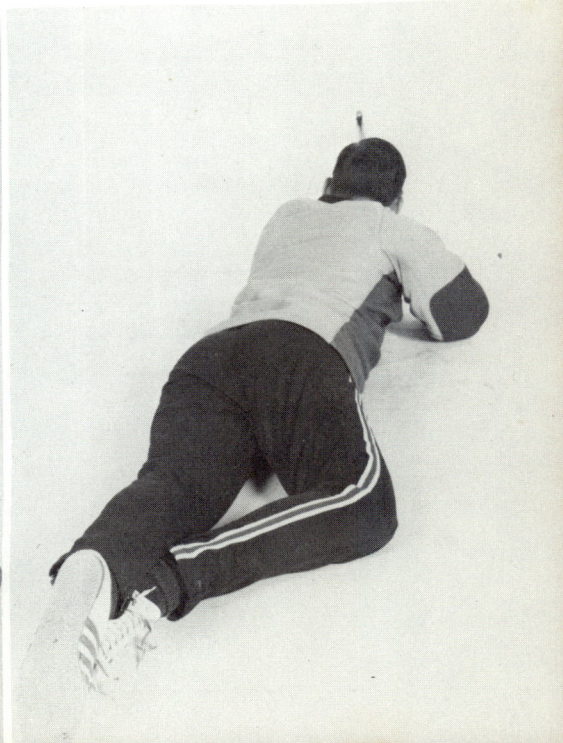

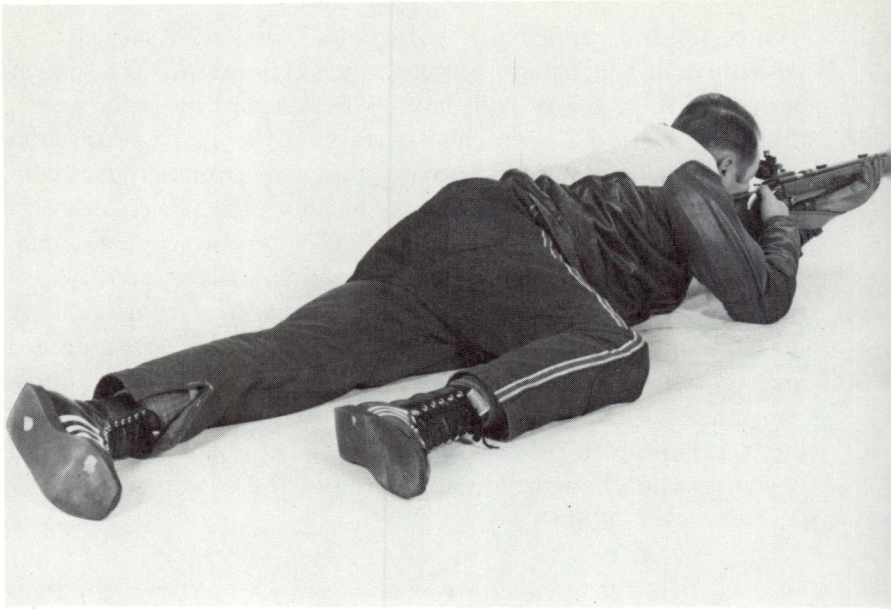

Other views of the position with the right leg brought well forward.

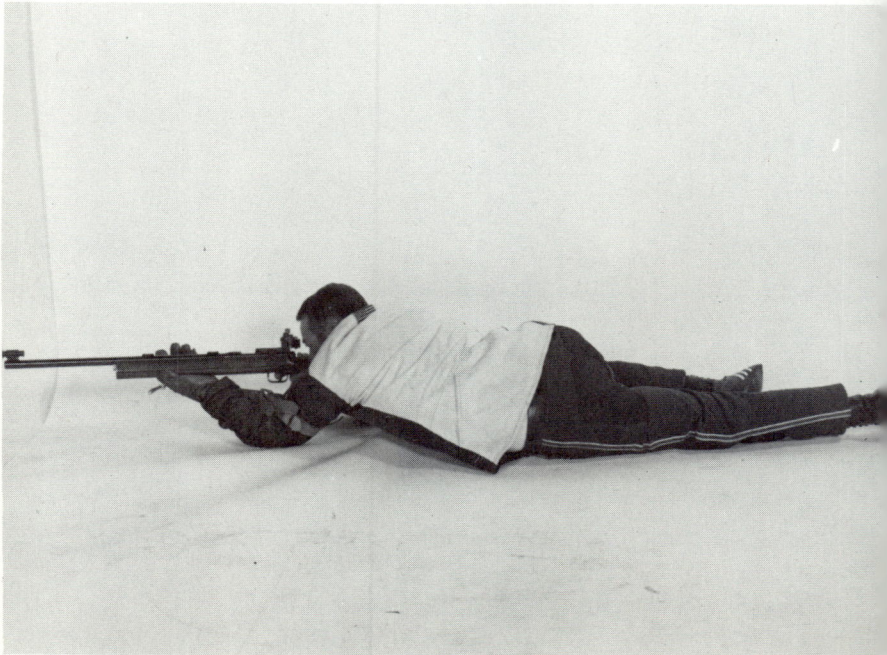

An orthodox position with a minor variation: the left foot rests on the toe rather than on its side.

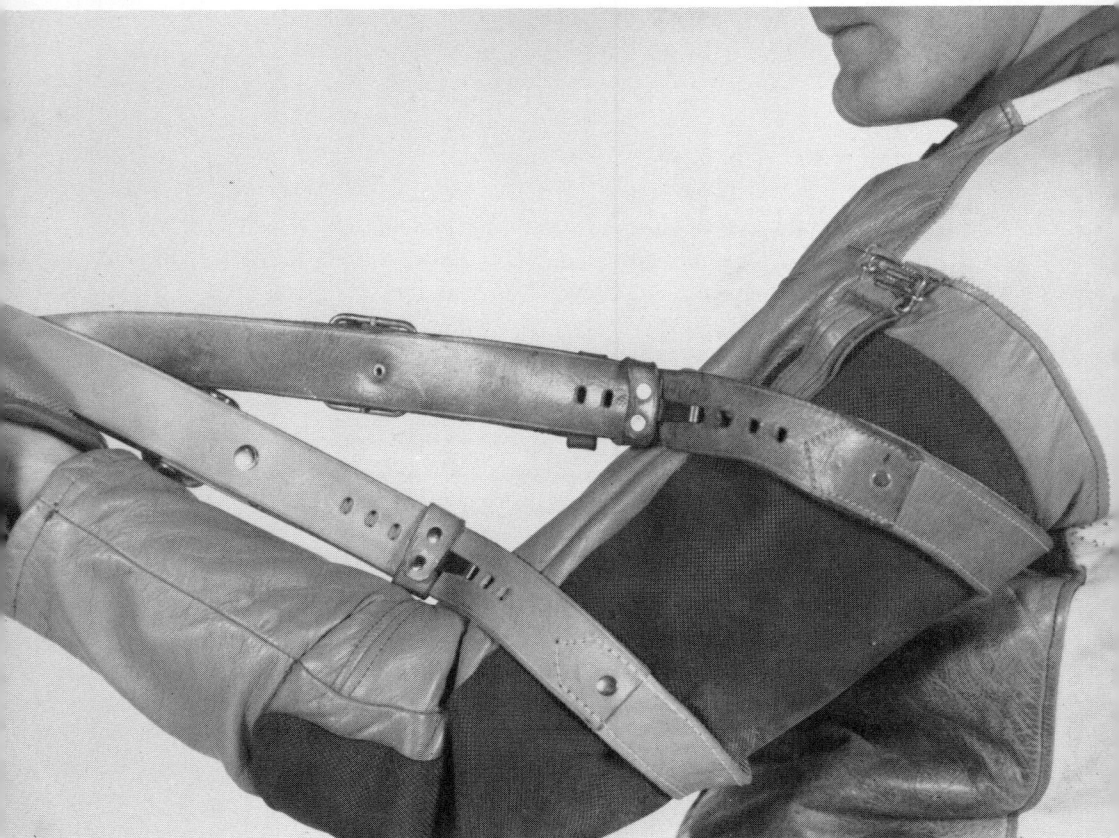

Above: Detail showing the proper sling positions—either high or low on the upper arm. Placing the sling in an intermediate position would cause it to pick up a stronger pulse beat, which would be transmitted to the rifle. The sling should be placed similarly high or low in the kneeling position.

Right. Detail of the prone position photographed from above. The sling is attached low on the arm. Note the properly relaxed left hand and the correct position of the left elbow, which is slightly to the left of the rifle.

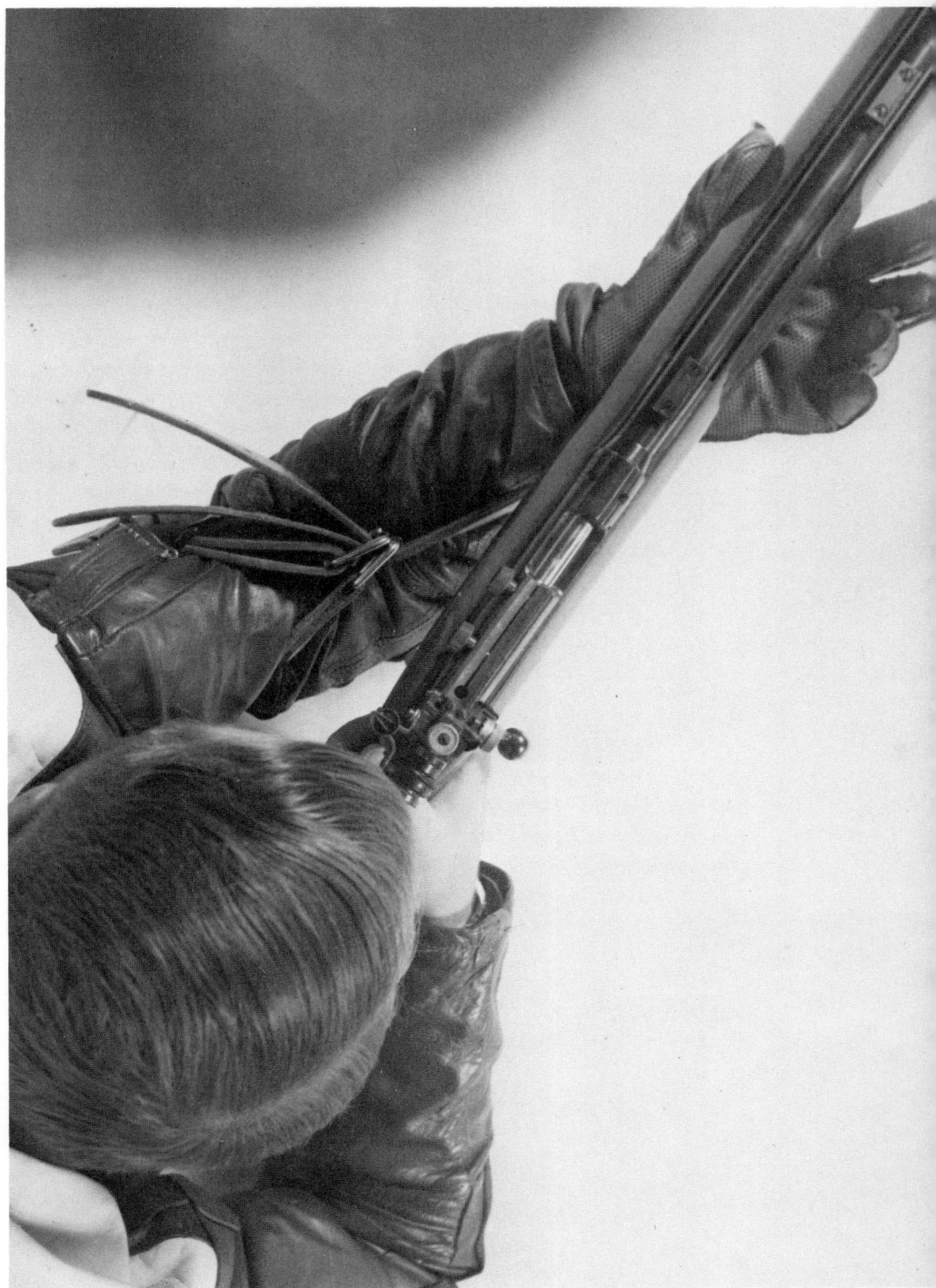

A view of the scope properly placed. The positioning of the hands, arms, and head are quite good. This shooter is using what is probably an average eye relief. Note the use of the butt-hook.

Gary Anderson, who is left-handed, uses an orthodox position. Note, however, that the position is probably higher than average, which allows his forward hand easily to clear the minimum legal distance from the ground allowed in ISU competition.

KNEELING

The evolution of scores in the kneeling position shows clearly how psychological barriers set the limits of physical performance. Before the late 1950's, riflemen in the United States used either of what are now known as the "forward" or the "low" variations, and kneeling scores of about 370 were considered the upper limit of performance. Then in the late 1950's and early 1960's, the so-called "high" variation was used to set a new record in world competition; good shooters everywhere went almost exclusively to the high variation, and kneeling scores improved considerably. By the middle 1960's, kneeling scores had climbed to low 390's in world competition, and the high kneeling position was the only one used by successful competitors. Today, kneeling scores below 395 are almost certainly out of the running, and these new high scores have recently been fired not only from the high variation, but from the old forward and low variations as well! Scores are now higher not so much because positions have improved, but because we have accepted the idea that good scores can be fired from the kneeling position.

No one person can fire equally well from all three of the basic variations, however. The variation which works best for an individual is the one which takes the greatest advantage of his individual body conformation. The reason for this should be quite clear: kneeling is the only position in which proper positioning of the rifle in front of the eye is dependent upon the length of various parts of the arms and legs in relation to the length of the torso and neck. This placement is complicated by the fact that the structure of the entire body, when the arms and legs are positioned to place the rifle in proper relation to the eye, must make full use of bone support, must be balanced, and must be capable of producing a 10-ring hold. Obviously, since individuals vary greatly in the proportionate lengths of their arms, legs, torsos, and necks, and moreover in the distribution of muscle bulk and weight over their skeletons, the same kneeling position will not work equally well for all individuals. Each rifleman must choose the one that is best for his physique. Some experimentation will be required to make an intelligent choice. If a statistical average were established on the practice of successful shooters, it would probably indicate that something like 65 percent of them now use the high variation, 25 percent the forward variation, and 10 percent the low variation. The three variations described here are basic positions. They are good places to begin experimenting, but few individuals will make maximum use of the principles stated in the theory of positions without making individual adaptations based on body conformation. The variations are assumed as follows.

Positioning the sling.

The sling is most easily attached to the rifle if the shooter kneels or squats and places the butt of the rifle on the shooting mat. It is helpful to have masking tape along the fore-end rail and to mark the correct placement of the fore-end stop for the kneeling position (as opposed to prone) once this point has been found. Similarly, the correct placement for the sling buckle in the kneeling position should also be marked. The length of the sling should be such that it comfortably supports the weight of the rifle once the shooter is in position. The exact placement of the left hand, and the length of the sling, will depend upon the length of the individual's arms and legs in relation to his torso and neck. The left hand should be snug against the fore-end stop, and the rifle should, when placed against the shoulder, feel reasonably, comfortably tight, but muscles should nowhere be cramped and circulation of the blood should nowhere be impaired.

The sling should pass flat over the outside of the left wrist, without twisting. On the upper arm, the sling should be buckled tight enough to prevent it from sliding down the arm, but loose enough to allow for free circulation of blood. The sling must be either high or low on the arm; if it passes over the triceps, it will pick up a heavy pulse beat from the back of the arm. The sling should not be too low, or it will lose its support value. It should carry the entire weight of the rifle. It will usually pick up some pulse beat, but the extent of this movement diminishes as the arm becomes accustomed to the sling. A sweatshirt with good cushioning qualities is helpful in reducing this movement even further.

Orienting the position.

With the sling positioned and adjusted, the next procedure is to orient the body to the target and position it over the kneeling roll. How this is done depends upon the variation being used. In all variations, the spotting scope should be adjusted to a height to meet the eye and placed within easy reach before the position is assumed.

The high variation. This variation is assumed by placing the body at an angle of 45 to 60 degrees away from the target. The knee of *the right leg* is placed on the mat at an angle of about 60 degrees to the line of fire, and the right foot or ankle is placed over the kneeling roll. The most widely used type of roll in this variation is a small roll, 3 to 4 inches in diameter, with very loose stuffing that easily loses its shape and compresses almost flat. With the use of such a roll, the toe of the foot is pointed so as to form almost a straight extension of the lower leg bone, and the top of the foot is now almost parallel to the shooting mat. The heel of the foot is placed between the buttocks and contacts the body at just about the base of the spine. The body then settles on the foot and kneeling roll, which bear about 75 percent of the weight of the entire structure. The right knee bears only about 10 percent or less, and the remaining 15 percent or so is borne by the left foot. *The left leg* is directed more toward the target, at an angle of about 30 degrees. The lower left leg is approximately vertical, and the left thigh is roughly on a line with the left forearm. Because the shooter is facing to the right of the target, it appears that he is firing across, rather than straight out of, the position.

The left arm is placed with the elbow joint just past the left knee; the upper arm is placed on the knee, not so far forward that the arm muscle is pressed against the knee, but only far enough so that the bony portion of the arm rests solidly in the hollow of the knee. The sling should support the entire weight of the gun. The rifle should rest on the heel of the left hand in a position that picks up the least possible amount of pulse beat. The fingers do not grasp the rifle, but are straight, to avoid creating a springing action. The left wrist is also straight, for the same reason. Some pulse beat movement in the rifle is probably unavoidable, but it should be no more extreme than that in the prone position. The proper technique is to fire between pulse beats, when the rifle is at a point of maximum stability.

The right arm is held at a comfortable angle from the body. The right elbow may be resting naturally against the side, or held higher, somewhat away from the body. The angle which gives the greatest degree of control in the right shoulder, arm, and hand is the angle to use. The butt of the rifle is placed comfortably against the right shoulder in a manner which gives the greatest amount of contact between the butt-hook or plate and the shoulder itself. This maximum contact, if maintained without change, helps ensure uniform recoil and muzzle jump. The right hand grasps the stock in the manner that is most comfortable to the individual and yields the greatest amount of control of the trigger finger. The thumb may be placed through the thumbhole or along the side of the stock, but the placement should be consistent each time. Neither the thumb nor any part of the right hand is involved in guiding or muscling the rifle into the 10-ring. The trigger finger is placed against the trigger at any point between the extreme tip of the finger and the first joint back from the tip.

The critical feature of the high variation is that *the back and spine* must be almost perfectly straight. The torso and head should be completely upright, with the center of gravity for the body almost directly over the kneeling roll. The weight of the rifle is supported primarily by the bones of the left arm and leg. This variation depends heavily upon establishing the body in a state of equilibrium. If this point of balance can be found, it is a truly excellent variation, and has a natural area of aim so small that it is almost a true point of aim, and is easily confined with the 10-ring. Its major drawback, however, is that finding the critical point of equilibrium is frequently difficult, and sometimes appears to be impossible. It is also the least stable variation under windy conditions.

The forward variation.   This variation is assumed by facing the target almost squarely. The knee of *the right leg* is angled away from the target at about 15 degrees; the right foot is placed on the kneeling roll in the same manner as in the high variation. The heel of the right foot is placed either between the buttocks or under the right buttock. *The left leg* is pointed almost directly at the target. The lower left leg may be vertical or at an angle, depending on the body conformation. Most of the weight of the position appears to be supported by the left leg and right knee, with very little weight on the right foot and kneeling roll. Viewed from behind, the rifleman appears to be shooting directly out of, rather than across, the position. *The left arm* functions in the same way as in the high variation, but the sling will generally be much shorter and the fore-end stop and left hand will be drawn back considerably toward the trigger guard. *The right arm* is used also in the same way, except that the right shoulder will be brought forward and will appear to "wrap around" the butt-hook or plate. *The spine* is inclined forward, but the head is maintained in an upright position to allow the best use of the vestibular apparatus and the eye. This position utilizes bone support, but relies less upon a delicate point of equilibrium because it takes maximum advantage of the cartilages, ligaments, and tendons which link bones together at joints, particularly those in the spine. It is *not* based upon strain or tension between the various parts of the body or between the body and rifle. This position has a natural area of aim that is somewhat larger than the natural area obtainable through equilibrium in the high variation, but it is nevertheless admirably suited to some body conformations and many individuals find that they can easily hold the rifle well within the 10-ring. It is a relatively stable position in the wind.

The high and forward variations are both classics, and are capable of combinations to produce various hybrid modifications which take advantage of certain features of both. Some excellent shooters have kneeling positions that are intermediate between high and forward. Different body conformations make it necessary for them to develop these variations in order to make maximum use of the principles stated in the theory of positions. Again, a position is judged not by what it looks like, but by whether it is legal, reasonably comfortable, and capable of producing a good hold.

The low variation. This variation is familiar to many shooters as the kneeling position they learned in junior programs. It consists of facing slightly to the right of the target and bending *the right leg*, so the buttocks can be placed squarely down on the inside of the right foot. The right foot may rest beneath the left or right buttock, and seems to bear the entire weight of the torso. Unlike the high variation, however, the spine is inclined forward, and this position also makes maximum use of ligaments, tendons, and cartilages to hold together the bone support structure. *The left leg* is pointed more or less directly toward the target, and the lower part of the leg is usually not vertical, but angled out from the body, so the left knee is much lower than in the other variations. *The left arm* functions as in the other variations, but the sling is usually much longer and the left hand farther forward on the stock. *The right arm* functions as in the other positions. The neck is bent comfortably back so the head is upright. For a small minority of shooters, this is an extremely stable position, with a small area of aim and a reliable consistency.

Final orientation of any of the kneeling positions is critical. In all variations of the kneeling positions, minor changes produce major results, particularly in the stability of the hold. Large horizontal changes should be made by rotating the position around the left foot. The configuration of the position should not be disturbed in this process, and the effect should be as if the shooting mat had been rotated without disturbing the shooter. Small horizontal changes can sometimes be effected by changing the angle of the left foot with regard to the line of fire.

Large vertical changes should be made by adjustments to the fore-end stop and butt-hook or plate in the high and forward positions, and by these adjustments as well as by moving the position of the left foot in the low position. Fine vertical adjustments are effected by breath control. Once the position is finally oriented to the target, the spotting scope should be placed to allow the individual to look through the scope with only a small movement of his head. The only change that should occur in body configuration while looking through the scope is the movement of the head.

Refining the position.

Once a kneeling position has been found, the shooter continues to refine it until his hold is as good as it is in the prone position. The process is continual, and is based upon analysis of performance and analysis of position. Ultimately, thorough concentration during shooting is necessary for either of these processes to be possible. Once again, an individual's progress in refining a position will be directly related to how well he thinks about the position.

Here's a woman shooter on the line with her equipment well organized. Note the position of the spotting scope, which allows for viewing the target with only a minimal movement of the head. The equipment box is used to keep ammunition, ammunition box, stopwatch, and other items within easy reach, which allows them to be used without disturbing the position.

Detail photographed from above, showing the placement of the left elbow and hand in the kneeling position. The elbow is almost underneath, but slightly to the left of, the bore of the rifle. Note the properly relaxed left hand.

These shooters illustrate the classic high kneeling position. Note the differences in eye relief, elbow placement, and position of the right hand. One figure has his head thrust forward and down, but it is still upright, as it should be. The other is holding his head in a more natural position and has raised the rifle to his line of sight by lowering the butt-hook. These photographs and the next three, taken in the mid 1960's, show the set triggers which were widely used then, but are less preferred today.

Other views of the classic high position. Note the almost perfectly vertical spine and lower left leg, and the upright head position used by both shooters. Both have most of their body weight balanced above the kneeling roll.

This sequence shows the modifications that have taken place in this Olympic champion's position over a period of years. The first photograph shows him in the mid 1960's in an orthodox high position; the other three show him in what is now more of an intermediate position, somewhere between high and forward, with weight shifted somewhat more onto the left foot. This shooter tends to face away from the target, shooting across his position more than straight out of it.

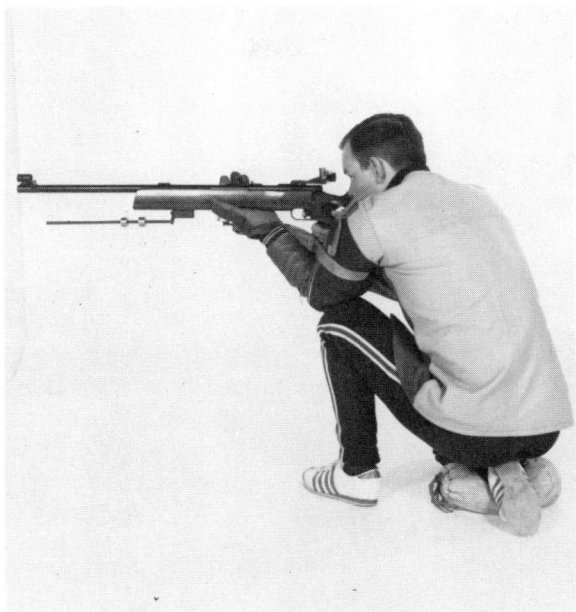

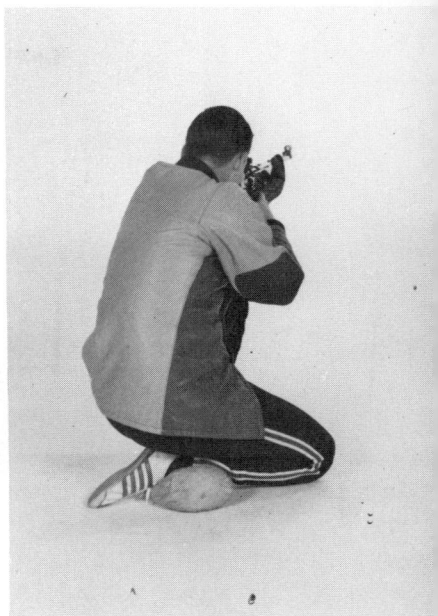

These shots depict a classic example of the forward variation. Although the left hand is well back, body weight is shifted forward onto the left leg, the spine is tilted toward the target, and the shoulders are brought forward to wrap around the rifle. This figure, instead of shooting across his position, is facing more toward the target and appears to be shooting almost straight out of the position.

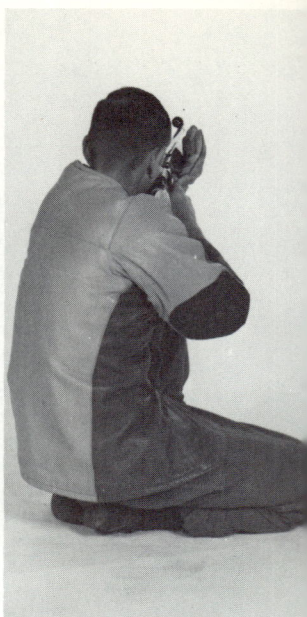

This sequence is of a classic low variation. No kneeling roll is used, in this case, and the rifleman sits on his right foot. The left foot and the left hand are farther forward than would normally be found in the other variations. Note that the left elbow is placed beyond, not on, the left knee. This old standard kneeling position is being adopted once again as it is a good, stable position.

These two photographs also illustrate the low kneeling position. This left-handed shooter, former world champion Gary Anderson, has recently been able to fire better scores in this variation than he could in the high variation he previously used. This indicates that the low position is better suited to his particular body conformation.

STANDING

As mentioned earlier, the standing position is the most important, because the scores in this position usually determine who wins a multiple-position match. Standing is the most difficult position for several obvious reasons. It has the smallest support area, or area of contact between body and ground, and the highest center of gravity; hence it is the most susceptible to loss of equilibrium. One of the major sources of bone support is the spinal column, a flexible series of numerous small vertebrae rather than the longer bones and fewer joints found in the arms or legs; moreover, instead of being arched in a single direction as it is in the kneeling position, the spinal column is bent into a less stable S shape in the standing position. Consequently, the torso can move easily in a number of directions, resulting in the position having a rather large natural area of aim rather than a natural point of aim. These factors combine to require the greatest degree of concentration on body control and performance: the kinesthetic sense must be aware of a much larger number of muscles directly involved in supporting the body, and concentration on hold must similarly be expanded to include holding almost all body muscles at a level of tension which will hold the body in equilibrium; and, because the body has a tendency to drift constantly out of equilibrium, this means that the level of tension in different muscles must constantly be changing to correct for changes in the center of gravity. The mental effort, or willpower, required by the position is greater, as the body must be *made to hold a point of aim in what is only naturally an area of aim.*

The only correct way to fire from the standing position is to hold the rifle still and pull the trigger without disturbing the hold. A dependable score cannot be fired by pulling the trigger as the rifle drifts across the 10-ring, for the changing recoil and muzzle jump incurred by such a technique will cause wide shots even if the shooter can time the trigger pull to coincide with the coming together of the 10-ring and the drifting point of aim. A beginning shooter has begun to establish a good position when he can consistently expect the rifle to settle somewhere within the 8-ring. As the position is refined, the rifle will come to rest consistently inside the 9-ring. Ultimately, the position can yield a 10-ring hold if the position itself is sufficiently refined and if concentration and will are strong enough to force the body-rifle structure to hold still in the correct attitude to the target.

Like the other positions, the standing position makes use of the principles of bone support, mechanical aids, and balance. To achieve maximum utilization of these principles, each individual must design a position that takes into account the features of his own, individual body conformation. This means that any two shooters who correctly design their positions will probably not have configurations that look exactly alike. However, they will undoubtedly share essentially the same basic position, for it is highly unlikely that there will ever be several successful basic variations as there are in the kneeling position.

The old "hip-slung" standing position attempted to make use of bone support, which it did in a limited respect, but it failed to make full use of the possibilities of bone support, because since the center of gravity of the body-rifle structure was displaced toward the target, muscles had necessarily to be quite actively involved in holding the body upright against the pull of the weight of the rifle. For international style shooting this is clearly inferior, as the muscles involved simply cannot sustain the necessary effort through forty shots without developing fatigue tremors. In addition, the hip-slung position probably has a larger natural area of aim than the back-bend position.

The only possiblity now of a new basic position rivaling or replacing the present one would be a new development in position theory. While such a breakthrough is always possible, it is highly improbable, as too many people have thought too long and hard about the standing position to have overlooked many of the possibilities. The position described below is the product of a highly refined theory. The basic position is assumed as follows.

Orienting the position.

The rifleman positions himself to face approximately 90 degrees to the right of the line of fire. *The feet* are placed in a natural, comfortable position, usually slightly less than shoulder width apart. As nearly as possible, weight should be distributed equally on both feet. However, experiments show that absolutely equal weight distribution is almost impossible to achieve, and that successful shooters usually have slightly more weight on one foot than on the other. It seems unimportant which foot bears the slight additional weight, as long as the position feels comfortable and stable. A type of shoe should be used which provides maximum ground contact with, and weight distribution across, the bottoms of the feet. Shoes which create pressure points on the bottom of the heel, or on the balls of the feet, create a more critical and unstable support area, and should be avoided. Many good shooters now prefer low-quarter tennis shoes made with thick innersoles that are contoured to fit the bottoms of the feet. The shoe is correct if it is legal and provides a solid support area and a sense of equilibrium.

The legs are held straight, but without the muscles "locking" the knees. The leg muscles must be somewhat tense to support the body; if the leg muscles are relaxed, even when we are standing without a rifle, we fall to the ground. However, the tension in the leg muscles is only slightly greater than the minimum amount necessary to support the body. This slight additional tension seems to facilitate both kinesthesia and hold, but does not appreciably incur fatigue. *The hips* are held level. It is possible by placing greater weight on one foot to throw the hip forward for use as a support for the left arm. However, this hip-slung position is both unnecessary and undesirable, as we shall see below. The hips should remain level and directly above the feet.

The spine, in the small of the back, is bent back over the hips and twisted to the left so the shoulders are made to face more in the direction of the target. In effect, the upper torso and head are placed behind and to the right of the pelvic bones. This twist and bend, it should be emphasized, begins *above* the hips, which remain level and facing 90 degrees away from the target. Moreover, the bend and twist should not place an unnatural strain on any part of the body. It will at first create soreness in the back muscles, and this soreness can become quite painful and will persist for several days. The only way the back muscles can be conditioned to the position is through training by holding the rifle in position. This should involve two or three hours of training each day. It is during this stage that many shooters lose courage and minimize the bend and twist by developing a hip-slung position.

The hip-slung position is not as painful at first, but in the end it is a much inferior position. Once the muscles have become accustomed to the bend and twist, the position becomes quite comfortable, and the muscles are easily kept in condition for it. The purpose of the bend and twist is to achieve a state of equilibrium by balancing the weight of the body and the weight of the rifle over the support area created by the feet. The bend and twist are correct if the rifle is brought into alignment with the target and this equilibrium is created. Beginners will generally create a state of equilibrium with little durability, but durability can be increased by refining the position. This will require time and constant analytical effort. Body sway in particular can be minimized by refining the position. Muscle movements within the position structure will be minimized primarily by developing improved equilibrium and increased control over the muscles.

The left arm carries the weight of the rifle entirely by means of bone support. The section of the arm between the shoulder and the elbow rests against the rib cage. The elbow may reach the hip bone, in which case the hip bone is used for support; but generally the elbow does not reach this far, and it does not need to, for the bones of the rib cage provide completely adequate support. The upper arm rests against the rib cage at a position that is comfortable, aligns the rifle on the target, and provides complete bone support so that no muscles are involved in lifting the rifle to the target during the hold.

The left forearm, hand, and *palm-rest* constitute one of the most critical structures in the entire position. The bones of the forearm serve to support the rifle and transmit its weight to the elbow, upper arm, and rib cage; no part of the left arm, then, is involved in active muscle support of the vertical alignment of the rifle. However, the left forearm easily pivots right and left over the elbow, and is thus very much involved in the horizontal alignment of the rifle. The muscles of the left arm are actually involved, not in holding the weight of the rifle up against the forces of gravity, but in holding the rifle in a precise alignment with the rest of the body. The effects of this are almost too complex to describe, for every remaining portion of the body becomes involved in adjusting to any such movement in the forearm in order to maintain the entire body-rifle structure in a point of equilibrium. If the forearm moves to the left, the center of gravity is shifted to the left and the whole position must therefore shift right in order to bring the center of gravity into a point of balance above the support area. But this function is also reversible: if the body sways right, the center of gravity which would otherwise move right can be maintained over the center of the support area by a compensating sway to the left by the forearm and rifle. The left forearm and rifle, then, are integrally and crucially involved in maintaining the equilibrium of the entire position. The automatic accommodation of the rifle to body sway is not only an aim reflex, but apparently also a balance reflex that helps to keep the body from moving out of equilibrium.

It is important to keep in mind, however, that the left forearm is not the sole means of effecting horizontal alignment of the rifle: the twist flexion of the spine affords a means of rotating the body left and right over the stable hip bones. Thus a combination of horizontal movements, located first in the lower spine, and second in the left elbow and forearm, are responsible for fine horizontal alignment of the rifle and target. The whole problem of the relationship of the forearm to the rest of the body in achieving rifle alignment and position equilibrium is much more easily understood through the feel of the position than through a verbal description.

Not surprisingly, the positions of the left hand and the palm-rest are quite important to the proper functioning of the left arm. The left wrist should not be bent or twisted in any unusual manner. It should bend naturally and comfortably, and the palm-rest should meet the hand in such a way as to feel solid and well balanced. The sole purpose of the palm-rest is to raise the rifle so the shooter can see through the sights without bending his head or using muscle support in the left arm. The palm-rest may be of any design that is legal, and many different commercially made shapes are available. Most people eventually create a grip of their own design, affixing it to the hardware of a factory-made palm-rest. Shapes range from the "baseball" grip to the "horseshoe" rest. The palm-rest should be adjustable in every direction, and capable of retaining an adjustment indefinitely. Some riflemen are now discarding the traditional palm-rest and resorting instead to building up the fore-end of the stock with a movable piece of solid timber, such as a length of 2 x 4, and supporting the rifle either with the fingertips and thumb, or with a closed fist. This technique may be used with either a straight rifle or a free rifle. This may well become the preferred method in the future.

The head is as erect as possible, with the eyes looking straight out of the sockets. The rifle should be brought into alignment with the head, rather than the head being tilted to align with the rifle. If the rifle is too low, generally the palm-rest and butt-hook should both be lowered, to raise the rifle in relation to the rest of the body. If the rifle cannot be brought into alignment by this method, some other mechanical means should be attempted. Raised or offset sight mounts may be used. Another method is to cant the rifle. Canting is not a desirable technique, since it creates problems with maintaining consistent recoil and complicates sight zero changes, but canting is nevertheless preferable to tilting the head. Most shooters do not have difficulty aligning the rifle with the eye, and only a very few cant the rifle. None of the really top shooters tilt their heads.

The right arm has no real purpose except to get the right hand up to the trigger. The angle at which the right elbow is held from the body is almost totally unimportant. Some shooters keep the elbow high, others low. The position of the right arm should be comfortable and allow for the greatest degree of control of the muscles of the shoulder, arm, and trigger finger. Beyond that, the only requirement is that the placement of the arm should be consistent. Changing the elbow from a high to a low position will probably result in a significant change in the center of gravity of the position, and will therefore cause a number of minor changes throughout the whole position. Certainly the position of the right arm should not be changed in the middle of a string of shots during a match. Perhaps the most important thing about the right arm is that it should be positioned in such a way that when the trigger finger moves, nothing else does.

The right hand functions merely to keep the trigger finger in position. The thumb may be through the thumbhole or alongside the stock. The fingers may grip the stock loosely or tightly. Again, the major considerations are consistency, and using the technique which allows the individual the greatest degree of control. The butt-hook should fit snugly and comfortably underneath the right arm and provide support for the rifle, keeping the butt of the stock both from tilting upward from the weight of the barrel pivoting down over the palm-rest, and from moving forward away from the shoulder. Another important function of the butt-hook is to provide a means of positioning the stock consistently against the shoulder each time the rifle is placed in position. The butt-hook should be adjustable both vertically and horizontally so it can be made to perform these functions. Most individuals find that the factory models are satisfactory, but a few individuals eventually design a special hook to their specific needs. All butt-hooks, of course, must meet shooting organization specifications to be legal.

Final orientation is achieved as follows. Major horizontal adjustments to the position are made by moving both feet in such a way as to keep them in the same relation to each other. The effect should be as if the position had been adjusted by rotating the shooting platform. Small horizontal changes are made by changing the amount of back twist, or by moving the left hand and forearm. It must be remembered that any change to any part of the position will probably result in a change of center of gravity and necessitate a change in the overall position attitude and muscle function to achieve a new point of equilibrium. Major vertical adjustments are made by raising or lowering the palm-rest grip on the shaft which attaches it to the fore-end rail. Changing the amount of back bend is *not* a satisfactory means of making vertical adjustments; the amount of back bend should always remain consistent. It frequently happens that shooters moving from one range to another encounter target frames of different heights. Unless these differences are recognized and compensated for by vertical adjustment to the palm-rest, great difficulties can be experienced in controlling the position, with the reason remaining obscure to the shooter. The reason is that the body is being moved out of its usual position and forced to assume an unnatural or unfamiliar back bend by the different target height. Small vertical adjustments are achieved by breath control. The easiest method is to take a deep breath and exhale, letting the rifle come down on the target. The flow of air from the lungs is cut off as the rifle enters the 10-ring. The left arm is never involved in making vertical adjustments.

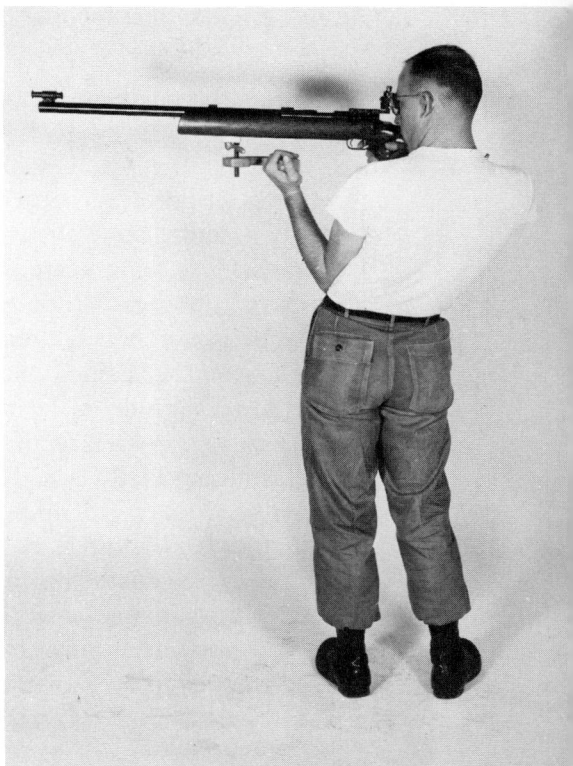

Here's a sequence of a shooter with an orthodox position. The left hip seems to be thrown slightly too far forward, but with this shooter the results are actually a fairly equal distribution of weight on both feet. Note the degree of back bend and twist.

Refining the position.

Refining the standing position is more of a challenge than refining either of the other two. It is a more complex structure, involving more bone segments stacked upon bone segments, and a much more complicated system of muscle involvement in the support function. Consequently more motor learning and an expanded awareness are required to gain control of the position, and mastery is gained more slowly. In refining the position, great care should be devoted to following all of the principles outlined in the theory of positions. Bone support, mechanical aids, and especially a highly refined equilibrium are extremely important. Each individual should concentrate on the correct principles and build a position that is legal, reasonably comfortable, and capable of producing a good hold and shot release. The fact that his position resembles or does not resemble anyone else's is totally irrelevant. His position should be built from the inside out, as it were, and if it is done so correctly, it will be a position that wins.

A classic position.

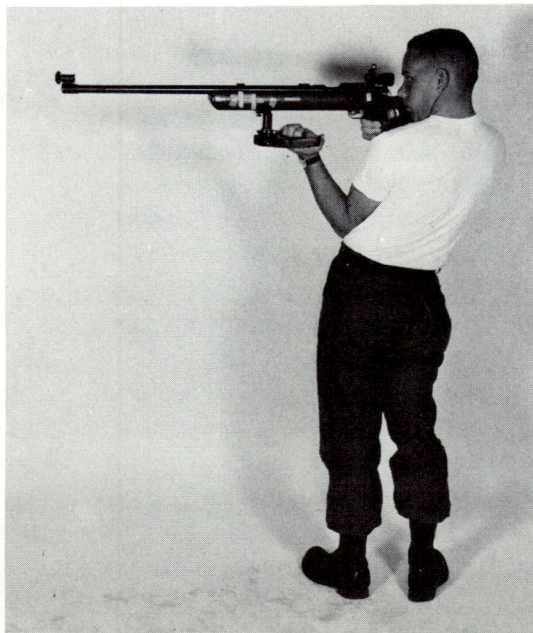

Here's an individual with a light body frame and weight. To achieve a proper balance with his body structure, he utilizes a pronounced bend and twist and places his feet relatively far apart.

Here's a very tall shooter who, though slender, has a heavier body weight. His bend and twist are not as severe. Note the high position of the right elbow, which is purely a matter of personal preference.

*An orthodox position: an individual
with a medium body build.*

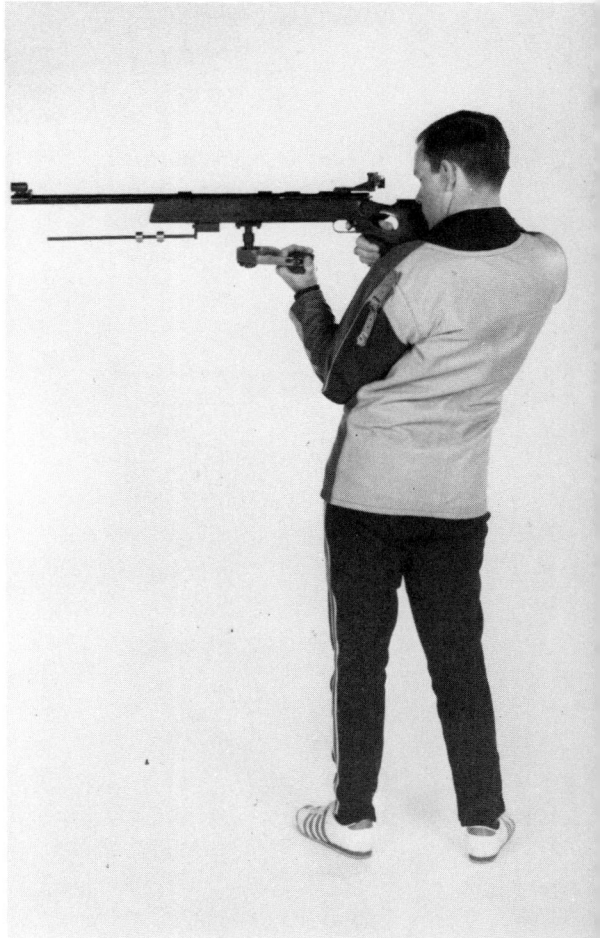

Another model position, again a person with a medium body build.

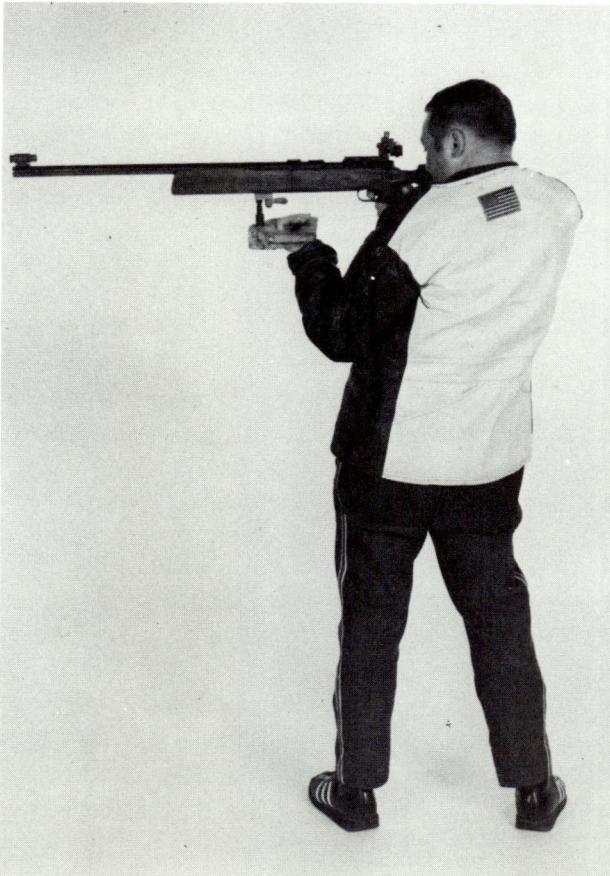

This position yields outstanding scores for this person with a stocky build. People with this general build usually have less back bend than do individuals with lighter body frames.

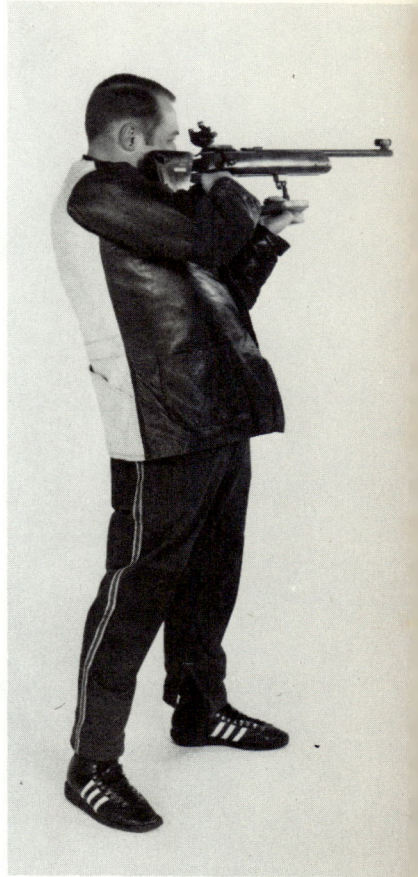

This sequence shows four different, widely used ways of supporting the straight rifle which has no palm-rest attachment. The rifle may be grasped between the thumb and fingers, may be balanced on the tops of the thumb and fingers, may be balanced on the fist, or may be rested between the first and second fingers.

Here's a shooter on a typical range for a 300-meter event. Note the low butthook, which allows for a very fine, upright head position. One can almost sense the balance in this shooter's position. He is wearing shooting glasses, which should always be worn when shooting centerfire cartridges.

Here's a smallbore shooter on the line with his equipment properly set up. The scope can be used without moving the feet.

These two photographs show left-handed Gary Anderson using a standard rifle. Note that there is no indication of a "hip-slung" position: the legs are straight and the hips level; the bend and twist begins in the small of the back, above the hips. In the close-up, note the built-up fore-end instead of a palm rest. This rifle qualifies for both standard and free rifle ISU smallbore events. The rifle is rested between the second and third fingers of the forward hand, one of several possible means. The placement of the trigger hand and the eye relief are orthodox, one could even say classical.

— V —

COACHING

This section is designed not for shooters, but for those who act in a coaching capacity or those who select or appoint coaches. Most shooters are from time to time involved in helping others of less experience, but this activity is coaching in only the narrowest sense of the word. In a much broader sense, coaching involves working with a team to build its strength, to keep it running smoothly, and to create and nurture its morale, its confidence, and its desire to win. On another but related level, coaching involves working with individuals to help them develop in such a way as to meet and overcome the personal challenges encountered in competition. Only when an individual is thus made ready to compete will he be capable of using fully the technical assistance a coach may give him with positions and techniques. This section will deal first with the broader aspects of team coaching, and will then consider the problems encountered in coaching an individual.

Coaching a Team

Building a team of shooters, whether in a military, varsity, or civilian club situation, always involves the processes of recruiting, selecting, training, and, where necessary, applying discipline to the individuals who comprise the team. The coach, in addition to being responsible for carrying out these functions, also plays a supporting role for the team. While all of these functions involve some personal relationships between the coach and the individuals he works with, the psychological rapport that characterizes the coach's relationship to the individual is not of central concern here. That relationship will be treated in the following chapter. Our primary concern here will be with the basic principles involved in the coach's relationship to the team as a whole.

RECRUITING

As a team can only be as good as the individuals who make it up, successful recruiting is extremely important. Every coach wishes to bring into his team the best shooters he can find. There are four basic techniques for recruiting available to most teams: personal contacts through all members of the team, publicity through means other than personal contacts, the use of tangible incentives to induce people to join the team, and the use of intangible incentives for the same purpose. Military teams may resort to a fifth method, which is to have qualified individuals passed automatically up to the team from some administrative point designed to spot talented shooters, such as a marksmanship program in an enlisted men's or officers' basic training school.

Personal contact, being direct, is one of the most persuasive means of bringing in new shooters, but is also one of the most risky when it used among young shooters. It may result in a young person recruiting someone simply on the basis of friendship, and then himself losing enthusiasm if the friend should be turned down for lack of talent. It also has the inherent danger of close friendships causing social cliques to develop among members of the team, creating undesirable feelings of enmity and divisiveness in the team as a whole. However, personal contact is certainly a useful method of recruiting, especially among more mature or advanced shooters, and every coach will probably want to have each member of his team on the lookout for new recruits.

A less direct means of recruiting new personnel is through the use of publicity that will draw attention to the team and make it known to potential members. Some simple devices for reaching the right people are recruiting posters, announcements to groups, contacts achieved by voluntarily conducting firearm safety classes, and publicity in newspapers, radio, and television, either in connection with shooting events, or with human interest stories on members of the team. For this reason it is helpful to any coach to get to know sports editors and reporters who work for both print and broadcast media, and to try to get them interested in the team and its activities. Inviting a reporter out for a day's shooting, and maybe even buying him a beer afterward, is not only ethical, but a legitimate way of helping reporters gather material. Such a gesture will not necessarily result in a story in the next day's paper, but it does give a reporter an additional source of potential material, and the coach a potential source of publicity. In short, both benefit.

A very effective recruiting method on high school and college campuses, and on some military posts, is to offer some tangible inducement to get indiviudals to try out for a team. On campuses this frequently involves granting academic credit for riflery through the physical education department. This is especially effective on some college campuses, where physical education classes are inconvenient or undesirable to students for various reasons, often quite legitimate. Both schools and military teams may offer inducements of expense-free or reduced-expense travel, free use of equipment and ammunition, and the possibility of winning trophies, medals, letters, or other distinguishing insignia. These latter, of course, may be offered by private civilian clubs as well. But perhaps the most effective recruiting process of all comes from offering the intangible reward of membership in an elite organization. All people take pride in being a member of a highly successful team, and such a team will seldom be without people wanting to try out for a position. It has the further advantage of motivating the present members to work hard to maintain, or raise, their own positions.

SELECTING

When the number of recruits exceeds the number of individuals a team can absorb, the coach must begin a process of selection to keep only the best prospects on the team. One way in which this works in practice can be demonstrated by a hypothetical example. Let's say that a team has ten designated members and facilities for five "try-outs," or prospective members, at any one time. Of the ten regular members, the four with the highest performance averages are usually designated as the first-string team, and the remaining members are constantly given the opportunity to "bump" a member from the first string by achieving a higher overall performance average for, say, a sixty-day period.

This has the effect of motivating the first-string shooters by keeping pressure on them from below, as well as motivating the other members to strive for a position on the first-string team. But the pressure should also be kept on the entire ten team members from below by the possibility of any one of them being bumped by a new recruit who achieves a higher performance average. It should be made clear to all shooters that this may happen any time a new recruit achieves, for a period such as thirty days, a performance average higher than one held by a team member. When the situation is structured in this way, the process of selection is more or less automatic.

However, in building a new team, or in filling vacancies with a long-range goal in mind, a coach will often choose to base selection on potential, rather than on accomplished, achievement. That is, he is taking on people who have little or no shooting experience and no performance average that is presently useful, but who nevertheless have the potential of becoming quite good shooters. This is essentially a screening process whereby individuals with the greatest potential are chosen from a field of new recruits. Among an average group of novices, quite probably the most important characteristic to look for is motivation and competitive spirit. When considering an individual, the coach may ask himself, "How much does this person want to become a winning shooter? How much effort is he willing to make in order to do so?" The novice shooter himself may not know the answer to these questions; nevertheless, the coach should himself make a considerable effort to evaluate the person's motivations. If the individual appears to have a high degree of motivation, he should be given serious consideration as a potential team member.

Other qualities are next considered. Two of the more important ones are physical ability and intellectual characteristics. It is obvious to anyone that different individuals possess varying degrees of what is usually called "athletic ability"—primarily overall health, muscular coordination, strength, and stamina. It is possible, and sometimes happens, that a person of lesser athletic ability can outshoot a person of superior athletic ability. But the probabilities lie in the opposite direction, assuming the two individuals are equally motivated. Generally speaking, the person with superior coordination and kinesthetic awareness will be able to progress more rapidly than the person with less ability in these areas.

However, even the person with superior physical ability must also possess certain definite intellectual characteristics. The more native intelligence he has, the better. Successful shooting, as we have emphasized throughout this book, is crucially dependent upon the individual's ability to think clearly and logically, and to analyze his own performance with complete accuracy and objectivity. The person who characteristically takes personal credit for any success he is even indirectly associated with, but rationalizes or excuses any failures he is directly responsible for, lacks the mental toughness to become even a moderately good shooter, much less a champion. A successful shooter will always have the mental characteristic of seeing himself, his successes and his failures, clearly and unemotionally. However, it should be emphasized once again that no amount of physical and mental potential is of real value unless the individual is also strongly motivated to become a successful shooter. The person with average ability and strong motivation is usually a much better bet than the natural athlete who has no real desire for success, or rather, no ability to sustain a training effort over the long haul necessary for success at a high level.

Many times, however, a team can benefit from having one member who is not satisfactorily motivated to win, but who is nevertheless of a very useful, easily recognizable personality type. This person is cheerful and well liked, and is usually extremely conscientious and makes every effort to do everything asked of him by the coach. If he is also a good natural athlete, he will usually unconsciously act as a bellwether for the other team members, leading them into good habits by his own eager and enthusiastic acceptance of training requirements and hard work. This type of individual seems to be highly motivated to do the right thing, but to lack some aggressiveness that is essential to defeating tough competition. His scores in training are usually quite good—often much better than his scores in competition—and he thus serves to motivate others in training by setting a high training standard of performance and enthusiasm. Such an individual can be a valuable asset to a team.

A coach will sometimes feel that an additional consideration in selecting individuals is their compatibility with other members and with himself. About his own compatibility with individual members we will have more to say later. About the compatibility of a new recruit with other members, several things need to be considered. If he is compatible, of course, there is no problem. If he is not compatible, and not a good shooter, he will probably only create unrest and dissension on the team. If he is not compatible, but a very good shooter, then he may have the effect of uniting the other members in an effort to outscore him in training and competition, and thus raise the level of performance, if not the number of smiles, throughout the entire team. This may not be the case, however, depending upon the group composition and the group dynamics. Unless he is too valuable to be dispensed with, an individual who creates dissension among others and destroys morale should be dismissed from the team. It is best to do this privately, as quietly and unobtrusively as possible.

TRAINING

Once team members are selected, they become the object of the coach's training efforts. These efforts embrace several phases, including supervision of the training program, instructing, motivating, stimulating, and disciplining the team. All of these processes are carried out on both a group and individual basis. Here we will be primarily concerned with the group aspect of these efforts.

Planning and supervising training.

The coach is responsible both for drawing up a team training schedule and for supervising training activities. Planning a training schedule involves, first, setting up a schedule of matches to be entered. Unless he is working with two or more squads who are independent of each other, he should not schedule more than two matches in any one month. A majority of the matches should be within a relatively short travelling distance, as extended travel tends to lower the level of a team's performance. Selecting matches to enter is greatly simplified if the team joins a regional conference or league; matches are then automatically scheduled at convenient times and places by the conference headquarters. The coach should also designate one match near the end of the season as the objective of the season's effort. This becomes the team's Big Apple. This will usually be, but does not have to be, the conference championship. For beginning teams, it might be simply a match against a strong rival at about their own level of achievement. For advanced teams, the goal of the season may be a national or even international championship which takes place after the conference season has ended. All other matches are then regarded only as training matches, and this fact is emphasized throughout the season to prevent performance slips after each match.

Second, the coach decides how many hours per week of training he will require. The amount must be realistic, but the training load should be as heavy as the shooters can reasonably bear without becoming overtrained. Next, the schedule is put into operation by scheduling precise hours and days for each individual to train. Military coaches can simply issue orders directing the members to be on the range during certain hours. Civilian coaches must deal with the problems of team members having to attend classes or having to be on their jobs during different hours of the day. A good method here is to pass around a one-week calendar with the hours of the day (and, perhaps, the evening) written on it, and have each individual sign up to train during specific hours on certain days; this then becomes a continuing, weekly schedule. The coach then has to see that the range and equipment are available to the shooters when they come to train.

The coach's next important function is to supervise the training of the team. It will be greatly to his advantage if all of his directions to the team are phrased as simply and clearly as possible so that everyone understands perfectly what he wants when he puts a notice on the bulletin board or issues a spoken order. This way there can be no malfeasance excused by the shooter's saying, "But I didn't understand." Compliance should be demanded of each individual. If a directive is issued and individuals allowed to ignore it, then it will only be a short time until everything the coach says will be ignored, and he will lose his effectiveness. In issuing directives and supervising compliance with them, the coach should at all times be completely fair and impartial, and treat everyone alike. Unless there are valid reasons to the contrary, if he says that all members are to be on the range by eight o'clock, then any member who is not there by eight o'clock should be subjected to disciplinary action. If he directs that all shooters train so many hours a week, anyone who fails to do so should be disciplined. If he directs that all shooters participate in supplementary conditioning exercises, anyone who does not should be disciplined. All of this will work satisfactorily *if* his demands and directives are practicable and reasonable. If he shows favoritism to certain members of the team by allowing some members to ignore requirements that are demanded of others, he will create resentment among the other members and lose his effectiveness. To succeed fully with a team, he should always be clear, firm, and impartial.

He should display these same traits while working with individual shooters. Later we will discuss in detail the coaching of an individual, but for now we will consider this function as a part of a coach's supervision of the team. He will work with each individual separately, usually during each training session. He should, however, devote a roughly equal amount of time to each member of the team. He should not spend all of his time with the strong shooters and ignore the weak ones; nor should he spend most of his time with the weak or new members. Doing so could appear to be favoritism, even if it is not. He should spend some time with each person, even the member who he knows is going to quit or be dropped. The importance of this impartiality does not seem apparent at first, but experience shows that failure to observe it will almost certainly result in a dispirited team with low morale.

In short, among the members of the team, everyone is treated by the coach as equal to everyone else. This does not mean that he says the same things or deals in the same way with everyone—certainly he does not—but it means that he devotes the same amount of time, and displays the same impartiality, to everyone. At times this is not easy, because faced with a group of people, any human being is bound to like certain of them better than others. Yet it is possible to conceal these feelings from the entire group, and that is what the more successful coaches do.

Instructing.

One of a coach's basic duties is to instruct his shooters in the technical aspects of shooting. Instructing is a narrowly defined process, and quite distinct from *teaching*, a term which we reserve for another coaching function which will be discussed later. Instructing involves imparting specific, technical information about the fundamentals of shooting and training. The fundamentals have been discussed throughout this book, but perhaps the most important information for the coach to emphasize relates to positions, use of the eyes, trigger pull, training habits, and diet (see the bibliography at the end of this volume for suggested sources of information about diets and nutrition).

A good procedure is to use some time during each training session to talk to the group about some fundamental. This may even be presented in something approaching a classroom format. No matter how experienced or intelligent the members are, if these things are not constantly emphasized, fundamentals begin to get overlooked and concentration begins to weaken. The coach will find it very effective to put constantly before them something basic and specific. These discussions should progress, from day to day, in an orderly way through a complete list of fundamentals, but should also bring up any topics that need discussion at a particular time. There are so many fundamentals that a coach will rarely feel that he is repeating himself too frequently in matters of positions and physical training. However, in the area of mental training the coach can and should repeat himself frequently. He should never let up on the few primary fundamentals of psychology. Shooting is a game of very small details—and the more attention paid to details, the more success can be expected.

The coach should constantly keep talking to his shooters about the important details of concentration, and about how to keep concentration at a peak of effectiveness. He should see that a mental routine is established in training, and that this routine is adhered to in matches. He should be sure that his players are aware of the value of mental practice as a training technique. A good part of coaching, he will discover, is not so much helping a shooter make a correction in his position or techniques when a problem develops, *but simply in getting him to concentrate properly*, in which case the "problem" will disappear.

Motivating.

In a majority of instances, a team will possess only one or two individuals who are sufficiently motivated to need no training supervision. This highly motivated type will go after a first-place medal or championship whether or not he is associated with a team or club. The remainder of the team members will usually benefit if the coach can use their own personal identification with the team, and the group dynamics of the team, as tools to increase their level of motivation. There are no hard and set rules about how this can be accomplished, and perhaps a few tried and proven methods will suggest numerous possibilities to a resourceful reader.

In all efforts toward motivating the team, one cardinal rule must be applied: a coach cannot force a team to win a championship; he can only assist the individuals who want to win. Thus it is of primary importance that the coach create a situation in which the desire to win is fostered, encouraged, and rewarded. This desire to win *is* the team's motivation, and it cannot be imposed upon a team by direct authority; rather, it must be viewed as already existing within the individuals, though perhaps latent or asleep. The coach's job is to awaken that desire to activity without the shooters being aware that he is doing so. In other words, he must *appear* to be doing something else when he is really working to increase the motivation of the group or of individuals within the group. This, as will be seen, is not deception; it is merely the most successful technique of leadership, which *inspires* a group to work for a certain goal rather than *forces* them to work for it. It is a technique of leading rather than driving. In all cases, it must be emphasized, the coach is working with the *psychology* of the group and its component individuals.

It is an old cliché that nothing succeeds like success, and the saying has a basis in psychological truth: once we have gained a certain advantage, we realize that for us gains are possible, on the one hand, and, on the other, we don't want to give up the advantage we have already gained. Therefore we are willing to work to keep what we have; and we see clearly that with additional work we can gain more than we already have. We gain confidence and, expressed in its crudest form, a certain amount of greed. And the greed for winning is exactly what a coach wants to inspire in his shooters.

The atmosphere which fosters this kind of greed should be nurtured and heightened. It has its beginnings seemingly far away from any match or medal or championship. It begins when the coach establishes high standards for the team that have an important long-term effect upon their psychology. He begins by telling the group that he wants high scores—say scores of at least 1170 from each individual if it is an advanced team—and that they are capable of shooting these scores. He does not state this as a command, but as a quiet announcement as if "This is what we should be doing." In many instances, especially with younger shooters, this announcement will be greeted with gasps and scoffs and a certain amount of derision. They may be shooting 1130's, and believe that 1170's are totally out of their reach. But their belief that they *cannot* shoot high scores is certainly a major factor in holding back their performance. The coach attempts to overcome this mental arthritis and get the team to thinking of 1170's as within the range of their own capabilities. He must recognize that he cannot do this overnight. It will take time—weeks, months, perhaps even a year or more—but by constantly talking 1170, by gently but constantly holding the goal of 1170 in front of them, a subtle alteration takes place in their thinking, and gradually they come to believe that 1170's are possible for *them* if they work hard enough. Once this occurs, they start working toward that goal and making gains toward it. Then the psychology of success takes over—they begin to see that gains are possible, and they become greedy for success. This change, it must be emphasized, is a slow-working psychological process that must be given time, and the coach must exercise patience and work largely through intuitive psychology to bring the change to completion.

To help maintain the atmosphere of increasing success and high standards, a weeding-out process must be kept constantly in effect to keep the losers and unmotivated individuals out of the team. As far as possible, a coach should keep only top talent. It is ultimately damaging to keep an individual on the team merely because he is likable or a "nice guy"; unless he makes a positive contribution to the motivation of the team, he should be dropped if he has no real shooting potential. The weeding-out process should be thoughtful and objective. It is not a ruthless and indiscriminate process, but rather a very finely discriminating one based upon careful evaluation of a shooter's potential contributions in all areas. People who make no real contribution are dead weight and ultimately drag down the motivational level of a team. On the other hand, an elite group without dead weight inspires pride among its membership, which motivates them to work hard.

One of the frequently used motivational devices in many sports is the locker-room-style "pep talk." However, this technique works only in rare circumstances among the better shooters, probably because shooters really do not function as a group in the same way as other sports teams. They and their work are highly individualistic, and not susceptible to direct group treatment of this type, which is frequently designed to get a group angry and thereby increase its aggressiveness. But a shooter who is angry or in any way emotional simply cannot function at peak efficiency. A much more effective technique of dealing with a shooting team, it has been discovered, is to work toward motivating the group by dropping suggestions and comments to individuals during the time spent with each one during the training sessions. For example, it is quite useful to say to one shooter, "So-and-so has picked up ten points in his standing scores this month. You can do the same thing by the end of next month if you work at it." This comment is delivered not as a command, but simply as an observation—a statement of the coach's belief and confidence in his shooters. This is merely an example, but techniques similar to this have worked successfully over and over again. Implicit in the example is also another technique—that of keeping the whole team striving to equal the highest gains by any one person on the team. If one person gains considerably in the prone position, suggest to everyone else—privately—that they can make similar gains. If another shooter makes a good gain in the standing position, suggest that everyone can of course do the same thing. It is particularly important to make maximum use of achievements made within the team, as these achievements realized at home seem to other members to have an immediacy and attainability that achievements made by others, who are remote and personally unknown, do not have. Shooters sometimes have difficulty relating to the achievements of a world champion they have never met; but they can easily relate to and identify with the achievements of a teammate.

In the early and intermediate stages of a training cycle, a coach should keep his emphasis on performance, not on winning matches. He keeps reminding his team constantly, when they enter matches, that these are training matches only. The purpose is to gain match experience. The goal is a good performance from each individual. Winning is an issue that is more or less set aside. This way the level of performance is allowed to move steadily upward as the training program progresses, without experiencing large drops after every insignificant match.

Toward the end of the training cycle, however, the coach may begin to talk to the team about winning in the match chosen as their match of the year. He should realistically assess what he believes to be the best that they can do, and then say that he expects them to do just that—place second or third, say, or win, by turning in a specified performance. If the coach is lucky enough to have a team with considerable experience at winning, he can keep the focus on setting new records. He conveys to them, without saying it, that he *knows* they will win the match—what he *expects* them to do, however, is turn in their best performance and set a new record. He conveys to them the sense that they *can* do it if they only *will* do it. Without taking the focus off of performance, he nevertheless allows them to savor the potential rewards of winning big. If the team is ready for this kind of motivation, it can work very well. It is futile, however, to attempt this process with a young and inexperienced team, as it will only result in frustration and demoralization.

Still another broad technique for supplying motivation is to rely upon group dynamics as a means of building team spirit. This technique will work best when a team has settled into a more or less stable membership, and, hopefully, has enough talent to make it a winning team at least part of the time. The coach then tries to give the individuals a strong sense of group identity by affording them opportunities to be together, to know each other, and to function as a group. A good way of doing this is to have dinners limited to the team members following each match, particularly when traveling. If this dinner can also be something of a victory celebration, so much the better. These social occasions offer the opportunity to relax and escape from the pressures of the match, and to participate in the group experience of reliving the match and sharing the dinner. Besides serving to build group identity, these occasions can also be fun and rewarding. Some of the more memorable social occasions in the authors' experiences have been dinners such as these.

A similar effect can be achieved by the very useful device of having the team sit down, during the next training after each match, and as a group analyze their performances. A great deal of useful analysis comes out of these discussions, heightened awareness is created in individuals regarding their own experience of the match, and all of this formulates information and ideas that can be incorporated into future training efforts. These discussions, too, help to create a sense of group identity. And the strong team spirit that can evolve out of such dynamics helps to give enthusiasm and confidence to the individuals of the group, and to motivate them to sacrifice a bit more for the sake of the team than they would for themselves alone. The team members will "talk it up" among themselves, and tell a member who is in trouble, "Come on, Charlie, we know you can do it." Often, this kind of bolstering by teammates makes the difference between Charlie doing it and not doing it.

Finally, to increase rather than diminish motivation and team spirit, the coach should always allow all the honors and applause to go to the team, not to himself. Even if he made the team what it is and knows it, he should always quietly disappear during awards ceremonies, picture taking, interviews, and any other occasions which grant rewards to the team. If he takes personal credit for their victories, they are going to be resentful, and he is actually working against his own best interests as a successful coach.

There are certainly many other techniques for increasing a team's motivation. These are basic techniques and can be used by almost anyone. Most coaches eventually develop their own special methods that work successfully for them, but would be unsatisfactory for anyone else. No matter what particular techniques are used, however, we would emphasize the importance of this cardinal principle, which has been verified time after time by educational psychologists: students—as members of a class or as members of a team—tend to perform as the teacher/ coach *expects* them to perform. The teacher or coach does not have to announce his expectations verbally—his actions, his attitude, the tones of his voice, will convey them. If he expects his students to do poorly, they usually will. If he expects them to do well—if he *believes* in them—they will do well.

Stimulating.

A coach may frequently have in his charge two or three people who are highly motivated and who work hard. He may be able to create the right atmosphere and team spirit to instill motivation in the rest of his team. But all of these individuals, more than likely, will at various times need to be stimulated into *doing* something about realizing their ambitions. All sorts of motivational energy can be siphoned off into planning and talking and daydreaming about big successes that never materialize because the actual training effort necessary to achieve them is never made. A coach will have to keep this energy loss to a minimum by constantly keeping his shooters applying their energy in the form of training activity. Keeping them physically engaged in training is only part of this job. The more important part of it lies in stimulating the thinking of the individual shooters. A shooter's progress is always directly proportionate to how well he thinks, and the coach's most important role, perhaps, is to stimulate the shooter's thinking, his analysis of performance and position. Only then will the shooter make progress. A very successful way to stimulate progress, it has been found, is to allow the shooter to believe that he came up with all of his own solutions to his problems, even though the coach actually led him to the solution.

There is no set way for *how* a coach stimulates his team to work. Essentially he just keeps at them, nudging, pushing, setting requirements, doing whatever he can to keep every individual training as hard as he should. He wants to do this, of course, without rubbing any of the shooters the wrong way. As all of us have at least some experience at eliciting cooperation from other people, almost any coach can draw on his past experience and figure out ways to keep the members of his own team actively working to improve.

Disciplining.

For any team to be run in an orderly fashion, there must be a system for meting out discipline. The coach should *not* be the person to dispense discipline. He may be the one who decides what discipline is to be applied to whom, but someone else should hand it out. Every team should have one person who takes this thankless job of being a hard-nosed disciplinarian. In the military this might be the unit commander. In the military organization the machinery of discipline already exists; the coach merely has to obtain cooperation from the proper quarters and then make use of that machinery. The situation is less clearly defined in civilian teams, and any civilian coach might do well to have an experienced, capable adult associated with the team in the capacity of "manager" or "director" or "club president" or some other title, whose function actually is to act as team disciplinarian. Freed of the disciplinary role, the coach can avoid too strong friction with his shooters and maintain his position as someone who can listen sympathetically to the shooters' gripes and complaints.

Supporting.

A coach plays a supporting role for his team in a number of ways. He should be thought of by his team members as their advocate in any area where they might need one; but they should not have to ask him to act as advocate—he should usually speak up on their behalf without being asked. In the normal, day-to-day conduct of the team, for example, he should see that all members have the best rifles and accessories the team can afford; that they have adequate range facilities; that the range is free from distracting noises or interferences during training hours; that record-keeping errors, either in shooting, academic, or military organizations, are speedily corrected; that team planning and schedules are made with the convenience of the individual members in mind; that proper match entries are made in advance; and that travel, lodging, and food arrangements are made ahead of time. During a match, a coach should be near his team and provide any kind of psychological and even logistical support he deems necessary. He should take full and complete responsibility for all administrative details, and thus leave the shooting as the only responsibility falling on the team. He may even assist the shooters in the preparation of equipment on the firing line, thus assuring and demonstrating his support before the match begins. He should take upon himself the responsibility of seeing that the range operation is in no way unfair to his shooters; that no one heckles or distracts or annoys them during the match; that they have all the items of equipment they need; that their targets are scored accurately and fairly; that they are given all the time allotted to them by match rules; that all procedures are properly followed; and that any rule violations by other shooters are brought to the attention of the match authorities. By thus assuming a support and advocate role, the coach builds for himself a position of both trust and authority in the eyes of his team, and this places them in a position to concentrate exclusively on performance, and himself in a position better to guide and direct them in their development.

SOME IMPORTANT DETAILS IN TEAM CONDUCT

As the person primarily responsible for a team's conduct, the coach must pay very careful attention to details in two important areas: safety and etiquette. Both areas demand that the coach instill, and insist upon, good habits among his shooters. In the area of safety, the usual range rules apply: rifles are to be pointed downrange only and are never to be aimed at anything except the target, and bolts are to remain open except when on the firing line. To back up these demands, the coach should *insist* that there is to be no horseplay around guns, and that there be no practical jokes played by the team members on each other. Practical jokes have a way of quickly getting out of hand. One joke requires that another, more elaborate one be played next, and soon the whole thing mushrooms to uncontrollable size, and around a rifle range someone is likely to be seriously hurt. The coach must keep discipline *very* tight on the matter of safety, and even if it is not an active issue, he should bring it up early in his relationship with the team, and then, if need be, follow through with rigid disciplinary measures. This is one area in which he should personally handle discipline instead of relegating it to someone else.

In the area of etiquette, again the coach must work on little details, but again he should do so thoroughly and with rigid insistence on compliance. First, he should require that each member of his team know the rule book thoroughly, and then that they violate none of the rules, either in training or in a match. He may even hold formal classes to familiarize everyone with the rulebook. In addition, he, and they, should see that competitors do not violate rules during a match. Second, he should insist that his shooters observe the more informal rules of range etiquette. Each individual cleans and polices his firing point after he has finished shooting, either in training or in a match. Each individual respects the rights of others on the range to shoot without the interference of unnecessary noise, movement, or other distraction. No individual is rude to other shooters or range officials. No individual harasses or otherwise annoys the target scorers, or even asks these usually very busy men a question until they have finished scoring the targets and are available for challenges.

Finally, the coach will insist that the following miscellaneous specific habits are developed by everyone on his team. Each shooter double-checks before each match to see that he has the right targets, and the right target for the right match. After firing he avoids handling the target in any way that might cause the suspicion of his tampering with the target. When firing, he always pushes the round completely into the chamber with his hand—pushing it in with the bolt may strip the lead and cause an erratic trajectory. Each person keeps a strict account of the number of rounds he has fired in each position. On the firing line, no one uses his scope to look at anyone else's target—each person concerns himself only with his own. Scores should always be checked after they are posted to see if they are correct; if they are not, the coach should be informed, and *he* should make any challenges. Most important, each person must be constantly thinking, must have a plan of action in mind at all times immediately before and during a match, and must be always abreast of the situation.

The coach can help his shooters to be free to concentrate on the match if he will get them to the range at least one day before record firing begins. Then, he and they can use this time to see and speak to old friends that must be greeted, to check the height of the target frames, to fire a few shots and get the feel of the range, and to study the effects of wind and mirage on that particular range.

The coach who pays attention to these details will have a team that is more settled, that is more mature, that respects itself, and ultimately one that performs better.

CHAPTER
13

Coaching the Individual

We will now be concerned with the coach's relationship to individual shooters. This relationship exists even if he is working with the shooter as a member of a team. It is necessary to recognize that even the shooter who is a member of a team is essentially an individual player, and is in some ways painfully isolated. The shooter who is going after a first place score or a world record is, on the line, utterly alone and in many ways defenseless—there is nothing he can do to influence the performance of his competition, there is no way he can play against their weaknesses, there is no way he can match his skills to the complementary skills of a teammate, there is no way he can pass the ball to another friendly player. He is there alone, battling really against the weaknesses and fears in his own nature. It takes an individual of exceptional psychological strength to want to perform under these conditions and to do it successfully. The coach who finds an individual under his care who possesses championship potential has a great opportunity and also a great responsibility. To nurture and develop this potential is an extended process which depends upon establishing and maintaining a sometimes very delicate psychological rapport with a strong-minded player. It can be one of the most demanding jobs in coaching—and also one of the most rewarding, for the success of such an undertaking sees not only the development of a technically competent shooter, but the development of a mature individual as well.

The demands made upon a coach by such a relationship are considerable. These demands are usually made not so much upon his knowledge of shooting as upon his understanding of human nature. Earlier we talked about the coach's role as instructor. His job as instructor is to impart technical information about the specifics of shooting. We will come back to that again at the end of this chapter. But now we are ready to talk about the coach's role as *teacher*. The coach's job as teacher is to instill a set of values, inculcate certain habits of mind, foster a set of attitudes, and in other ways aid the individual to realize more fully his potential for maturity as a human being and as a shooter. This does not depend upon a factual knowledge of shooting, but rather on something much broader and more difficult to pin down.

The importance of what we have called the teaching role of the coach is evident even where his relationship is primarily with a group rather than an individual. Technical knowledge of a sport is not the key to successful coaching. It is a necessary part of a coach's equipment, but it is far from the most important. This would be evident if we could take ten men, all of equal technical knowledge, and put them in coaching positions in the ten teams of a sports league, and also have the teams equally matched. Of these ten coaches, one would emerge over the season as the best, one as the worst, and the others would arrange themselves in some order in between. But the differences among them are not, we remember, differences in knowledge of the sport. The differences are in their ability to create psychological conditions favorable to the development of the players both as individuals and as a group. In short, the very successful coaches are those who understand people.

Exactly what enables a coach to create these conditions and build this kind of relationship with his players is difficult, if not impossible, to isolate. Perhaps it is, as many people argue, a matter of the coach's personality, that indefinable something which determines how other people perceive him and feel about him. In part, perhaps, a successful coach must be born with certain personality traits. However, it is probably also true that no one is born with all, or even many, of the traits that make a successful coach. Ask one if his work is easy, and he will undoubtedly say that it is not, that he has to work at it harder than most people work at their professions, and that he has learned by making many, many mistakes along the road to his present success. The personality of a successful coach is formed from within, consciously, by self-analysis, self-control, self-sacrifice, and by exercising almost infinite patience—patience with other people because of their different personalities, different opinions, shortcomings, confusions, and mistakes. This is not to say that a coach should be weak or tolerant of ineptitude or satisfied with low standards. On the contrary, he should have the highest standards and the greatest regard for success in his sport; but he must have the patience and self-control to get his players gradually to accept the same standards and goals, and then the patience and self-control to get them to work for those goals, and work in such a way as to succeed.

The fact that personality seemingly plays an important role in coaching is reflected too in the fact that certain individuals can be highly successful coaches at certain levels, but are ineffectual at others. Some individuals are very good with new shooters; others are most effective with intermediates; and still others seem able to work best with champions or probable champions. Experience in observing coaches suggests that these types may not be interchangeable—that is, that the type who is good with beginners may be very poor with champions, and vice versa. Whether this is a difference in personality, or a difference in teaching methods, is uncertain, because trying to separate personality and teaching methods is another area where confusion reigns. But the individual who is considering accepting a coaching position, or who is appointing the coach, should consider in his evaluation what kinds of shooters are to be coached—beginners, intermediates, or advanced players—and then judge the fitness of the prospective coach accordingly.

BUILDING A WORKING RELATIONSHIP

Within the framework of the team, the coach is going to have to develop fairly close personal relationships with each individual member. Early in those relationships, he is going to have to decide how to treat each individual. Some individuals respond best if they are criticized directly; others respond best to gentle suggestion; still others respond best to criticism delivered in a joking or sarcastic fashion; many additional variations are possible as well. The approach that is taken toward each individual should be determined early and then should be followed without exception.

Unquestionably, the coach is going to make some mistakes in this area by occasionally choosing an approach that will not work with a particular individual; unfortunately, these mistakes will sometimes have to be written off as losses. These losses are perhaps unavoidable, for it is of paramount importance that a shooter come to see his relationship with his coach in a certain way, and then know that his relationship will remain constant. If he cannot depend on this consistent relationship, he will not be able to develop personal trust in the coach, and this is an absolutely necessary ingredient for success. The coach who treats an individual courteously one day, and screams at him the next, cannot inspire personal trust in his players and will not succeed with them fully. A successful coach may be the quiet, courteous type, or he may be the screaming, rude type, but he is always consistent.

It should perhaps be emphasized here that even though the coach takes a different approach to each individual, he still, within the framework of the group, treats them all alike in terms of asking them all to meet the same training requirements, spending the same amount of time with each one, treating them all fairly and without bias. The different approach taken with individuals does not negate the fact that he treats them all impartially.

The fact that the coach enters into a relationship of trust with his shooters implies that they must get to know him individually. It is for this reason that he should spend some time with each individual shooter during every training session. However, while the player should trust the coach as an individual, he should not come to be seen as an "equal"; the coach should be both a trusted figure and an authority figure. He must, if he is to be effective, have the power to correct, to order, to direct; and he must be able to enforce his will. Maintaining the image of authority without remaining too aloof to inspire trust and

242   Position Rifle Shooting

confidence is a difficult task and undoubtedly requires experience and practice.

Another factor which inspires trust among the shooters is the personal integrity of the coach. Is he honest? Is he dependable? Does he possess moral integrity? A coach is constantly trying to instill these qualities in his shooters. If he preaches the value of these characteristics, but does not possess them himself, he is not likely to be effective as a teacher of these precepts.

After a coach develops a clear style in his approach to an individual and wins his confidence and trust, he begins to direct the development of this individual in certain specific ways. He is working, of course, to make the individual a champion shooter. But the qualities that make a champion shooter are also precisely those that make him a mature individual. If the coach has a potential champion on his hands, he is going to prepare that individual for the time when he may go out on the firing line and, without help from anyone, shoot a new world's record by performing in a way that no other human being has ever performed before. To do that, the rifleman must have technical knowledge, confidence, and developed skills; he must be able to think for himself, to rely on himself, to make decisions probably of a very crucial nature, and to exercise complete self-control. He must, in short, be a mature human being. These qualities are not possessed only by world champions. The shooter who goes out to win a small local match for the first time should have exactly these same qualities.

How does one person direct the development of another person in this direction? The first and cardinal precept is that a shooter cannot be forced to become a champion or forced to become mature. The coach's role is to act as a kind of psychological midwife—he assists in bringing into life the personal, psychological potential that lies dormant within the individual. This process can be effected by a shooting coach only if the player *wants* to be a shooting champion. The coach cannot perform this function with an unmotivated individual. However, if the player is motivated, the coach can do specific things which will foster this development. Perhaps the most subtle of these things is to instill a set of values in the player. These should include, first of all, a high regard for excellence in every field. Admiration should be conveyed—not by long speeches, but by simple remarks dropped in conversation—for the athlete or anyone else who performs exceptionally well, who makes sacrifices to achieve those ends, and who sets new records by breaking through previously existing limits.

The man who excels, and as a very minimum does exceptionally well, should become the standard of comparison for activity in all areas. This gradually becomes a part of the psychology of the shooter—he comes to believe quite naturally that nothing less than the best is acceptable. Moreover, the player should come to value the styles of certain athletes. He should be guided into admiration for those who play fairly and exhibit good sportsmanship. Of particular importance, he should value the ability to remain cool and calm and cheerful in losing, in winning, and in moments of crisis. The shooter who gets rattled when he falls behind is going to lose; the shooter who throws a temper tantrum when a target fails to operate properly is going to lose. A good baseball player, because of the nature of his sport, may allow his temper free rein when he strikes out, and still perform well in his next turn at bat. But because of the nature of shooting, a rifleman who allows emotions of any kind to take control of him during a match is not going to be able to perform well on the next shot. The coach should convey the value of the cool style without preaching about it. Also, it is highly desirable to teach the value of winning without becoming boastful or conceited. Besides being objectionable to everyone else, the person who allows success to go to his head after a good season is likely to have finished the best part of his career, at least for a couple of years.

Aside from instilling certain values, the coach also fosters a certain set of attitudes. Values and attitudes are to some extent inseparable, but to separate them at least for purposes of discussion will be useful. Unquestionably the most important attitude is the one a shooter holds towards the *how* of achieving the goals he values so much. Specifically, his attitude must be that the way to achieve success is through hard work. The work of training is to be undertaken conscientiously—it is to be performed exactly as called for by the training schedule, with great thoroughness and care. Ultimately, a person with the right attitude comes to take pride in the excellence with which he approaches the task of training. He actually enjoys the work and goes about it cheerfully. A coach will find that some individuals possess this attitude naturally; in others it must be patiently cultivated, more by setting an example than by preachments. A shooter should believe the old truisms that anything worth doing is worth doing well, and that a man who takes pride in his work is a happy man.

Another attitude must also be fostered to bring the values and attitudes we have been discussing into balance. This is the attitude that human beings, by their very nature, are imperfect and prone to make mistakes, and that these flaws and weaknesses must be taken into stride. The individual should be made to see that he will have bad days, that he will occasionally shoot bad shots, that his coach will sometimes make mistakes, that his friends will make mistakes—in short, that everyone will occasionally fall short of perfection; and that these mistakes, which sometimes seem designed specifically to frustrate him, do not mean that he is worthless or that his coach and friends are worthless or turning against him. If he can discriminate between malice and simple human weakness, he will see that usually when the people around him commit some error, they do so not out of malicious intent, but out of human frailty. And he can come to see that his own mistakes are not signs of worthlessness, but products merely of normal human error. This acceptance of the imperfect world is a vital step in the development of a mature, compassionate individual who perceives himself and the world in realistic perspective. It is also incidentally quite important in helping the shooter overcome the psychological effects of the wide shot that may occur during a match.

In addition to values and attitudes, the coach as teacher also cultivates certain habits of mind in his players. These habits may involve mentally putting to use certain of the values and attitudes already discussed. Among the more important of these mental habits are the ability to see himself as his real competitor, the ability to think positively about his performance, and the desire to go only for the top medal. Each of these habits of mind has rather broad implications, and they in fact have been the subject in one way or another of most of this book. A brief review here, however, might be in order.

First, the shooter should develop the habit of consistently

seeing himself as his real competitor rather than someone else on the firing line. He does this by concentrating on his own performance, and by seeing his responsibility as controlling his own actions, not defeating someone else. If he thinks about someone else, he is not thinking about—and is not controlling—his own performance. His real competitors are the forces within himself that could possibly interfere with his turning in the best performance he is capable of. To be effective under match conditions, this way of perceiving the realities of a match must be rehearsed during training until it is an almost unshakeable habit.

Second, the individual must habitually think about his performance in positive terms. His thought patterns should be, "First, I will do this, and then I will do that." They should never be, "If I don't do this, then I might do that." Negative thinking will inevitably lead to exactly the mistakes which the rifleman fears he might make. Positive control over performance is the result of the mental habit of thinking in positive, not negative, terms, and this habit too is acquired by rehearsal, training, and conscious effort.

Third, the individual must learn to think in terms of winning the top medal. We said earlier that a shooter profits by learning to value excellence; but those values will be useful to him as a shooter only if he applies them directly to himself and to his own performance in a match. The person who does not try for first place probably will not win it. Particularly in the sport of shooting, trying for second place is not good enough, even if second place requires an excellent score. Winning first place is the name of the game, and an individual will develop most rapidly, and will win most consistently, *only* if he goes for first place. This habit must be cultivated even in the seasoned champion shooter. He may have set a new record last season, but unless he improves, he will not keep the record this season, because someone else is going to beat the old record. The coach has to stimulate all of his players to keep contending for first place, or even his brightest champions will tarnish into obscurity.

A coach also plays a protective role in his relationship with the individual shooter, primarily in protecting his self-confidence. The coach works with an individual over a long period, building a rapport with him, providing technical advice, imparting values and attitudes and habits of mind, and generally supervising his development into, hopefully, a champion. But this process takes place over a period of months, at the least, and more likely over a period of years. Unquestionably, the individual shooter is going to have setbacks, some of them serious, and they are going to affect his self-confidence. Here the coach must be a kind of amateur psychiatrist.

If the player "sticks" in training, for example, and seems incapable of making a gain despite the hardest effort, the coach must help him see that this is not the end of the world, that every athlete experiences similar difficulties, and that the problem is in fact quite normal. The coach might point out that the learning curve always involves plateaus, and that it might be helpful to the individual to attempt only a "holding action" for a week or two, and perhaps lighten his training schedule for a while, before expecting further gains to take place. Similarly, if the individual turns in a really bad, ego-deflating performance in a match, the coach should point out that this too is fairly normal during a shooter's development. He might take the attitude of "Well, this had to happen to you sooner or later; just be glad it finally happened." By thus protecting the shooter's sense of worth, the coach is actually laying the groundwork for the shooter's sense of confidence in himself as a human being, which is necessary for his confidence in himself as a shooter. A sense of personal worth is necessary for a healthy maturity.

In addition, the coach takes another, very specific kind of protective action that is of utmost importance: he protects the shooter's confidence from the effects of an inaccurate rifle. One of the worst things that can happen to a rifleman, psychologically, is to turn in a good performance, even in training, and have a score way below par. The frustration of this experience gnaws away at the very basis of his self-confidence. It should be entirely the coach's responsibility, and none of the shooter's responsibility, to be on the lookout for a bad rifle and to spot a rifle's loss of accuracy the same day it occurs. Under no circumstances should the shooter be allowed to continue training with a bad rifle, for he will begin to excuse his own mistakes by placing the blame on the gun. The rifle should be taken away from him immediately and either repaired or replaced as soon as possible. If rifles are kept in accurate condition, shooters will tend to focus on performance, rather than equipment, and their confidence will remain undamaged.

A coach will have to deal with a shooter's confidence in other ways, too. He must remember that as an important authority figure in the player's life, everything he says and does will carry psychological weight. His comments to the shooter should be positive and encouraging. Negativism in his own approach will inspire negativism and self-doubt in the player. He should provide encouragement by verbally recognizing the individual's achievements. Small amounts of praise, distributed carefully and judiciously, work very well; failure to praise the shooter at all is unfair, and praise too lavishly distributed soon becomes meaningless. On the other hand, the coach shouldn't hesitate to puncture the overinflated ego that comes with overconfidence. A sharp, derisive comment may wound an overconfident player temporarily; but, if the criticism is in fact accurate, it will usually put things back into a healthy perspective for the shooter and will not do permanent damage to his relationship with the coach. A coach has got to field the problems that go with the area of self-confidence in a creative fashion, as they are never quite the same from moment to moment or from individual to individual. Work in this area, however, will eventually pay off in handsome dividends.

Finally, the coach should provide a sympathetic audience for a player who is in difficult circumstances. In many instances, a player who is under the pressure of intense competition becomes irritable and begins to develop a large number of complaints about his health, his equipment, the range, the conduct of the match, and various other problems, almost all of them imaginary. The coach should develop in his shooters the habit of talking to him in private to air their complaints about events related to the match. His role is to listen sympathetically and let the shooter get the problem off his chest; he may even agree that the problem exists and assure the shooter that he will do something about it, even though he knows the whole thing is imaginary. The shooter, however, having thus rid himself of some of the internal pressures by voicing his complaints, is free to go on to concentrate on his performance. Scolding him for his imagined complaints would send him to the line with bottled-up feelings of anger and frustration, and lessen his chances for success.

The very successful shooters are frequently individuals with firmly set opinions and a strongly held confidence that their opinions are right. This is at once desirable and undesirable. It is desirable because a good shooter must be decisive and have complete confidence in himself. It is undesirable because if the shooter's opinion is wrong, and the coach wishes to correct it, he faces a somewhat delicate task if he is to maintain good relations with the shooter. The only thing he can do is work on the basis of a very thorough knowledge of the individual. It is here, perhaps, that success in coaching really lies. A coach must really know, and really be interested in, an individual before that person will respond to him in such a manner as to become a champion shooter under his guidance.

PROVIDING TECHNICAL ASSISTANCE

Most people think of coaching as instructing an individual or group in how to perform a certain task. A shooting coach has this function to some extent: he regularly gives instruction to the team, as a group, as a means of keeping fundamentals consistently before them. He also gives instruction to beginning shooters on an individual basis—instruction which is usually designed to help the individual assume a correct basic shooting position.

But beyond the point of disseminating information about basics and fundamentals to the group, or to individual beginners, a shooting coach in working with individuals rarely *instructs*, as that word is normally used. Instead, he *assists* his players in their continuing education about technical matters. On reflection the reason becomes quite clear. To develop properly, a rifleman must begin by adopting as nearly as he can the classical techniques and positions; however, he must then begin to modify the basic position to suit his own individual body characteristics in order to make maximum use of the principles of bone support, balance, and hold. As the coach cannot himself feel the kinesthetic sensations of the shooter, nor see through his sights, he cannot *tell* the shooter what to do to bring about an improvement in his position. He can only assist the individual to analyze his performance and his position, and assist him in making improvements by suggesting possibilities. It is for these reasons that an individual cannot be *made* into a successful shooter; he can only be *assisted* in a developing self-analysis, the motive force of which is the shooter's own desire for improvement.

In this respect, the shooting coach's most important function, as we have said before, is to stimulate the shooter's thinking and to teach him how to think in the right way. As we have said several times—for it is worth repeating—a shooter's progress is directly proportionate to how well he thinks. Within the narrow limits of technical matters, a coach's role, then, *begins* with *telling* a new shooter what to do; but, as the shooter develops, the coach's role progresses toward questioning, probing, suggesting, tentatively analyzing, and, ultimately, with the real champion, perhaps merely supporting what the shooter himself does.

How does the coach prepare himself to perform these functions? The first step is to acquire a thorough knowledge of the technical aspects of shooting. This book might be a good place to start acquiring that knowledge, but knowing everything in it would only be a start, for there is always more and then more to be learned about the highly complex skill of shooting. Knowledge can always be expanded by reading articles and books, and by talking to shooters and coaches, and by constantly observing, observing, observing. And of course there is the ongoing job of developing new knowledge by thoughtful analysis of all that one reads, hears, and sees, and separating the good from the bad.

The second step in providing assistance to an individual shooter is to learn with absolute thoroughness every detail of his positions and techniques. This may take some time, but the ability quickly to do so can be developed with experience. The method is simply to watch the shooter perform. He need not be made too self-conscious by this close observation. The coach may sit or stand in the shooting booth, or behind it, and give the impression that he is primarily interested in watching the target or the wind conditions through a spotting scope. He should actually use the time, however, to observe the shooter's performance. He may also ask questions, from time to time, to discover how the individual is using the trigger, what his kinesthetic perceptions are, where his concentration is, and other details that may not be apparent to an observer. Every detail should be carefully stored in the coach's memory. Then, later, he will find that quite often he can help the shooter in a number of ways. When the shooter is one day unable to perform satisfactorily because "something" is wrong, the coach may observe his performance for a time and discover that he has unconsciously made some change in his position or technique that is adversely affecting his performance. Or, the coach may discover that the shooter has all along been doing something incorrectly, and may then be able to guide him into seeing that possibly an improvement could be made in this particular aspect of his position or performance.

The approach taken to the shooter may be direct or indirect, depending on the relationship the coach has worked out with him. Experience indicates, however, that an almost universally successful technique is to guide the individual into seeing the possible improvement himself, without actually telling him what to do. There are several advantages to this. One, the shooter's pride is not injured. Second, the shooter learns in the process correct analytical techniques as the coach guides him through an analytical process. Third, the shooter does not acquire a psychological dependence upon the coach to do his thinking for him. Additionally, there are probably some indeterminable advantages to be gained in morale, enthusiasm, and motivation by using this technique.

In the final analysis a shooter is not molded from without in the same way as a champion gymnast or diver, for example, is molded into perfect form and appearance by his coach's instructions. By contrast, a champion shooter must develop primarily through an expanding awareness of his own internal environment, and his external appearance, aside from various requirements for legality, accounts for very little. The importance of this interior world to the shooter's performance is what makes the work of the shooting coach so vastly different from that of other coaches. It is true that a gymnastics coach or a diving coach must develop motivation and confidence and self-discipline in his pupils; the shooting coach must do these things too. But the gymnastics or diving coach can look at his student and say definitely, "Your steps here are too short," or "Here you arch your back too much." But the shooting coach cannot do these things, beyond the initial stages of position building, for what wins a shooting match is not the shooter's appearance, but his performance as measured by his score on a target some 50 meters away, and there is no single standard of appearance which will yield a good score. One shooter may attain perfect balance by standing with his feet wide apart; another may attain it by placing his feet close together. One shooter may get the best bone support in the high kneeling position, another in the forward kneeling position. One shooter may get the best hold in the prone position with his right leg drawn way forward, another with his right leg almost parallel to his left leg. There is no way a coach can look at a shooter's position, so long as it is legal and seems to make use of the correct principles, and pronounce it "right" or "wrong." The best he can say is that it is "classic," or "orthodox," or "unorthodox." He can get some idea of whether a position is wrong for the shooter if it is obviously unsteady; but if it appears to be steady, the only way he can get an idea of whether it is right or wrong is by looking at the shooter's targets. If an unorthodox appearance allows the shooter to perform exceptionally well, then the position is right for him even though in appearance it is quite unusual.

From the standpoint of the technical knowledge or information required, the task of coaching shooters is probably not appreciably more difficult than any other coaching job. In any area of athletics, there exists at any one time a limited amount of technical knowledge that the coach must have to stay competitive. The amount of such information needed by a shooting coach is just as manageable as the information needed by coaches in most other sports. But coaching shooters probably does require—at least as far as we are aware—more skill in working with human psychology than any other sport. For this reason it is in the final analysis probably more difficult than most coaching jobs. And considerably more interesting.

Appendix A

The Sitting Position & Training for the Four-Position Match

Though the sitting position is not used in international-style riflery, it is sometimes found in other styles of competition, and a discussion of it is therefore included here. We are keeping the discussion relatively brief, however, because to a much larger extent than in the other positions, variations in the sitting position are so pronounced from individual to individual that a detailed discussion of any one variation of the position would be practically worthless to a majority of shooters. The best course seems to be to deal in broad generalities and allow the reader to work out a specific form of the position suited to his own body conformation.

We said earlier that kneeling is the position used in inter-national-style shooting which depends most heavily upon the relative lengths of arms, legs, and neck in relation to the length of the torso. These structural relationships are even more crucial in the sitting position, and are evident to the shooter himself in much more dramatic form. Moreover, the flexion arcs of bone joints in the legs and hips are also a considerable factor in determining which variation of the position works best for a particular individual, and these flexion arcs vary widely from one individual to another. These factors combine to demand that each shooter work out a highly individualized position based upon the length and flexion characteristics of bones and joints in his own legs and torso.

In practice, the sitting position is possibly for most people the easiest one to "find." This is true simply because if a particular variation will not work for an individual, the inappropriateness of the variation is so vividly evident as to be unmistakable. If a person cannot get into the crossed-legs variation, for example, there is no mistaking it: he simply cannot get into the position, or else cannot achieve enough comfort to allow for adequate mental concentration. He will in fact be forced to try another variation.

The three basic variations are the crossed-legs, the crossed-ankles, and the open-legs configurations. All three are capable of producing holds equal in steadiness and durability to the prone position. From the standpoint of theory, they arrange themselves in an order of descending preference, based upon the height of the torso from the ground, as follows: the crossed-legs, the crossed-ankles, and the open-legs. As the center of gravity is lowest in the crossed-legs, it is the most stable *if it can be assumed comfortably*; however, if it is not comfortable, the crossed-ankles variation is probably almost as good, and the open-legs variation is not much inferior.

All three variations make maximum use of bone support and, where applicable, balance. Balance is hardly a factor at all if the center of gravity is relatively low and the support area large; in the open-legs variation, and in rare instances in the crossed-ankles variation, balance is sometimes a consideration, but this is more the exception than the rule. Muscles should never be involved in holding the aim in the bull's-eye; all three variations are capable of producing a natural point of aim, and bone structures alone should support the weight of the rifle and align the point of aim with the center of the bull. Except in the open-legs variation, muscle tension throughout the body should generally be light, as holding the body still in the sitting position requires relatively little muscle tension if the position is correctly built.

The crossed-legs variation.

In this variation the shooter sits facing approximately 25 degrees to the right of the target. The feet are pulled up into a crossed-legs position so that each knee rests upon the inside of the foot or ankle of the opposite leg, thus forming a stable platform in which each foot transmits the weight of the opposite knee directly and solidly to the ground. On this stable structure the elbows will be placed, positioned directly on, or very near, the joints of the knees. In this variation the sling must usually be placed very high on the arm and adjusted to be quite short; the fore-end stop will usually be drawn back relatively close to the trigger guard. If a butt-hook is used, it must usually be positioned low on the stock, and the extensions drawn in so as to shorten the stock considerably more than in other positions.

Once the shooter is in position, the weight of the rifle helps to pull the torso forward, and the elbows should rest easily and solidly upon the legs. If the rifle points naturally at the target and is high enough to allow for good head and eye placement, and if the position is reasonably comfortable, it is probably the one the individual should use, though preference may lead him to another. It is a very stable position, however, because the weight of the rifle is transmitted to the ground by way of a structure that is in effect almost solid.

Adjusting the point of aim vertically is achieved through adjustments to the sling, fore-end stop, and butt-hook. Small vertical adjustments are also made by crossing the right leg over the left, or the left over the right. Very fine vertical adjustments are made by breath control. Horizontal adjustments are made by rotating the entire structure.

Many people cannot use this variation because when they assume it the gun points naturally to a spot on the ground about 10 feet in front of their knees. They must try another variation.

The crossed-ankles variation.

This variation is assumed by facing almost directly toward the target and sitting with the ankles crossed directly to the front of the shooter. The buttocks and heels are firmly upon the ground, but the back of the legs at the knee joints are above the ground. The distance will depend upon how far away from the buttocks the feet are placed, and how far the knee and hip joints will allow the legs to rotate outward in bowlegged fashion. If the feet and legs can be positioned so that the knees form supports of the correct height for the elbows and the point of aim is vertically adjusted to the bull, then the position will be stable *provided the leg muscles are completely relaxed and the rifle is supported by bone structures alone.* If the flexion arcs of the knee and hip joints are so great that the knees will turn out too far to provide an adequately high platform, the position should in no case be used, for leg muscles are brought into play to support the rifle, and these muscles will quickly tire and begin to tremble.

In this position the sling is usually placed very high on the arm; vertical adjustments are achieved by moving the feet toward or away from the body, or by crossing the right leg over the left, or the left over the right. Changes in the position of the legs will usually necessitate corresponding adjustments in the length of the sling and the position of the fore-end stop, and possibly the butt-hook or plate. Fine vertical adjustments are made by breath control; all horizontal adjustments by rotating the position.

The open-legs variation.

In this variation, the shooter sits facing slightly to the right of the target and places his feet in front of him, a comfortable distance away, with the soles of his shoes flat upon the ground. The left elbow is usually placed on the shin just below the left knee, the right elbow on or just above the right knee. The feet should be placed so that the legs are stable and, with the weight of the arms and rifle upon them, completely free of wobble. The weight of the rifle should be supported by the sling and left arm as it rests upon the left knee. Though the amount of muscle tension used throughout the body to support the position may be considerably more than that used in the crossed-legs variation, muscles are *not* used to support the rifle; bone support alone should perform this function.

Vertical adjustments may be made by moving the feet toward or away from the body, and by changing the position of the elbows on the legs. Sling, fore-end stop, and butt-hook adjustments may also be used. Fine vertical adjustments are made by breath control; all horizontal adjustments by rotating the entire structure.

TRAINING FOR THE FOUR-POSITION MATCH

Many quite good shooters whose primary interest is international-style shooting, after once mastering the sitting position, frequently enter four-position matches with little or no training time devoted to sitting performance. The reason for this is probably that the position resembles prone so closely: it has a low center of gravity, a large support area, both elbows are placed upon stable supports, and the position of the torso is very solid. It also resembles the prone position in that the same problems of breath and eye control, sling adjustment, and wind-watching are encountered, and the same techniques of trigger pull can be used. Therefore, training which improves or sustains prone performance has great value for sitting performance as well.

Initially, of course, everyone will have to train in one of the variations of the sitting position in order to build a solid structure and refine the hold to within 10-ring limits. If the individual is a beginning shooter, and plans regularly to use four-position matches either as program goals or training vehicles, he may wish to make training for the sitting position a regular part of his program. A suggested program is as follows.

For the beginner:

Phase I: progress in standing performance.

Phase II: progress in kneeling, 10% of training time devoted to maintaining proficiency in standing.

Phase III: progress in sitting, 10% of training time devoted to maintaining proficiency in standing, 10% to maintaining proficiency in kneeling.

Phase IV: progress in prone, 10% of training time devoted to maintaining proficiency in standing, 10% to maintaining proficiency in kneeling, 10% to maintaining proficiency in sitting.

Phase V: consolidation; 40% to standing, 30% to kneeling, 15% to sitting, 15% to prone; *or* 40% to the position that offers the most difficulty, 30% to the next most difficult, and 15% each to the remaining positions.

A more advanced shooter who plans regularly to enter four-position matches and wishes to train for all four positions might devise a training plan such as this:

For the experienced shooter:

Phase I: progress in standing, 10% each to maintaining proficiency in kneeling, sitting, and prone.

Phase II: progress in kneeling, 10% each to maintaining proficiency in standing, sitting, and prone.

Phase III: progress in sitting, 10% each to maintaining proficiency in standing, kneeling, and prone.

Phase IV: progress in prone, 10% each to maintaining proficiency in standing, kneeling, and sitting.

Phase V: consolidation; 40% to standing, 30% to kneeling, 15% each to sitting and prone; *or* 40% to the most difficult position, 30% to the next most difficult, and 15% each to the remaining positions.

The shooter who is primarily interested in international-style shooting, however, as we said above, may devote less regular training time to sitting, after he has mastered the position, and practice it only for a short time prior to entering a four-position event.

Appendix B

Shooting Limited-Time & Rapid-Fire Matches

Almost all that has been said in foregoing sections of this book assumes that the shooter is performing in international-style events where enough time is provided for each player to turn in his best possible performance, unhindered by the need to hurry. International-style events are in a sense limited-time matches, for the performer must complete the course within a specified time; usually, however, the time is more than adequate for even the slowest shooter. There are other forms of matches, however, that require the shooter to complete his performance within a narrowly restricted time span. At one end of the spectrum in this category are events that require the shooter to complete ten record shots in, say, ten minutes; these, for our purposes, will be called limited-time matches. On the other end of the spectrum are events that require, say, ten record shots fired within ten seconds; these may be described as rapid-fire matches. We do not wish to enter here into a detailed discussion of the problems posed by such matches, particularly the complicated areas of legal positions and equipment. However, we would like to offer these general suggestions which provide means of using to best advantage the principles set forth in other parts of this book.

The first major consideration is that limited-time and rapid-fire matches do not last very long, nor do they require a large number of shots. Consequently, a person who is well conditioned physically may use muscles in his performance without necessarily incurring damaging fatigue. However, we offer this observation: The fact that muscles may be safely used does not negate the usefulness of bone support. Whenever possible, the principles of bone support and balance should be utilized to fullest advantage, simply because a position based upon these principles is inherently more stable and steady than another position without bone support. Bone support, if present, in effect necessitates that the position be well designed. If it is well designed and if it does make maximum use of bone support and balance, then overall muscle tension may be increased throughout the body, and a faster, more deliberate control of the body/rifle structure can be used, a situation which allows for superb functioning for a short time, or until fatigue begins to set in. The potential is far greater under these conditions than if no bone support or balance is used and the rifle is simply muscled into the target.

An allied principle is that a position may be "tightened up" whenever a sling is used by shortening the sling. In a limited-time match where it is impossible to wait out unfavorable wind conditions, this procedure may be used to diminish the effects of wind blowing upon the body; and in a rapid-fire match to diminish the effects of both wind and recoil upon the position. Usually a sling tightened to create greater tension in the positon structure will also create discomfort, and even become unbearable after a time; but in a string of fire of short duration, the tension and pain are usually bearable if the sling is tightened within reasonable limits.

Anyone expecting to encounter the obstacles posed by limited match time should design his training program to help him prepare for these challenges. Training sessions should include periods devoted to shooting with increased muscle tension throughout the body so as to familiarize oneself with the different sensations and problems, and to condition the muscles to perform in a state of greater tension. Some conditioning should also be done to accustom the body to the pressures of increased sling tension.

Training for limited-time and rapid-fire matches should also aim for three additional goals: developing efficiency in the performance of physical activities, developing a pace or rhythm, and developing an accurate sense of time. Developing physical efficiency means simply learning how to perform all the actions of shooting without letting wasted motion consume time. For example, one should learn to assemble and operate the spotting scope with a minimum of time and energy, and learn how to position the scope so its use requires a minimum of movement and disturbance to the position. Similar efforts should be made toward improving the handling of all equipment and honing down all the movements made in shooting. The fewer motions involved in the process of shooting the more efficient the performance.

Developing a pace or rhythm is relatively easy for most people, and of paramount importance. In training sessions, make yourself shoot the required number of record shots without hurrying, but with speed enough to leave a reasonable safety margin or remaining time after you have completed your string of fire. Do this at first with the aid of a clock or stopwatch until you can pace yourself accurately almost without thinking about it. Both psychologically and physically, this internalized rhythm seems to become quite powerful and quite helpful, for once developed it seems to relieve some of the effort of shooting when it is allowed to control the frequency of shots. Always attempt, however, to leave a reasonable margin of time at the end of your string of fire; this can be invaluable if something unexpected or unavoidable should occur to interrupt your rhythm or put you behind schedule. The spare time allows you the opportunity to get back into your rhythm and finish your string without feeling panicked by lack of time.

A third training goal should be to develop an accurate sense of time. By this we mean that a shooter should be aware that he can, in an emergency situation, get off a normal, perfectly controlled shot in a matter of seconds. Frequently matches are lost by the leader when he finds himself with one shot to go in the final few seconds of legal time, and he throws the shot completely off needlessly in a wild lunge to beat the clock. These occurrences can be prevented if the shooter learns to act quickly and efficiently, and also develops an accurate sense of time so that he can, under the pressure of time running out, judge exactly how much time remains as he squeezes off the shot. If five seconds remain, and he still needs to improve the aim, there is no need to jerk the trigger; there is plenty of time left both to improve the aim and to release the shot smoothly. Knowing that, and being able to judge the passage of time accurately, will enable him to do so. Obviously, one wants to avoid these last-second situations if at all possible; but since unforeseen circumstances can force one into them, it is best to be prepared by training for the eventuality.

A moment of reflection will show that the principles outlined in this appendix do in no way undercut nor negate the principles set forth in the main sections of this book; rather, the principles and techniques outlined here for shooting limited-time or rapid-fire events can be used in conjunction with, or in addition to, the principles of international-style shooting when match regulations require a faster shooting pace.

Appendix C

Suggested Reading

TECHNIQUES OF POSITION RIFLE SHOOTING

There are many scattered magazine articles on position rifle shooting, many of them quite good. Also, the armed forces of several nations have produced manuals on the proper techniques of firing military rifles from various shooting positions, but these manuals would be of only limited value to a person interested primarily in three- or four-position shooting. To our knowledge, no full-length study of position riflery is available to the general public aside from this present volume. It is known that the Russians produced a book on international-style riflery back in the 1950's, but copies have not been generally available outside the Soviet bloc. The United States has seen two works worthy of mention. One, recently published, is *Marksmanship*, by Gary L. Anderson (New York: Simon and Schuster, 1972), published as the present book was undergoing final revision. We have been unable to obtain a copy in time to prepare an adequate review; but according to the author, it is a brief book aimed primarily at the beginner. The information in it, however, is undoubtedly quite sound. A second work, available for years, has been a pamphlet, *International Rifle Marksmanship Manual*, produced by the U.S. Army. As both the present authors were

responsible for the production of that manual at one time, it is
the acknowledged forerunner of this book, and we are grateful
to those who worked on that publication both before and after
us for the contributions they have made to the present state of
shooting knowledge. Pirated reproductions of the booklet
sometimes appear on the market at expensive prices, but copies
can be had free for the asking: they are available upon request
from Commanding Officer, United States Army Marksmanship
Training Unit, Fort Benning, Georgia 31905. New editions
appear at frequent intervals, and both the length and the quality
of the work vary widely among different editions.

PHYSIOLOGY

There can be no doubt that the greatest lag in applying
existing knowledge to shooting is in the area of physiology.
Technical knowledge relating to guns and ammunition finds
application on the firing line within months of its discovery; but
great masses of data on physiology and physiological function
remain relatively unexplored for possible application in shooting. Following, in alphabetical order by authors' names, are four
books dealing with various branches of physiology. All but Miss
Gross's book contain rich bibliographical references, and are
good places to begin investigations into the wealth of research
findings.

Graham, Clarence H., editor. *Vision and Visual Perception.*
New York: John Wiley & Sons, Inc., 1965. 637 pp. Chapters by Clarence Graham, Neil R. Bartlett, John Lott
Brown, Yun Hsia, Conrad Mueller, and Lorrin A. Riggs on a
variety of subjects concerning the eye, vision, and perception. Necessarily technical in places, but readable and com-
prehensible to the well-educated nonspecialist. Most of the
material is general in nature; almost all of it could be related
to shooting, if only indirectly. Particularly of interest are
chapters 1, 2, 5, 6, 9, 11, 17, 18, and 19.

Gross, Nancy E. *Living With Stress.* New York: McGraw-Hill,
1958. 207 pp. A readable, nontechnical account of the
research leading to the modern understanding of the
psycho-physiological causes and effects of stress. Though
the book never refers to the sport of shooting, a reader may

readily see that "match pressure" is an instance of the kind of stress Miss Gross discusses. Some suggestions on how to cope with stress, though not as many, perhaps, as the title would suggest. Short, easy.

Morgan, Clifford T. *Physiological Psychology.* 3rd edn. New York: McGraw-Hill, 1965. 627 pp. A remarkably comprehensive survey of the research into the physiological basis of human behavior. The book quickly covers elementary facts and moves on to more advanced considerations. It is avowedly designed for "undergraduate and graduate students preparing for psychology, physiology, and medicine and as a reference book for graduate students and other workers in the field," and so is predictably technical. While it never mentions shooting, almost everything it discusses could be related to shooting by a thoughtful reader. Difficult, but dense with valuable background information. Contains an invaluable bibliography.

Singer, Robert N. *Motor Learning and Human Performance: An Application to Physical Education Skills.* Toronto, Ontario: The Macmillan Co., 1968. 354 pp. Provides a basic survey of how motor skills are learned and what factors are involved in, or affect, the learning process in which muscles acquire the ability to perform certain functions. Useful in providing an introduction to and overview of the present state of knowledge on motor learning, and of some value to the person interested in improving his training techniques. Like most books on this subject, however, it reveals how little is really known about why some individuals readily learn certain skills and others do not; and although it is one of the most widely read books on motor learning, many readers will feel that it tends to emphasize the obvious.

Some additional books of minor interest in this area include Bryant J. Cratty's *Movement Behavior and Motor Learning* (Philadelphia: Lea and Febiger, 1964), 332 pp.; and *Psychology and Physical Activity* (Englewood Cliffs: Prentice-Hall, 1968), 214 pp. Also of some value is Joseph B. Oxendine's *Psychology of Motor Learning* (New York: Appleton-Century-Crofts, 1968), 366 pp. These books are similar in many respects to Singer's, though they seem to be less comprehensive.

NUTRITION

In the United States the standard work is the Department of Agriculture's *Agricultural Handbook No. 8: Composition of Foods*, available in the reference section of most libraries, or it may be purchased for a modest fee from the Superintendent of Documents, Washington, D.C. 20402. Anyone who wishes to gain a scientific understanding of basic nutritional principles should begin by familiarizing himself with this work. Another useful government publication is the volume *Food: The Yearbook of Agriculture, 1959*, available at the same sources.

Two readily available books on food preparation and nutrition are Adelle Davis's *Let's Cook It right*, revised edition, 1971, 572 pp., and *Let's Eat Right to Keep Fit*, revised edition, 1970, 334 pp., both available in hard cover or paperback editions from Harcourt Brace Jovanovich, New York. *Let's Cook It Right* contains sound information on the proper methods of preparing foods to conserve nutritional value, and any athlete might read through the chapter leads himself and possibly give a copy to the cook in the family. *Let's Eat Right to Keep Fit* is somewhat controversial because it has been identified in some minds with the health-food fad, and some of the writing does seem a bit too vivid. However, beneath the astonishing case histories are probably some valuable observations and recommendations if the reader is capable of studying the book carefully before using her ideas and then following her advice with prudent judgment.

TECHNICAL: GUNS, AMMO, ETC.

This is a nonbibliographical commentary, because we are purposefully not mentioning titles under this heading. In fact, we are including the heading only because omitting a reference to the subject area might appear to be an oversight.

The data surrounding gun design, ballistics, etc., is already so massive, and technical revolutions occur so rapidly, that any recommendations we make could only be partial and would likely be outdated by the time this book gets into print. But we are deliberately withholding recommendations in this area for another, more important reason: A shooter should get the best equipment available, and then forget about it. His whole effort should be directed toward improving his own performance. Unless he has unlimited time, almost any shooter who gets himself involved in pursuing the technical problems of gun design, modification, etc., is almost necessarily going to find the focus of his attention sidetracked from performance to equipment, where it does not belong if he is seriously interested in becoming a good performer. Shooters of high-power rifles may find hand-loading profitable if they can develop one or two satisfactorily accurate loads and then stop experimenting. But otherwise our advice is this: Keep abreast of new developments which make equipment perform better, but don't be overly concerned with *how* or *why* the equipment is improved. If the improvement is an authentic, significant breakthrough, take advantage of it; otherwise, don't be concerned. If the trend of the last two decades continues for the next ten years, and we believe it will, by far the more important advances in shooting scores will come not from improved equipment, but from improved performance. In shooting performance, the great unexplored frontier still lies in the area of unrealized human potential.

Index